CONSUMER GUIDE®

Fix-it

By the Editors of Consumer Guide®

Library of Congress Cataloging in Publication Data
Main entry under title:
Consumer guide fix-it.
    1. Dwellings—Maintenance and repair—Amateurs'
manuals. I. Consumer guide.
TH4817.3.C66   643'.7   75-31731
ISBN 0-671-22249-X
ISBN 0-671-22226-0 pbk.

Trade distribution by Simon and Schuster
A Gulf + Western Company
Rockefeller Center, 630 Fifth Avenue
New York, New York 10020

Publications International
Skokie, Illinois

Fix-it

Maintenance By The Calendar

IF YOU DO maintenance chores on a calendar basis, you can keep your home in top shape and prevent small problems from growing into major ones. By establishing a schedule of tasks to accomplish during each season, you can fix the damage done by the previous season and take steps to prevent any ill effects from the upcoming elements.

Another big plus to your doing home repairs at various times throughout the year is that you spread the expense over twelve months. If you wait until your fix-it tasks become critical, you might discover that several projects need doing all at the same time.

Then your financial position could suddenly become in need of repair as well.

Naturally, the maintenance calendar that you establish will be different from those of homeowners in different parts of the country. Nevertheless, the following season-by-season guide should be of some help when you set up your own schedule. Why not read through the guide and then make up your maintenance calendar before another day goes by in which you say "I wish I had done it earlier"?

Autumn

THE FALL SEASON is generally one in which you

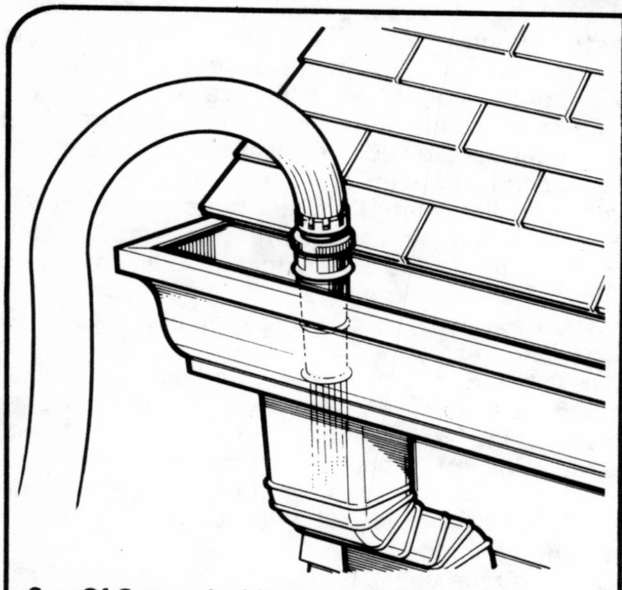

Care Of Gutters And Downspouts (Page 24)

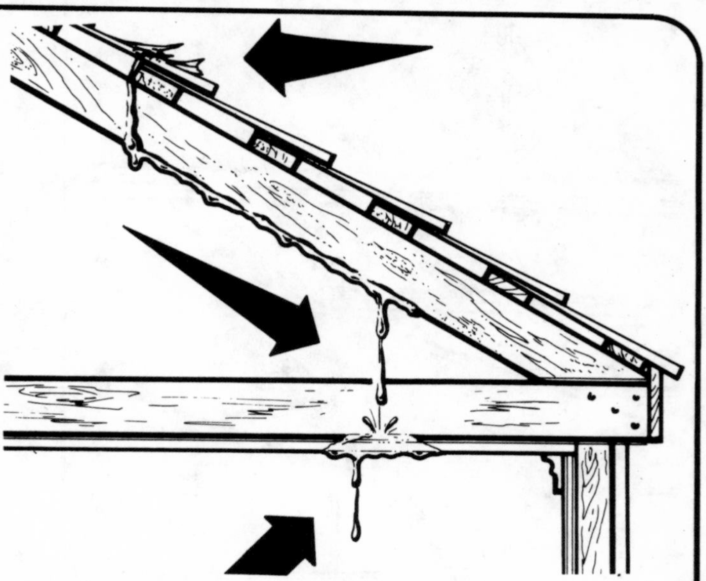

Repairing A Roof (Page 20)

Caulking (Page 25)

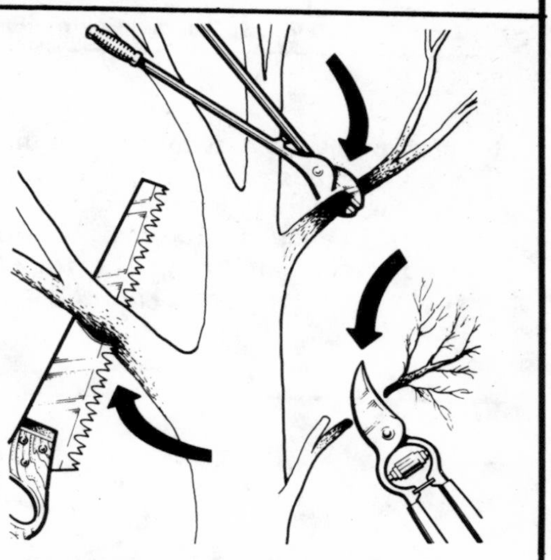

Pruning Your Own Trees (Page 17)

should prepare for winter. The protective measures you take during the mild autumn weather may well prevent having to deal with emergency conditions when the temperature dips below freezing.

The first thing to check is your heating system. Make sure it is working well before the time you actually need it. If you have a central heating system, make sure that all components are clean. Dirt is your heating system's worst enemy. If you have the disposable type filters, purchase enough to last you through the winter. Furnace filters are so inexpensive that you could install a fresh one every month without ever feeling a financial pinch. If you have the permanent type filters, take them out and clean them well before the mercury starts plummeting.

The fan or blower in a forced air system needs to be cleaned and lubricated annually. If the blower is of the squirrel-cage type, use a vacuum cleaner and a stiff brush to get all the dirt out from between the blades. Once these fins get clogged, the blower cannot move as much air, and the efficiency of your heating system goes way down while the cost of its operation goes way up. Remember, of course, that before you do any furnace cleaning you should turn off the gas and electric power to the unit.

Check the thermostat as well. Remove the face

WINTER MAINTENANCE

How To Install A Suspended Ceiling (Page 96)

clean. Usually brushing and vacuuming will do the job.

Now that you have the heating unit clean, inspect the area around it. Make sure that there are no items near the furnace that could pose a potential fire hazard or that might restrict the free flow of air to the system. Wall heater units must also have a free flow of air or they could become hazardous. Turn both the pilot and the burner off, and use a vacuum cleaner to remove all lint from all accessible surfaces. While you are vacuuming, check for any soot marks. Soot deposits are an indication that insufficient air is going to the heating unit, and you must correct the situation yourself or call in a heating professional to service the heater.

That should take care of your heating problems. Now move to your roof and check for any loose or missing shingles. Inspect the flashing for leaks, and look for signs of water spots in the attic. While you are on the roof, you might want to examine your TV antenna to make sure that it is secure and aimed in the right direction.

Once you are confident that the trees are finished shedding their leaves, clean all gutters and downspouts. Inspect the weatherstripping around all doors and windows, and replace the screens with storm doors and windows. Then make a complete tour all around the house to be sure that all caulking is sound. Bring in the garden tools, and drain and store the hoses. You should clean all the tools, protecting metal parts with a coating of oil or grease and rubbing wooden handles with a light coat of linseed oil. Power mowers and edgers should be drained and winterized.

plate, and gently blow away any lint that may have collected there. Just a little lint can destroy the accuracy of this delicate instrument. Inspect the pilot and burners for accumulated dirt, and if you find any, brush and vacuum it away. The registers for the forced hot air and for the cool return air must also be

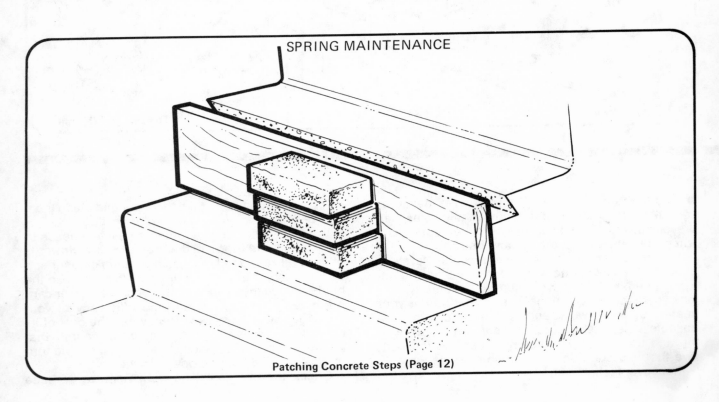

SPRING MAINTENANCE

Patching Concrete Steps (Page 12)

Install covers over all window air conditioning units and over all crawl space vents. Inspect all trees and remove any limbs too weak to withstand the weight of heavy ice and snow. Be sure that all outside faucets are turned off or properly protected so that they will not freeze, and check the main water cutoff to make certain you can shut it off should a plumbing emergency arise. Wrap any pipes that tend to sweat during the winter.

Winter

NOW IS THE time to keep busy doing all the inside repairs. Clean, repair, and repaint your patio furniture. Take care of any cracks or holes in your home's interior walls. If you have been wanting to panel some walls or install a suspended ceiling, winter is a good time to get the job(s) done.

Check your heating system on a regular basis during the winter. Make sure that motors are running properly and that they are well lubricated. There should be a clean filter in the heating unit at all times. Keep your home's humidity up to a comfortable level, but eliminate any condensation problems as they arise.

Spring

THIS IS THE time to repair all the damage done by winter weather and to prepare for the onset of summer.

Examine all masonry and brick work, walls, patios, the foundation, driveways, and all other exterior areas for cracks and holes. Repair any damage immediately. Inspect the roof once again for loose shingles, and look for potential problems that might crop up in your gutters or downspouts. Remove any rust and refinish all bare spots.

Repair and replace screens as you take down and store storm windows and doors. Store the storm windows and doors carefully to prevent any breakage.

Since spring is also the time when insects abound, check for signs of termites and keep a watchful eye for wasps starting nests in or near your home. Make certain that there are no unwanted openings in your home's exterior through which bugs could enter.

Spring is the best time to paint the outside of the house. Do it as soon as the weather turns warm enough but before the temperature gets too hot.

Inspect trees and shrubs, and cut off any broken limbs. Consult your nurseryman or county agent about proper spring feeding of your lawn, and plant seed in any bare spots. Prepare your power mower and edger for a season of hard work. If you have been thinking about planting a vegetable garden, spring is the time to start growing many types of vegetables.

Inspect the air conditioning system and get it ready for the hot days ahead. Remove all covers from window units and from crawl space vents. Clean out the fireplace, close the damper, and inspect the chimney to see whether it needs cleaning.

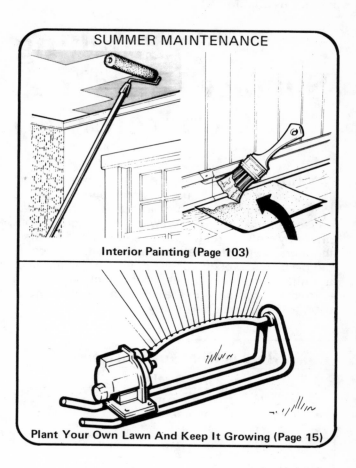

SUMMER MAINTENANCE

Interior Painting (Page 103)

Plant Your Own Lawn And Keep It Growing (Page 15)

Move all leftover firewood out away from the house before it can become a haven for bugs.

Summer

THE GOOD OLD summertime is a fine time for interior painting because you can keep the windows open. But try not to paint on excessively hot or humid days.

Check the basement for sweating pipes, and wrap any that might prove troublesome. Remove any standing water around your house before it can become a breeding ground for mosquitoes, and launch your program to combat the insects that can ruin your garden.

Be sure to keep your lawn, trees, and plants watered. If you are planning a vacation, arrange for a neighbor to water while you are away. Speaking of vacations, take steps to assure your home's security when you are gone. Arrange for mail and papers to be picked up, for the lawn to be mowed regularly, and for the neighbors to watch your place during your absence.

By observing this annual checklist you will find that home maintenance need never become a crushing burden. If you take care of your home's season-by-season requirements, you can save plenty of money and reduce your annual quota of homeowner headaches.

1. Patching Surface Holes In A Concrete Slab

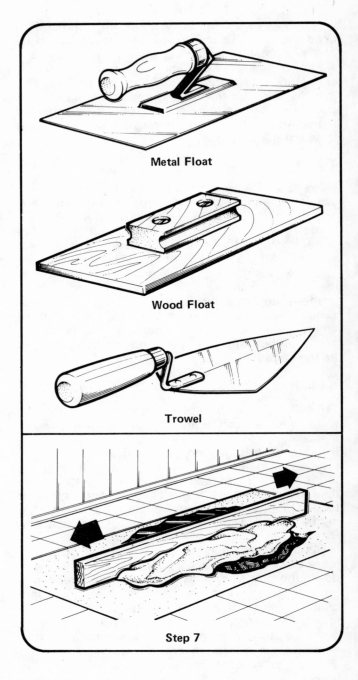

Metal Float

Wood Float

Trowel

Step 7

QUITE FREQUENTLY, the surface of a concrete drive, walk, or patio gets crumbly, and before long you notice some big holes. Such holes can cause sprained ankles, and when they occur in your driveway they are rough on tires. You would be wise, therefore, to patch small holes before they become big problems. Most patches, though, come out after a while, and then you are right back where you started. Do it right with the following method, however, and your patch will stay put.

Here Is What You Will Need

Materials

- Ready (sand) concrete mix
- Concrete bonding agent
- Tarp or plastic sheet

Tools

- Hammer
- Chisel
- Garden hose
- Paintbrush
- Metal wheelbarrow
- Trowel
- 2x4
- Wooden float
- Metal float
- Push broom

1. Remove every last bit of the loose concrete, and then hose out the cavity until it is perfectly clean.
2. Get a sack of ready mix (called a sand mix) and a small can of a bonding agent. The bonding agent is the key to creating a patch that is bonded permanently to the old concrete. You can buy patching mix that includes a bonding agent, but if you are patching many holes, the cost of the mix might be prohibitive.
3. Remove any standing water in the hole.
4. Brush on the bonding agent, following the manufacturer's directions.
5. Prepare the sand mix according to directions. Make sure that each grain of sand is coated with the gray mix, and make sure to use only the prescribed amount of water. A watery mix may be easier to work with, but it loses much of its strength. A metal wheelbarrow makes an ideal container for mixing.
6. Pour the mix into the hole, and then use a trowel to poke it in place completely.
7. Rake a 2x4 across the top to level the patch.
8. When the water sheen disappears, start to smooth the patch with a wooden float. You will soon see some water back on the surface, and when you do notice a sheen again stop the smoothing process.
9. If additional smoothing is necessary, wait until the surface sheen goes away again, and then smooth with a metal float. Remember, though, that most outdoor concrete projects should have a fairly rough finish for better traction. Pulling a push broom across the surface gives you the kind of finish you generally need.

10. When the water disappears again, cover the patch with a tarp or a sheet of plastic.
11. Remove the tarp or plastic sheet every day, adjust the nozzle on a garden hose to fine mist, and spray the concrete lightly. If possible, repeat this process for six days, recovering the patch after each spraying. What you are doing is letting the concrete cure. Curing is very important, since those who fail to do it — permitting the new concrete to dry out too fast — end up with a new crop of holes to patch in very short order.

2. Cracks In Concrete

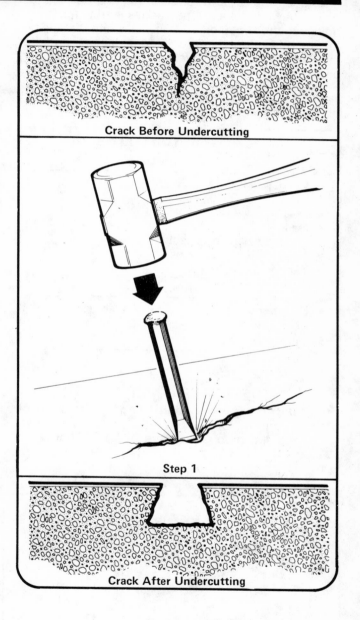

Crack Before Undercutting

Step 1

Crack After Undercutting

CONCRETE CRACKS just grow and grow. The small crack running across the patio today will become a chasm between two smaller patios in very short order. Moisture and temperature changes push at the sides of the crack as more of the surface inside comes loose, and before long you have your own Royal Gorge. Patching can stop the crack's progress. So get cracking and start patching.

Here Is What You Will Need

Materials

- Portland cement or concrete bonding agent
- Plastic coffee can lid
- Sand or gravel mix
- 2x4

Tools

- Cold chisel
- Hammer
- Goggles
- Stiff broom
- Garden hose
- Small trowel or putty knife

1. Use a cold chisel to convert the crack to a groove which is at least an inch deep and ½ inch wide. When chipping concrete, always wear goggles to protect your eyes. In addition, cut an "X" in a plastic coffee can lid and slip it over the chisel to shield you from flying fragments.
2. Undercut the groove to make it wider at the bottom; undercutting helps lock in the patch.
3. Brush and wash out all the loose concrete with a stiff broom and strong spray from your garden hose. If the crack goes all the way through the slab, tamp in a sand base.
4. Leave all surfaces wet, but get rid of any standing water.
5. Coat all surfaces with a creamy mix of portland cement and water, or use a bonding agent.

6. Prepare either a stiff sand mix or one with small gravel.
7. Tamp the mix into the crack with a small trowel or putty knife.
8. When the new concrete begins to stiffen (usually about 45 minutes later), smooth it with a trowel or a 2x4.
9. Let the patch cure six days.

3. Patching Concrete Steps

THE EDGES OF concrete steps receive a great deal of wear and rough treatment, and in most cases they can take it. Once edges start to fall apart, however, they keep on until after a while there is not much left. Not only do crumbled steps look bad, but they also pose a real safety hazard. Since patching damaged concrete steps is a fairly easy repair, why not fix them up now? Here is all you do.

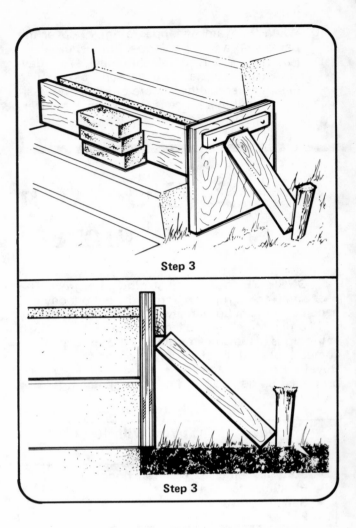

Step 3

Step 3

Here Is What You Will Need

Materials

- Wood planks
- Bricks
- 2x4
- Nails
- Concrete bonding agent
- Ready-mixed concrete
- Tarp or plastic sheet

Tools

- Hammer
- Cold chisel
- Garden hose
- Paintbrush
- Trowel
- Wooden float

1. Undercut the crumbling edge with a hammer and cold chisel. Undercutting is the process of cutting a "V" back into the solid concrete so that the patch will have a better chance of locking in place.

2. Remove all loose concrete, and clean the area thoroughly with the strong spray of the garden hose.
3. Build a form by placing a board against the riser and securing it with several bricks; that

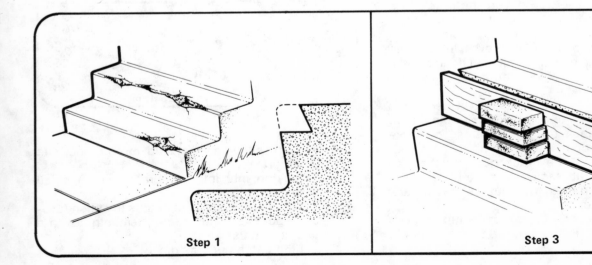

Step 1

Step 3

should hold the board firmly in place. Select two planks that are wide enough and tall enough and place them against the sides. Then angle a 2x4 as a brace, and nail it in place. Make sure that the top of your form is level with the step.

4. Paint the area to be covered with a concrete bonding agent, following the directions on the can. You can find concrete bonding agents at any hardware store.

5. Use ready-mixed concrete of the sand mix formula. Add no more water than the directions specify, and mix completely until every grain of sand is coated with the cement.

6. Use a trowel to poke the concrete mix in place, and check to be sure that you leave no air spaces back in the "V."

7. Finish off the concrete patch so that it is level with the rest of the step. You can use your trowel or a wooden float to get the patch level.

8. Make the patch match the texture of the rest of the step, and then cover it with a tarp or a plastic sheet.

9. The next day, and each succeeding day for five days, lift the cover and spray the new concrete with water. Adjust the hose nozzle to its fine mist setting.

You can remove the forms as soon as the concrete patch sets up, but by leaving them in place during the curing process, you reduce the likelihood of someone accidentally stepping on the patch before it is fully cured.

4. Replacing A Brick

A LOOSE BRICK should be reattached and a damaged brick should be replaced. Just buy a sack of mortar mix and you are ready to go to work. After you mix up a batch of the mortar, you should be able to get the loose brick back in place before it falls out and creates an even bigger headache.

Here Is What You Will Need

Materials

- Mortar mix
- Mortar coloring
- Replacement brick
- Bucket

Tools

- Hammer
- Cold chisel
- Wire brush
- Garden hose
- Trowel

---

1. Remove the mortar around the loose or damaged brick with a hammer and chisel. If the brick is already damaged, you can use a chisel to break it up too. If the brick is just loose, though, be careful not to break it as you chip the mortar to get it out. You will want to use the brick again in a few minutes.

2. After the brick comes out, chip away all the mortar that is still clinging to it.

3. Drop the brick into a bucket of water.

4. Go back to the hole and chip away all remaining mortar. You may have to use a wire brush to get the hole really clean. When you get all the mortar out, hose down the cavity.

5. Mix the mortar, adding coloring to shade the mixture so that it matches the rest of the wall.

6. Lay a bed of mortar down on the damp floor of the hole where the brick will go.

7. Take the brick out of the bucket of water, but do not dry it; just shake off any surface water. Butter the two ends and the top of the brick with mortar.

8. Insert the brick in the hole and press it in place, lining it up with the other bricks.

9. Use your trowel to force back into the cavity all the mortar that was pushed out when you inserted the brick.

10. Clean away any excess mortar.

11. Now — before the mortar sets up — make the new joints match the old ones. Remember that mortar dries faster on a hot or windy day.

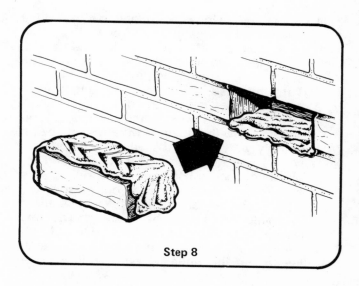
Step 8

5. Tuck-Pointing Loose Mortar Joints

Tuck-POINTING is sort of a weird name for removing old mortar between bricks and replacing it with new. Loose or crumbling mortar must be replaced or it will allow moisture to penetrate, and moisture can damage the interior wall. In addition, one loose brick tends to cause more crumbling and loose mortar outside. The next thing you know, you will have a whole wall of bad mortar joints to fix. Therefore, go ahead and fix them now, before the situation gets any worse. Just buy a sack of mortar mix that has everything already in it except the water, and your tuck-pointing should be a snap.

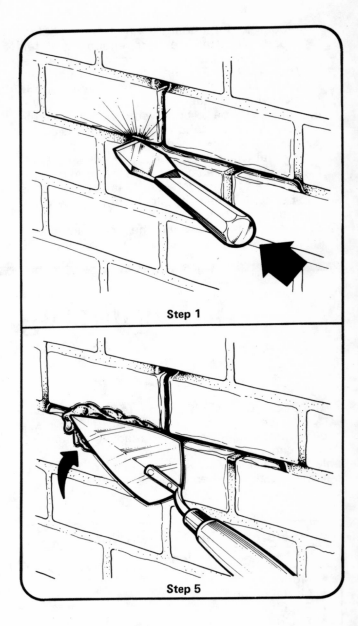

Step 1

Step 5

Here Is What You Will Need

Materials

- Mortar mix
- Corrugated cardboard
- Mortar coloring

Tools

- Cold chisel
- Hammer
- Safety goggles
- Garden hose
- Trowel
- Jointer tool or short piece of pipe
- Stiff brush

---

1. Clean out the loose or crumbling joints with a cold chisel and hammer. Cut down to a depth of at least a half inch, attacking the vertical joints first and then the horizontal ones. Be sure to wear safety goggles.
2. Turn the hose on the cleared joint to flush away all loose mortar and dust.
3. Now you are ready to mix the new mortar. You should know that the mix will probably be an entirely different shade when it dries than when you first mix it. Mix a trial batch and apply it to a piece of corrugated board. The porous cardboard will suck out most of the water, and the mortar that is left will be about the same shade it will be when dry. The next step is to add some color (available at hardware stores) to the mortar so that it will match the rest of the walls. When you arrive at a

match on the cardboard, you will have a good idea of what the wet mix should look like to achieve the desired results.
4. Dampen the joints to be tuck-pointed.
5. Force mortar into the joints with a trowel, filling the vertical joints first and then the horizontals. Press the mortar into the new joints firmly to make certain that you leave no cavities.
6. Now — before the mortar sets up — you must make the new joints look the same as the old. On a hot or warm and windy day, the mortar will dry out quickly, so you must work fast. Scrape off the excess mortar before you start pointing, and then use a jointer tool or a trowel to achieve the desired effect.
7. After the mortar sets up, take a stiff brush and clean the face of the bricks.

6. Plant Your Own Lawn And Keep It Growing

Having a green lawn does much more than just make your home look attractive. A good lawn fights air pollution, prevents soil erosion, helps to dampen sounds, and manufactures oxygen. Of course, most people who have nice lawns work at them primarily for the beauty only a well-manicured lawn can provide. It is a pretty way to set off any style house.

The type of grass that does best in your area varies with the climate, moisture, and soil. You can and should talk with experts, but the best way is to pick out several healthy looking lawns in the neighborhood and ask the owners what they did to achieve such great results. Find out what specie of grass is most successful and how much trouble it is to keep up. The owners will be flattered, and you will learn a great deal.

After you select which type of grass you want, learn which time of year is the best for planting. Here are some general steps to follow when putting in a new lawn.

Till Soil To Marble-Sized Lumps

Use Spreader to Distribute Seeds

Here Is What You Will Need
Materials

- Lime or gypsum
- Peat moss
- Grass seed
- Fertilizer
- Chemical weed killer

Tools

- Tiller
- Spreader
- Rake
- Roller
- Sprinkler
- Mower

1. If the grading has not been done yet, you should have it done or do it yourself. The ground should slope gradually away from the house in all directions.
2. After grading, check for low places by turning on a sprinkler and looking for spots where water collects.
3. Next, check the soil; it should have the proper PH. The only way to find out about the soil's PH is to test it. Most county agents and many seed stores will test your soil at no or very little cost to you. Lime is added to soil that is too acid, and gypsum is added to soil that is to alkaline. The soil should also be crumbly. Squeeze a handful tightly in your fist and release it. If the blob falls apart, the soil is too sandy. If it looks like a mud ball, the soil contains too much clay. In either case, three to four inches of peat moss will correct the soil situation.
4. Make whatever soil additions are indicated by the tests, and then till the soil. You can rent a

tiller if you do not wish to buy one. When tilling, avoid making the soil too fine. Marble-sized lumps are better than fine dirt.

5. Wet the soil to pack it down, and then wait 24 hours.
6. Spread the seed at the rate recommended for the specific variety of seed you are planting. Do not spread the seed too thickly; if you do, the young seedlings will compete for nutrients and most will die.
7. Rake the ground lightly to cover the seeds partially with soil.
8. Go over the ground once with a roller to press the seeds into the soil. Do not try to bury them.
9. Feed the lawn as soon as you finish the seeding. Use the fertilizer recommended for your variety of grass, and follow the directions on the bag.
10. Water as soon as you finish fertilizing. During the next two weeks, water two or three times a day, keeping the top layer of soil damp at all times. When the seedlings are up, cut back to regular morning watering.
11. Wait until the sprigs are two inches tall, and then mow. Mowing will help to spread the root system and make the lawn thicker.
12. Mow weekly until you note the proper thickness; then mow as needed.
13. Never use a weed killer on new lawns. Pull the bigger weeds, and mow the rest. As your lawn thickens, many of the weeds will be choked out. You can use a weed killer the second year your lawn is in.

The maintenance of your lawn depends on the specie of grass you planted, the soil condition, and the climate. A lawn specialist or the county agent can tell you what type of fertilizer you should have and how often you should apply it. He can also tell you how much water you should be using.

If your existing lawn is shot, try to renovate it. If there is at least 50 percent of the area still covered with grass, plant new grass in the bad spots. Here are the steps to follow.

1. Get rid of all weeds. Apply a chemical weed killer according to directions.
2. Mow the existing grass very close.
3. Rake the yard to remove all clippings and leaves and also to loosen the surface of the soil. Test the soil as described earlier.
4. Follow the same steps (6 through 13 above) suggested for a new lawn in order to seed the bare spots.

One thing many people fail to realize is that grass cannot grow in total shade. You may have had a good stand of grass several years ago, but now it is all dead around the trees. Years ago the trees probably were not as thick; now they keep the sun out completely. You can thin out the branches to let

Steps 7 And 8

Step 9

Step 10

Step 11

more sunlight through, and you can try one of the species of seed that grows well in partial shade. Those steps should put you on the way to a greener and more beautiful lawn.

7. Pruning Your Own Trees

YOU SHOULD PRUNE trees for several reasons. Pruning gives trees a more desirable shape, strengthens them by improving their structure, removes dead limbs and diseased portions, and increases the production of foliage, flowers, and fruit. Here are the basic steps for pruning your trees.

Here Is What You Will Need
Materials
• Tree paint
Tools
• Sharpened pruning tools
• Paintbrush
• Ladder

1. All pruning tools should be as sharp as possible. Dull tools lead to ragged cuts, and ragged cuts can lead to problems.
2. Use the right size and type of tool for your trees. Too large or too small a tool can make ragged cuts.
3. Make all cuts as close as possible to the base of the piece being removed without damaging the larger limb to which it is attached.

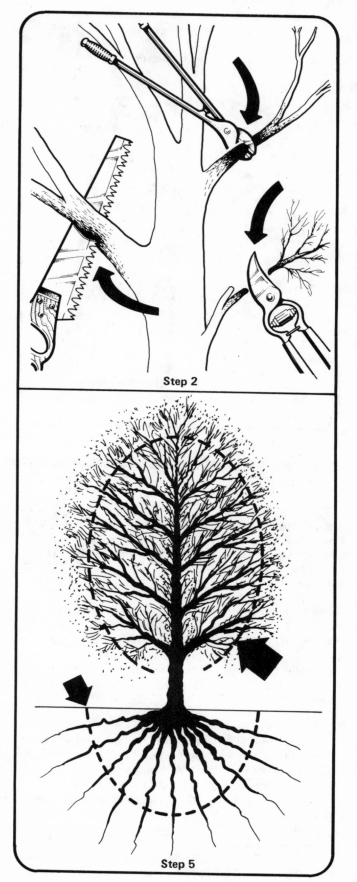

Step 2

Step 5

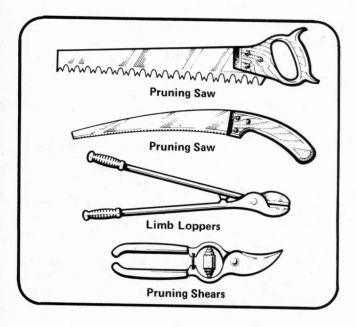

Pruning Saw

Pruning Saw

Limb Loppers

Pruning Shears

Step 4

4. Seal all cuts with tree paint.
5. Because their root systems have usually been greatly reduced, newly transplanted trees should be pruned no matter what the season of the year.
6. Winter is the best time for pruning most trees because that is when the trees are dormant. Naturally, trees that exude sap during the winter should not be pruned until the following spring.
7. You can prune most trees lightly for shaping during the spring.
8. Remove broken limbs anytime of the year, but prune dead limbs in the fall.
9. When heavy pruning (the removal of as much as a third of the tree) is needed, do not perform all of the pruning during a single season. Do it, instead, in stages over a two- or three-year period.

Above all, try to do as much of the pruning work as possible while standing on the ground. When you must work from a ladder, never try to reach very far; move the ladder frequently and make certain that it is always on solid ground. Position yourself and your ladder so that the limbs you prune fall free and nowhere near you, and if you are cutting away large limbs, make certain that there is no chance of them falling against power lines.

8. Fixing A Leaky Garden Hose

I T IS A rare homeowner who has never mowed across a garden hose hidden in the grass. Unfortunately, most people who take a chunk out of a hose just toss it away and invest in a new one. They obviously do not know that they can mend the break easily with a device that is available at any hardware store.

1. Cut out the section with the hole in it and take it to the hardware store. The hardware dealer will sell you a mending unit of the correct size for your hose. Although some mender manufacturers claim that their products can be used on both plastic and rubberized hoses, you should buy the one made especially for the type of hose you have.
2. The mender for a rubber hose has a short corrugated nipple or tube that you slip into each end of the cut hose.

Here Is What You Will Need
Materials
• Mending unit
• Hose coupling
• Washer
Tools
• Knife
• Hammer
• Screwdriver
• Soldering iron

3. When you get the tube snugged up all the way on both sides, place the mender on a wood block.
4. Take a hammer and start tapping the claw-like fingers on the flange of the mender down against the hose. When all of the prongs are resting securely against the hose, the leak is mended.
5. The mender for a plastic hose is a tube that fits

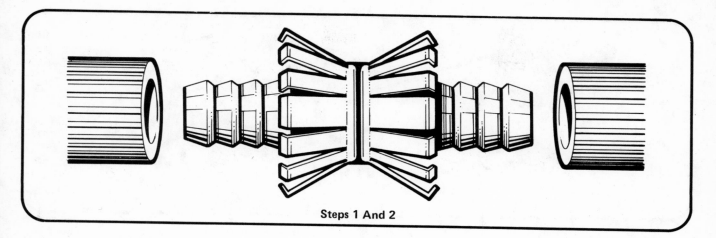

Steps 1 And 2

inside with threaded screw clamps that go over the hose. As you tighten the clamps, the threads tighten into the hose and hold it against the tube. To make a plastic hose more pliable and easier to work with, hold the ends in very hot water before inserting the tube.

6. You can sometimes mend a tiny hole in a plastic hose by touching a hot soldering iron to the hole. The heat will melt some of the plastic and close the hole.

7. You can replace hose couplings, but before you replace a coupling because it leaks, check to be sure that the washer is all right. Even if the washer looks good, it may be compressed and not able to provide a tight seal. Therefore, try a new washer before you install a replacement coupling.

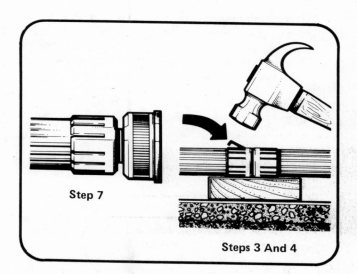

Step 7

Steps 3 And 4

9. Repairing Blacktop Surfaces

THE SAME PROBLEMS — ruined tires and sprained limbs — that accompany holes in concrete also present themselves with holes in an asphalt driveway. In a sense, however, the asphalt problems are worse. Once asphalt starts to slough away, the hole spreads, and before long you have a major resurfacing project on your hands. Fortunately, you can buy blacktop cold patch in a bag that requires no mixing. You just pour it from the sack to stop the spread of holes in blacktop.

1. Chip away at the loose asphalt material until you reach a solid surface.
2. Brush out all of the loose material.

Here Is What You Will Need
Materials
• Blacktop patch
• Blacktop sealer
• Sand
Tools
• Chisel
• Brush
• Shovel or rake
• Trowel

3. Pour in the blacktop patch from the sack, adding enough to make the patch about a half inch higher than the surrounding area.
4. Use the back of your shovel or rake to pack the patch down thoroughly. If you can pack

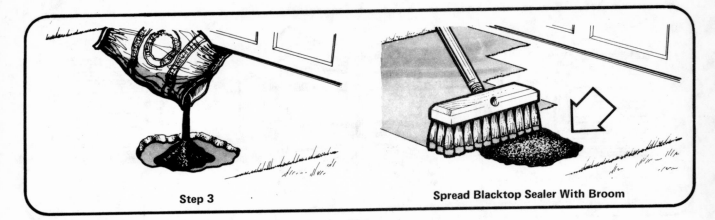

Step 3 | Spread Blacktop Sealer With Broom

the patch material below the surrounding surface, pour in more and tamp it down. Just make sure that the patched area is level with the rest of the driveway. You can drive your car over the new patch immediately.

There are blacktop sealers on the market that will prolong the life of your driveway. They come ready to use and require no heating (as did the old-fashioned asphalt toppings). Nonetheless, you will get a better seal if you apply the material during a summer heat wave. Most blacktop surfaces should be sealed about every two years. The sealer can also be used for filling wide cracks. You just mix the sealer with sand to form a slurry mix, and then force the mix into the crack.

10. Repairing A Roof

Here Is What You Will Need

Materials

- Flashing or asphalt roofing paper
- Asphalt roofing cement
- Shingles

Tools

- Garden spade
- Hacksaw blade
- Propane torch

ROOF LEAKS can do all sorts of damage inside your home. Fixing the leak is often an easy task, but — since leaks are very elusive — locating the leak can take forever. Water can enter at one point in your roof and follow a rafter for many feet before it drips down onto the ceiling. Sometimes a leak occurs only when the wind is blowing from one direction and with enough force to blow rain in under a broken shingle or through some crack. You frequently have to be in the attic when it is raining in order to track down the spot, but the leak may even be in a place where you cannot spot it from inside the attic; then you have to look outside — but not while the roof is wet. Look for such things as missing shingles, split shingles, loose nails, or bad flashing. Once you find the leak, mark it well so that you can know where to go to work when the roof is dry.

Assuming that you have located the leak, you are ready to make some actual repairs. The following instructions are for a wood shingle roof.

1. You can either replace a split shingle or stop the leak in the old one. If you decide not to replace the shingle, try slipping a piece of flashing under the split or inserting some asphalt roofing paper under it. First, pry up the overlapping shingle with a flat garden spade, using your foot on the handle to apply pressure. If you cannot get the patch as far back under the shingle as you think it should go, use a hacksaw blade to cut away any nails that are in the way. Then apply asphalt roofing cement to anchor the patch. If you need to drive new nails that leave exposed heads, put a dab of the cement over each head.

2. Replace any missing shingles as soon as you notice their absence. Pry up the overlapping

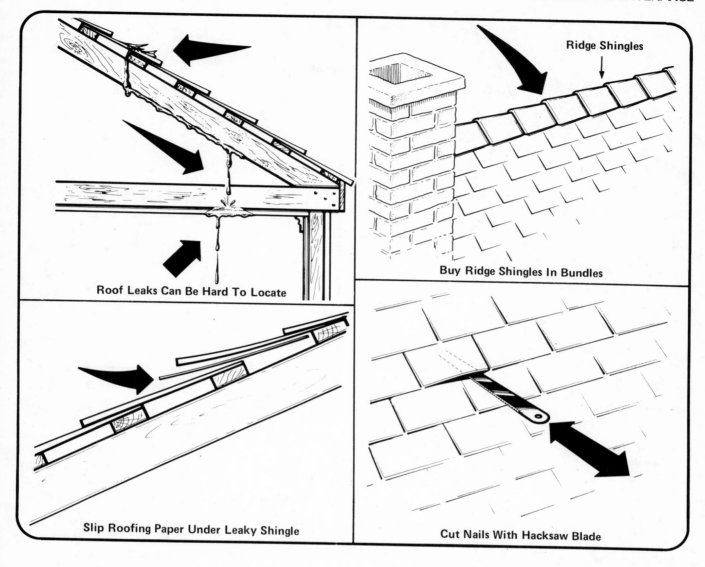

Roof Leaks Can Be Hard To Locate

Buy Ridge Shingles In Bundles

Ridge Shingles

Slip Roofing Paper Under Leaky Shingle

Cut Nails With Hacksaw Blade

shingles, saw away any nails that prevent your getting the new shingle in far enough, and use a combination of cement and nails to anchor the new shingle.

3. If the problem involves the ridge shingles, your best bet is to go to a lumberyard and buy a bundle of ridges rather than try to piece them together.

For repairs on composition roof shingles, follow these instructions.

1. Asphalt shingles with curled corners can be tamed easily by putting a dab of asphalt roofing cement about the size of a quarter under each and pressing the corner down.

2. You can patch many holes or rips with roofing cement. Just lift up the shingle, dab the cement under the hole, and press the shingle back down.

3. If you must replace a shingle, you can usually get to the nails holding the faulty shingle by raising the overlapping shingle. Raise it gently so as not to crack the shingle. Then loosen and remove the nails, and slip the bad section out. Put the new one in its place and renail using only two nails. Dab cement on the nail heads and on the overlapping shingle to anchor it down. You will find that warm composition shingles are much more pliable and, therefore, easier to work with. If you cannot do your roof repair work on a hot day, try running the flame from a propane torch across your shingles if they seem too brittle.

You can patch most flashing problems with asphalt roofing cement. The problem here is in locating the trouble. A gap in a flashing joint is easy to spot and easy to patch, but detecting a nearly invisible pinhole is something else again. When you see any spots that might possibly be such pinholes, cover them with cement. In addition, dab a little cement on any exposed nails in the flashing.

11. Installing Gutters And Downspouts

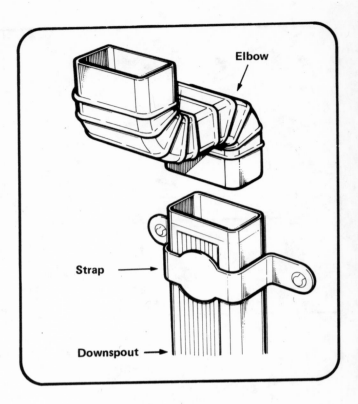

NOT HAVING good gutters and downspouts can wash away your soil and your plants, cause water problems under the house, rot out parts of your home's foundation, and create other problems too numerous to mention. If you lack gutters or if those you have are inadequate, by all means put on new ones. You can make it a do-it-yourself project by just following these directions.

Here Is What You Will Need

Materials

- Gutter sections
- Slip connectors
- Outside or inside corners
- Downspouts
- Drop outlets
- Elbows
- Downspout straps
- Strainers
- End caps
- Supports
- Caulking
- Chalk
- Wood block
- Masonry nails
- Concrete mix
- Zinc chromate primer
- Exterior house paint
- Asphalt roofing paint

Tools

- Hammer
- Drill
- Fine-toothed hacksaw
- File
- Paintbrushes

the house, and another elbow to carry the water away from the house. Downspouts also come in ten foot sections, and each downspout should be secured by at least two straps. A strainer should go in each downspout, and end caps go over each end of each run of guttering; end caps are made for use on right and left ends. Supports should be placed about every 36 inches. By careful planning you can avoid delays, save trips to the supplier, and cut waste to a minimum.

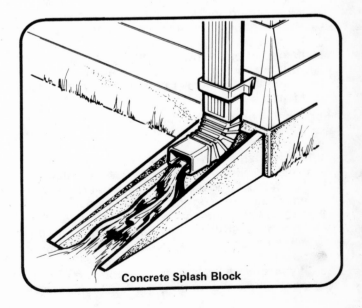

Concrete Splash Block

1. Make a sketch of the roof. From this, you can determine the number of sections you will need. Standard gutter sections are ten feet long, and each section is joined to the next with a slip connector. Where the gutter turns, there must be either an outside or inside corner. A downspout should be installed at least every 35 feet, and for each downspout you will need a drop outlet, an elbow to reach back to

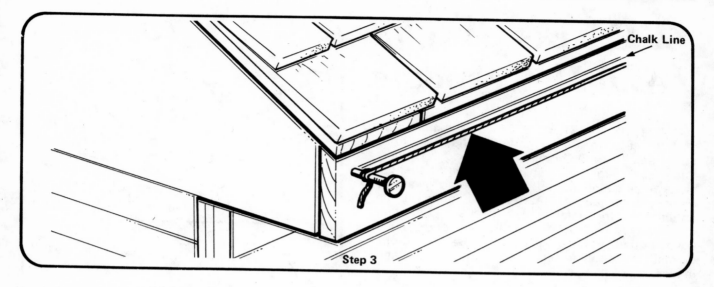

Step 3

Chalk Line

2. After you have purchased the materials, lay them out on the ground around the house to be sure you have everything you need.

3. Establish a chalk line so that the gutters will slant toward all downspouts at a slope of about a quarter inch per ten foot section.

4. Start with the end of the gutter farthest from the downspout.

5. Apply caulking to the end cap, and slip it in place.

6. Drill the holes for supports if necessary before raising the section.

7. Attach the section by installing supports every three feet; make sure that the gutter follows the chalk line.

8. Connect each section or different component with a slip connector that you have caulked along its edges.

9. If any cutting needs to be done, use a fine-toothed hacksaw and support the gutter from inside with a block of wood. File off any burrs to make installation easier.

10. Use a support on each side of a corner section.

11. When all of the guttering is up, slip elbows in place over the drop outlet.

12. Slip the downspout section in place, and install the straps near the top and bottom of the section to hold it flat against the wall. Use masonry nails if the wall is brick or concrete.

13. Attach elbows to the bottom of the downspout to lead water away from the house. Use as many extensions as are required, and pour concrete splash blocks if necessary.

If you buy prefinished guttering, then your work is done. If it is not painted, however, you must paint it yourself — that is, unless you installed galvanized metal sections. Galvanized metal does not accept paint until it has weathered for several months, and you should ask your dealer how long galvanized

guttering should weather in your area before painting. Use a zinc chromate primer to prepare gutters for painting, and then apply regular exterior house paint. Paint the insides of gutters with asphalt roofing paint.

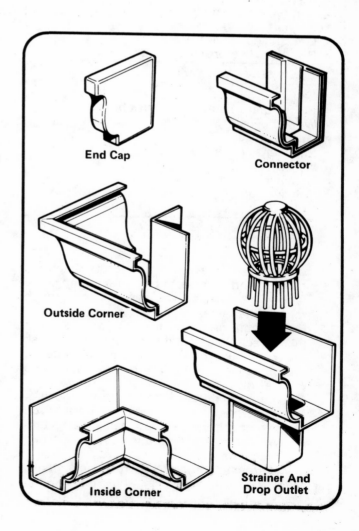

End Cap

Connector

Outside Corner

Inside Corner

Strainer And Drop Outlet

12. Care of Gutters And Downspouts

GUTTERS AND DOWNSPOUTS do require a little attention. Most importantly, they need to be kept clean. If the water cannot run along the gutters and pass through the downspouts, it will go over the sides and onto the ground. Gutters should always be cleaned after all the leaves have fallen in the autumn, and they may need to be checked at other times as well — depending on the type of trees you have around. For example, a mimosa tree drops blooms at one time, seed pods at another, and leaves at yet another.

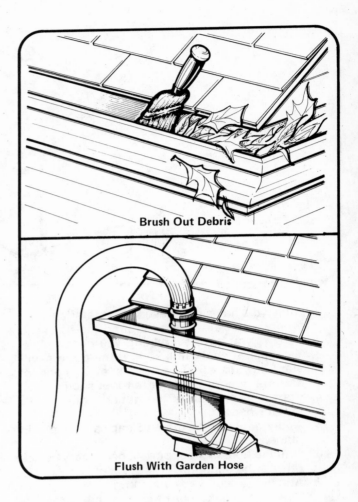

Brush Out Debris

Flush With Garden Hose

Here Is What You Will Need

Materials

- Paint thinner
- Window screen material
- Asphalt roofing cement
- Galvanized roofing nails
- Rivets or waterproof duct tape

Tools

- Ladder
- Plastic plate, scraper, or whisk broom
- Work gloves
- Garden hose
- Plumber's snake
- Wire brush
- Hammer
- Pop rivet tool
- Drill

1. Use a ladder that is tall enough to reach the gutters, and be sure to play it safe; move the ladder often so that you never have to reach far to either side.
2. Remove all the debris from the gutter. Use a discarded plastic plate scraper or a whisk broom to rake the leaves out of the gutter. If you clean the gutters with your hands, be sure to wear gloves.
3. Flush out the gutters with the garden hose.
4. Flush out the downspouts with the hose. If you discover that they are stopped up, use a plumber's snake to break through the clog. Then flush with the hose.

While you are cleaning, look for rust spots, holes, loose supports, and sags in the gutters and downspouts. Check the runoff to be sure the gutters are still pitched properly, and be sure the strainers are in place and unclogged.

Gutters with holes can be patched. For an easy way to patch them, follow these step-by-step instructions.

1. Remove all rust and any other loose metal by cleaning the area with a wire brush. Cover the bad spot with paint thinner.
2. Cut a patch from wire window screen material. The patch must cover the hole and extend about a half inch beyond it.
3. Coat the area around the hole with asphalt roofing cement.
4. Put the patch down over the cement and press it in place.
5. Brush the cement over the screen.
6. When the first coat sets up, cover it again with cement. You can patch tiny holes without using the screen; the cement will fill in by itself. You may have to apply several coats, however.

A gutter that sags usually has a loose hanger. There are three types of gutter hangers in use today. One type employs a gutter spike driven through a sleeve and into the roof board. If the spike comes loose, you can drive it back in with a hammer. Another type features a strap that is nailed to the roof under a shingle. Be sure to use galvanized roofing nails to resecure a loose strap, then put a dab of roofing cement over the heads and old nail holes. The third type of gutter hanger is a bracket nailed to the fascia under the gutter. Since you may not be able to get to the loose nails with this type of gutter hanger, add an auxiliary support of another type to eliminate the sag. Sometimes a gutter sags because it lacks sufficient support points. There should be support points about every 36 inches along the run of gutter.

If an elbow or a section of downspout keeps coming off, the easiest way to attach it permanently is with a pop rivet tool. This is an inexpensive tool that installs rivets from the outside without your having to reach the inside surface. To install pop rivets, follow these steps.

1. Place the two sections together.
2. Using a drill bit of the size specified to accommodate the size rivet you have, drill through both pieces. Make two such holes, one on either side or one at the front and one at the back of the downspout.
3. Insert the rivet into the hole in the tool, and then place the tip into the holes you drilled.
4. Squeeze the handles of the tool together until the rivet shaft pops off. The rivet will then be permanently in place.

If you do not have a pop rivet tool and do not wish to buy one, you can use waterproof duct tape to hold

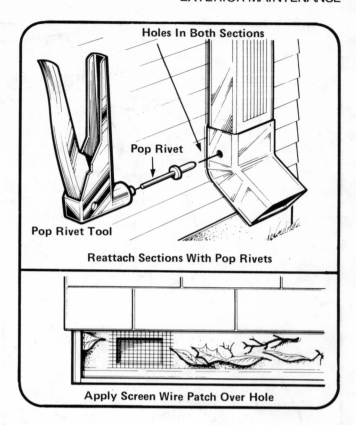

Reattach Sections With Pop Rivets

Apply Screen Wire Patch Over Hole

the sections together. Although the tape holds well, taped sections look far less neat and attractive than riveted sections.

13. Caulking

CAULKING IS important for three reasons. First, most uncaulked areas look bad. Second, uncaulked cracks can let cold air in and hot air out during the winter, and just the opposite if your house is air conditioned during the summer. And third, a lack of caulking allows water, dirt, and insects to attack your house's paint and framing.

There are five basic types of caulking compounds. Oil base is the least expensive, but it does not last as long as others. Moreover, you cannot paint oil base caulking compounds for 24 hours. A latex base is much longer lasting and can be painted almost immediately. It adheres to most surfaces, weathers well, and cleans up with soap and water. Butyl rubber caulk is also long lived, but it is best used on masonry to metal joints. It requires a solvent for clean up. Silicone caulks are excellent because they cure quickly and are long lasting. Polyvinyl acetate caulks, which are generally better indoors than outdoors,

lack the flexibility of other caulks because they dry hard and brittle. Silicone and polyvinyl acetate caulks are not used as widely as the oil, latex, and butyl rubber types. In fact, not many paint or hardware stores carry any but the first three types.

Here are some general tips on caulking.

1. Always clean away all the old caulking. It can be scraped, peeled, gouged, and pulled away.

Here Is What You Will Need
Materials
• Oil-, latex-, butyl rubber-, silicone-, or polyvinyl acetate-type caulk   • Cleaning solvent
Tools
• Knife   • Caulk gun

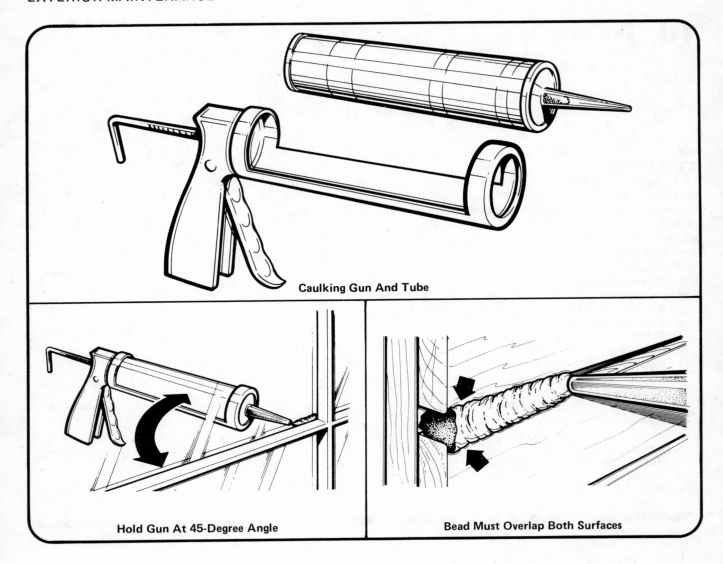

Caulking Gun And Tube

Hold Gun At 45-Degree Angle

Bead Must Overlap Both Surfaces

Once you get rid of all of it, clean the area to be caulked with a solvent. You want the area to be as free of dirt, oil, wax, and dust as possible.

2. Try to do your caulking work in warm weather. If that is not possible, warm the caulking tube itself before you apply its contents. In extremely hot weather, the caulking can get too runny; try placing the tube in the refrigerator for a brief period to slow down the caulk.

3. Cut the spout at a place that will give you the proper size bead for the job. The bead should overlap onto both surfaces. Make your spout cut at an angle.

5. Hold the gun at a 45-degree angle in the direction of your movement.

6. When you have to stop, twist the L-shaped plunger rod until it disengages in order to stop the caulk from oozing out.

Where should you caulk? As a rule of thumb, any place that has two different parts that come together with a crack in between should be caulked. Think particularly in terms of places where two different materials come together. Here is a sample list of caulking spots:

1. Around doors and windows where the frame and the side of the house come together.
2. At the point where the side of the house and the foundation meet.
3. In the joint where steps or porches and the main body of the house meet.
4. Where the chimney meets the roof, around the flashing, and the gap in the seam between flashing and shingles.
5. Where plumbing goes through walls to enter the house.
6. Along the seam formed at corners where siding meets.
7. Around the exhaust vent for the clothes dryer.
8. In the spaces between air conditioner window units and window frames.

14. Installing Your Own Underground Sprinkler System

WATERING IS one absolute essential to possessing a lush green lawn. In fact, it is so essential that some people spend nearly half of every summer day moving hoses and sprinklers around so that all of their yard gets watered. You really need not invest all that time, though, because underground lawn sprinkler systems are now available for do-it-yourself installation. The advent of plastic pipe and fittings has made the installation of an underground sprinkler system a project that is certainly within the capabilities of most homeowners. Here is how to put one of these systems in your yard.

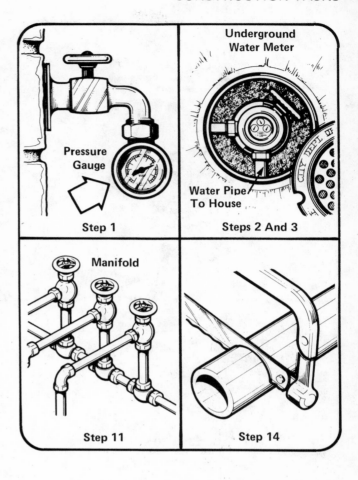

Step 1 — Pressure Gauge

Steps 2 And 3 — Underground Water Meter / Water Pipe To House

Step 11 — Manifold

Step 14

Here Is What You Will Need

Materials

- System kit or components
- Stakes
- Plastic pipe
- PVC solvent
- PVC pipe dope
- Sandpaper

Tools

- Water pressure gauge
- Trenching machine or straight spade
- Trenching nozzle
- Garden hose
- Hacksaw

---

1. You should first check the water pressure. In many areas, the local water company can give you the average pressure in PSI (pounds per square inch). Or, you can install a pressure gauge on an outside hydrant and take a reading with the valve open but with no water running in the house.
2. You also need to know the size of your water meter. If the size is not stamped on the meter, again ask the water company.
3. Determine the size of the pipe coming from the meter in your house.
4. Make a scale drawing of your lawn, showing walks, drives, trees, shrubs, and any other obstructions.
5. Check your local building code to find out what is required of an underground sprinkler system.
6. Tell your sprinkler system dealer all this information, and let him figure out what materials you need.
7. Stake out your yard, using a stake at each sprinkler head location.
8. Assemble a sprinkler head and riser to use as a depth gauge for trenching. If you have a new lawn that is not yet seeded, set the heads between 1/2 and 3/4 of an inch above the soil level. If the lawn is or will be sodded, set the heads two inches above the soil.
9. For the actual digging, you might wish to rent a trenching machine. If not, use a straight spade to dig a V-shaped trench to the required depth. If you already have grass, save the sod you dig up for replacement later.
10. To trench under walks, obtain a special nozzle that uses water pressure to get through obstructions. Attach the nozzle to the length of pipe, and attach the pipe to the hose. Work from both sides to trench under the walk.
11. Assemble the sprinkler system's control valve (manifold) system according to the procedure set up by the dealer. The control valves vary in number depending on how many separate circuits there are.

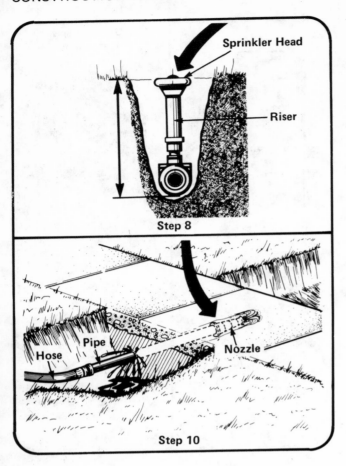

Step 8

Step 10

12. Shut off the water at the meter, and make the connection to the water line at the point prescribed by the dealer.
13. Lay out the pipes, fittings, and heads along the trenches.
14. Assemble the separate components into a system. PVC plastic pipe can be cut with a hacksaw. Sand the pipes inside and out to deburr, and then brush PVC solvent (cement) on all surfaces to be joined. Apply a thin coat of solvent inside the fitting and a heavier coat outside the pipe. Push the pipe all the way into the fitting with a twisting motion, and hold it there for about 15 seconds. That is all there is to joining plastic pipe, but handle the joint with care during the next 30 minutes. Rub any threaded connections with PVC pipe dope, not with the solvent.
15. When the lines are all hooked together, connect them to the manifold.
16. Remove nozzles from heads, and then — provided you have waited at least an hour since you cemented the last joint — turn on the water in the system. The water cleans any dirt from the lines, and allows you to check closely for any leaks.
17. Fill up the trenches and replace the sod, if necessary.
18. Test the system with the nozzles in place to see if the pattern is correct. You can adjust the heads to create the pattern you want.

15. Building A Fence

THERE ARE hundreds of ways to design a fence and dozens of different materials to use. Some fences are for protection, some for privacy, some for appearance, and, of course, some accomplish all three purposes. Before you decide on a specific fence design, check the local building code. It may restrict you to a certain height, style, materials, and positioning in relation to property lines. No matter what kind of fence you decide to put up, though, the key to durability is the proper installation of the posts. Here are some hints for installing fence posts the right way.

1. Stake out your fence. Tap short sharp sticks into the ground, and then run strings from one stick to the next.
2. Using the strings as a guide, drive additional

Here Is What You Will Need

Materials

- Short sharp sticks
- String
- Fence posts
- Wood preservative
- Asphalt paint
- Gravel
- Portland cement
- Sand
- Fence sections

Tools

- Measuring tape
- Paint brushes
- Post-hole digger
- Shovel
- Level
- Outrigger braces
- Wheelbarrow

Step 4

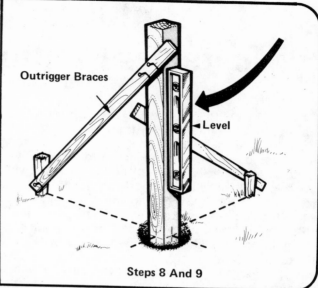

Steps 8 And 9

stakes to indicate where each post goes. The spacing depends on the type of fence, the terrain, and the purpose of the fence. As a rule of thumb, posts should range from six to eight feet apart.

3. Select wooden posts of a rot resistant wood like redwood, cedar, or cyprus. If you choose any other kind of wood, be sure to treat the posts with a preservative. Even the rot resistant woods benefit from a preservative treatment. Coat metal posts with asphalt paint to prevent rusting.

4. Dig the holes with a post-hole digger. If you have many holes to dig, look into the possibility of renting a gasoline powered post-hole digger. Dig only the corner posts at first.

5. Try to have about a third of the total length of the post underground, particularly at the corners and at any gates. In-between posts can still be solid, though, as long as they are in the ground to a depth of at least two feet.

6. After you dig the hole to the proper depth, flare it at the bottom with a straight shovel.

7. Put about an inch or two of gravel in the bottom of the hole for drainage purposes.

8. Position the post in the hole, and use a level to get it plumb.

9. When you get it straight and at the proper height, rig outrigger braces to hold the post in place.

10. Mix just enough concrete for this one post. Use a mix of one part portland cement, two parts sand, and three parts medium-size gravel. A wheelbarrow makes a handy mixing place. Use only enough water in the mix to coat the sand and gravel with cement.

11. Shovel the concrete into the hole around the post, poking the mixture to eliminate any air bubbles.

12. Add enough concrete to fill the hole slightly above the ground, and then slope the concrete away from the post for drainage.

13. Set the other corner posts the same way, and stretch taut cords between them. Now you can line up all the other posts that come between the corners.

14. Let the concrete cure fully before building the rest of the fence. If you wait six days, you can then build whatever fence you want with the assurance that it will last for quite some time.

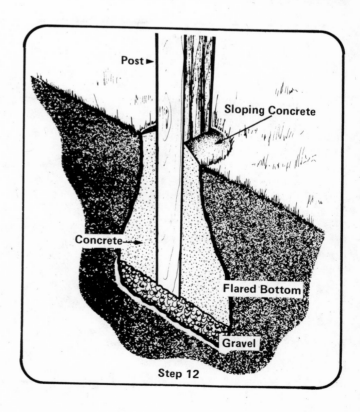

Step 12

16. Building A Mortarless Patio

PLENTY OF PEOPLE would like to have a brick patio, but they shy away from building one due to the challenge or mortaring the bricks together. What would you say if someone told you that you could build a patio without any motar?The following procedure will produce a long-lasting patio that has proven itself for many homeowners, and the ease with which you can make it will boggle your mind.

Regarding the bricks to use, the only thing of which you must make certain is that the bricks are SW (severe weathering) grade. Beyond the grade, only your personal taste and the availability of bricks in your area will dictate what you get. Since the bricks will be walked on, you should consider a darker shade that will show less dirt. Used brick is fine if you can locate what you want at a wrecking yard.

Pick out the spot where you want the patio to go, and make a rough layout with boards to see if the shape looks about right. You can estimate how many bricks you need just by determining the square footage. Since there are no motar joints in this patio all you have to do is measure the brick and see how many it will take to equal the square footage you measured. Now you can build your new patio.

Here Is What You Will Need

Materials

- SW grade bricks
- Wooden boards
- Redwood
- Sand
- Plastic sheet
- Nails
- Stakes
- Dry cement

Tools

- Measuring tape
- Shovel
- Garden hose
- Hammer
- Broom

1. The first step is always the hardest. In this case, it is time to do the excavation. You need to dig down far enough to accommodate the thickness of the brick, plus a two-inch bed of sand. At the same time, you must keep water run-off in mind. Therefore, slope the area you are digging. The slope should be about a quarter inch per foot.
2. You should have a border around the perimeter of the patio to prevent bricks along

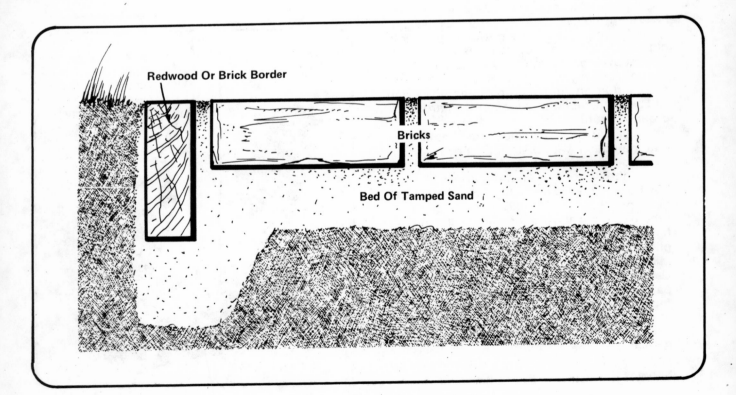

Redwood Or Brick Border

Bricks

Bed Of Tamped Sand

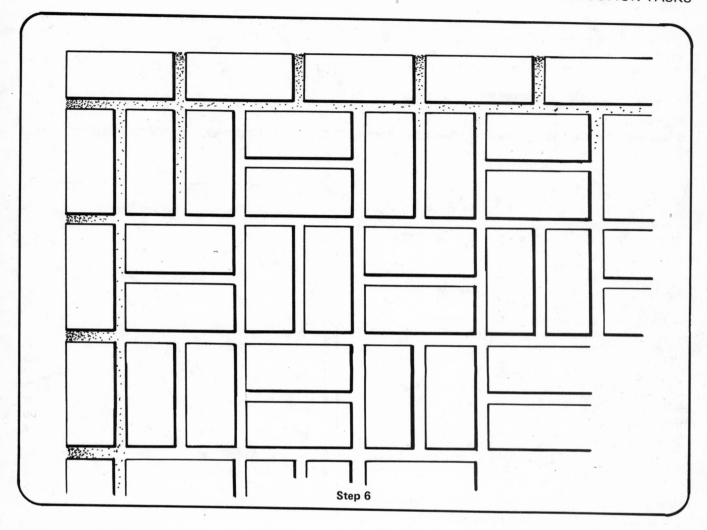

Step 6

the edge from sloughing off. You can elect either to stand the bricks on edge or to construct a redwood border. Whichever one you choose, dig a trench around the perimeter to accommodate the border plus a two-inch bed of sand.

3. Pour in the sand and tamp it down completely. When you get through, the compacted layer should be two inches thick. Dampen the sand as you tamp, but use only the fine spray adjustment on the garden hose nozzle.

4. At this stage, many people like to put down vapor barrier plastic sheets to prevent weeds from growing through their patios.

5. Put down your border for two sides of the patio only. If you are using bricks for your border, merely butt them end to end as you lay them on edge. Some people mortar the border, but you do not have to do so. If you are using redwood or another rot resistant wood for your border, just make a 2x4 frame by nailing the corners together in a butt joint. If stakes are necessary, put them on the outside and below the surface so that you can cover them.

6. Start laying the bricks from the corner, and work outward to cover the entire area. Use any pattern that you like, butting the bricks against the border and against each other as you go. If you notice any uneven places, take up the brick and either tamp in more sand or take some away to level the area.

7. After you lay all the bricks, you can install the other borders. By waiting until then, you make certain that the border will be as close as possible to the patio itself.

8. Now take handfuls of dry sand, scatter them over the patio, and sweep back and forth. The sand will go into and fill the cracks between the bricks.

9. Adjust your garden hose nozzle to its fine mist setting and spray the entire patio. The water will cause the sand to wash on down into the crack and out of sight.

10. When the surface is dry, repeat the sand treatment, sweeping and then spraying.

11. Next, mix dry cement to three parts sand. Sweep the mixture into the cracks and spray mist it down as you did the sand.

That is all there is to it. You now have yourself a patio that will last for many, many years. If you ever notice any areas that start to sink or if you spot a damaged brick, you can replace or repair such areas (even an individual brick) easily. Just take up the low or damaged bricks, add and tamp the sand underneath, and put the old bricks or their replacements back in the patio. Then, all that remains is to follow steps 8 through 11 — but just for that area. Incidentally, you can use the same technique to render a quick but beautiful brick walkway.

17. Building A Cedar Closet

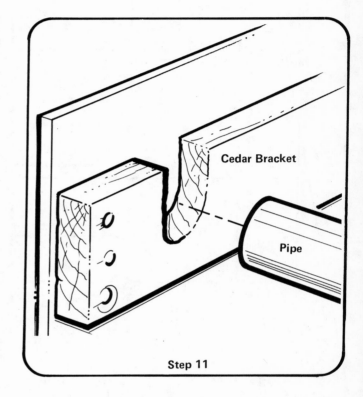

Cedar Bracket

Pipe

Step 11

THE TIME TO build a cedar closet, of course, is before you have a moth problem. The cedar aroma does not kill moths, but it does repel them. Just make sure that your clothes are moth free before you put them in the closet.

The cedar closet is an exceptionally easy project now because there are companies that package cedar planks in bundles. Each bundle contains 40 board feet of aromatic red cedar, which covers 30 square feet. The planks come in random lengths from two to eight feet, and in widths from two to four inches. All the strips are 3/8 of an inch thick.

This project involves the creation of a new closet; if you have an existing closet that you want to line with cedar, skip over steps 1 through 3, and start with the lining of the closet. By selecting a spot in which you can use existing wall, you will save quite a bit of framing. The following instructions are for doing it the hard way: building a complete closet out in the middle of the floor in either a basement or an attic. Here is how it goes.

Here Is What You Will Need
Materials
• 2x4's
• 3/4-inch plywood
• Nails
• Hollow-core door
• Cedar strips, moldings, shelves, brackets
• Finishing nails
• Weather stripping
• Pipe
• Sandpaper
Tools
• Hammer
• Saw
• Nailset
• Drill

1. Build a framework for the closet — the size will depend on the available space — out of 2x4's. Frame it as you would a house, with the studs and floor braces on 16-inch centers. Make sure that the frame is structurally sound and that it is tall enough so that any family member can walk into it without ducking.

2. Add floor, sides, and ceiling. Three-quarter inch plywood will do, but if the closet is to be in a basement or garage where moisture could be a problem, you should use exterior grade plywood.

3. For doors, you can either use more plywood or pick up used hollow-core doors at a wrecking yard. Frame around the doors for as tight a fit as possible.

4. Now you are ready to start installing the cedar strips. As mentioned before, the bundles contain boards of random lengths, and you should apply the strips in a random pattern. Start at the floor and work up, installing the strips horizontally. Start the tongue-and-

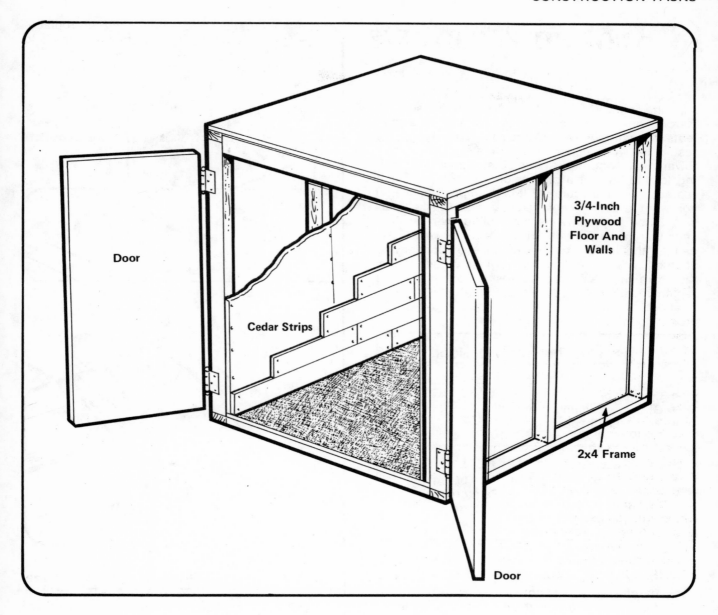

Door

Cedar Strips

3/4-Inch Plywood Floor And Walls

2x4 Frame

Door

grooved strips with a grooved edge down. Start in any corner, use 4d finishing nails, and drive the nails below the surface with a nailset. Work all the way across, and cut end pieces to fit.

5. When you get the first course all the way across, work on up, doing one course at a time. The next course will interlock, tongue in groove, with just a light tapping. You need just a minimal number of nails because of the locking properties of the boards.

6. When one wall is completely lined with cedar, do the others in the same way. Then line the door(s).

7. Next, line the floor and ceiling in the same manner.

8. Install cedar molding at corners and where floor and ceiling meet walls.

9. Weatherstrip the door(s) to contain the cedar aroma.

10. Make shelves of cedar too.

11. Install a hanger bar; a length of pipe will do nicely. Use cedar for the brackets to hold the bar, drilling a hole in one bracket and cutting a slot in the other one.

12. Paint the outside of the closet if you wish, but never put anything on the cedar that would seal in the aroma.

Although you may need to adapt this plan to suit your needs and space, the general procedures for building the cedar closet will be the same. Incidentally, if the cedar aroma starts to fade after several years, you can restore it by lightly sanding all the cedar surfaces. In addition, keep the walls dust free so that the pores in the wood stay open.

18. Broken Windows

NO MATTER what time of the year it is, all across the country kids are trying to break either Hank Aaron's home run record or Joe Namath's passing feats. Usually, however, the only breaking that results is what occurs when a stray ball heads toward your windows. At that point, rather than calling for the help of a professional glazier, why not replace the pane yourself? It is a simple job, even if you want to cut the replacement glass to size yourself. Since any hardware store or lumberyard that sells you the glass will cut it to size, however, you can fix the broken pane without ever concerning yourself with the techniques of glass cutting. Here, then, are the basic procedures for painless pane replacement.

Here Is What You Will Need

Materials

- Linseed oil
- Glazier's compound or putty
- Replacement pane
- Paint

Tools

- Work gloves
- Hammer
- Chisel
- Propane torch
- Wire brush
- Paintbrush
- Putty knife

1. Remove all the old glass. Wear gloves and be careful as you wiggle the pieces back and forth until you free them. If there are pieces which are too firmly imbedded in the putty to come loose with wiggling, take a hammer and knock them out.
2. When the glass is all out, scrape away all the old putty from the frame. You can soften dried putty with heat from a propane torch, or — if you do not have a torch — you can brush the puttied areas with linseed oil and let it soak in. The linseed oil should soften the putty sufficiently to allow you to scrape it away. As you remove the old putty, be on the lookout for little metal tabs (in a wooden frame) or spring clips (in a metal frame). The tabs (called glazier's points) and clips are important later on when installing the new pane.
3. Use a wire brush to remove the last traces of putty, and coat the wooden area where the putty was with linseed oil. Just brush it on.
4. Measure the frame across both directions,

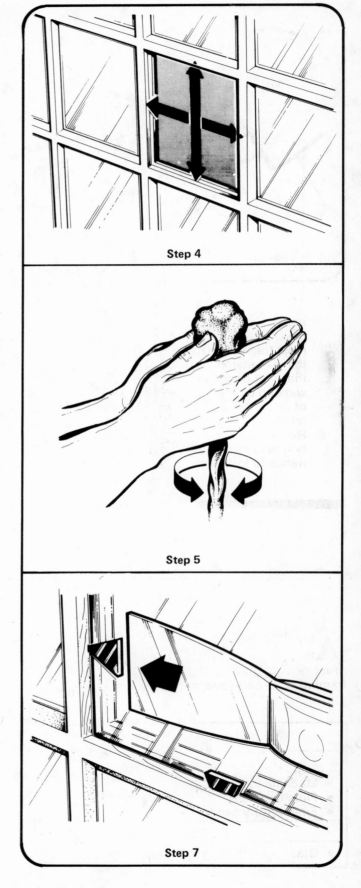

Step 4

Step 5

Step 7

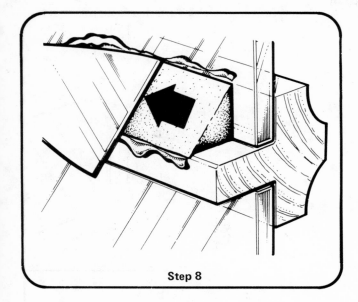

Step 8

and subtract 1/16 of an inch from each measurement to compensate for the fact that most frames are not perfect rectangles and for the expansion and contraction of the glass that will occur later on. In fact, if there is a wide lip on the frame, subtract as much as 1/8 of an inch from both the vertical and horizontal measurements.

5. Roll either glazier's compound or glazing putty (the compound is preferable) between your hands to form a string about as big around as a pencil. Press this string against the outside of the frame where the glass is to fit.

6. When the putty completely covers the lip of the frame, press the glass in place against the putty. Press firmly, and pay no attention to the fact that some of the putty is pushed out around the frame.

7. With the pane pressed firmly in position, insert the glazier's points or spring clips to hold the glass in place. The clips snap in holes, while the points must be pushed into the wood. Use your putty knife to push them in; they need not be pushed in very far. The points should go in about every six to eight inches around the frame.

8. Now you are ready to finish off the job by putting putty around the outside of the glass. The object here is to make your new bed of putty look like the others on windows around it. The best way to go about it is to place blobs of putty all around the glass against the frame, and then use your putty knife to smooth them out. If the putty knife seems to stick to the putty and pull it away from the glass and frame, dip the knife in linseed oil (or even water) to stop it from doing so.

9. Remove the excess putty from both inside and outside the frame, and put the putty back in the can.

10. Allow the putty to cure for three days, and then paint it. Paint all the way from the frame up to the glass, letting a little paint get over on the glass to seal the putty completely.

19. How To Cut Glass

ANY HARDWARE store that sells glass will cut it to your exact specifications, but if you do a great deal of glazing or if you do your own picture framing, you can save money by doing the cutting yourself. With a little practice, the right tools, and proper instructions, you can be cutting glass to size in no time. Just follow these steps.

1. Select a flat surface on which your piece of glass will fit.
2. Clean the surface of the glass.
3. Lubricate the tiny wheel on the glass cutter with machine oil or kerosene. You should also brush a film of the lubricant along the line you intend to cut.
4. Hold the glass cutter between your index and middle fingers, with your index finger resting against the flat area on the handle. Your thumb should be on the handle's bottom side. Grip the cutter firmly but not too tightly.
5. Place a straightedge along the line to be cut, and hold it firmly in place.
6. Position the cutter so that it is almost at a right angle to the glass.
7. Start your cut about 1/8 of an inch (or less) from the edge farthest from you. The stroke must be an even flowing motion toward you

Here Is What You Will Need
Materials
• Machine oil or kerosene
• Finishing nails
• Fine wet-dry sandpaper
Tools
• Glass cutter   • Straightedge

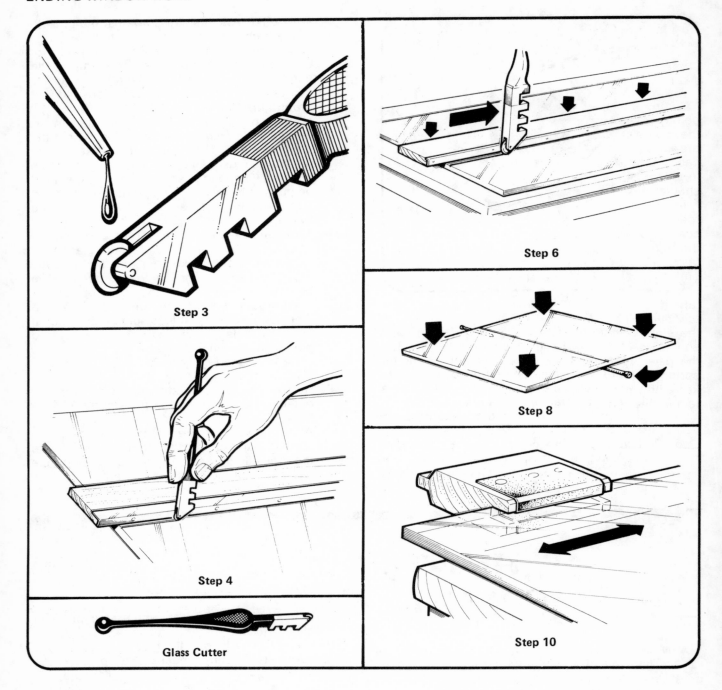

Step 3

Step 4

Glass Cutter

Step 6

Step 8

Step 10

that continues until the cutter goes off the near edge. The idea is not to cut through the glass, but merely to score it. Experiment with scrap pieces of glass to discover how much pressure you must apply to attain an even scoring. Never let up on the cutter and never go back over the line.

8. As soon as you score the glass, make the break. Glass heals, and if you wait too long it will not snap along the line. The idea in snapping is to provide a raised area under the scored line. Some people position the glass so that the cut is along the edge of the table, and then they snap the glass along the table edge. Others slip a pencil under the glass and center it on the line, while still others place finishing nails at each end of the scored line.

9. To make the snap, press down on the glass firmly on both sides of the line.

10. Smooth the newly cut edge with fine wet-dry sandpaper.

Keep the wheel of the glass cutter well lubricated between uses, and protect the wheel from anything that might nick or dull it.

20. Window Shades

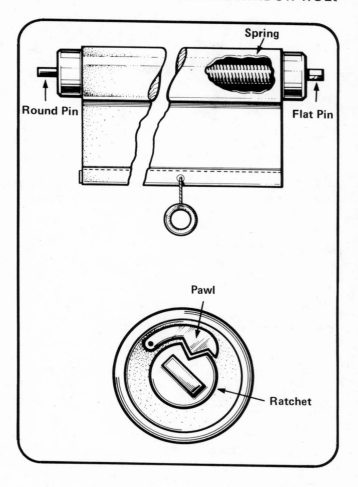

ANY SHADE THAT refuses to go up and down and stay up or down the way you want it is a pain in the neck. Some shades are so wound up that they could almost lift you off the ground, while others are so slack that they fail to go up at all. In most cases, the remedy is just a matter of adjustment; but in order to know how to adjust a shade properly, you should understand how one works.

Look at the deceptively simple looking wooden roller. One end of the roller is hollow, with a concealed coil spring in it. There is a pin at either end of the roller; the one at the spring end is flat and rotates, winding or unwinding the spring. When you pull the shade down, the spring winds tight. When you stop pulling, a littler lever — called a pawl — falls in place against a ratchet at the spring end of the roller. The pawl prevents the spring from winding the shade back up. When you wish to raise the shade, you tug down slightly on the shade, moving the pawl away from the ratchet and allowing the spring to carry the shade back up. Now that you know how a shade works, you should have no problem in figuring out what you have to do to adjust it.

Here Is What You Will Need

Materials

- Graphite or dry lubricant
- Cardboard shim
- Sandpaper

Tools

- Pliers
- Screwdriver
- Hammer

---

1. The shade that refuses to go back up as far as you would like obviously lacks sufficient spring tension. To increase the tension, first pull the shade about half way down, and then remove the flat pin from its bracket. Now roll the shade back up by hand. When you get it all the way up, put the pin back in its bracket and test the tension. If the shade still will not go up far enough, repeat this procedure until the spring tension is just right.
2. If the shade wants to pull you up with it, you must decrease the spring tension. To do so, take the flat pin out of its bracket while the shade is up, and unroll it by hand about half way; then return the pin to its bracket and see whether you have tamed your shade's spring tension sufficiently.
3. If the shade fails to stay down, you know that for some reason the pawls are not catching. Remove the metal cap from the flat-pin end of the roller; then clean and lubricate the pawl and ratchet mechanism. You can use either graphite or a dry lubricant.
4. A shade that wobbles when it goes up or down usually has a bent pin. Apply gentle pressure with a pair of pliers to straighten the pin.
5. When a shade falls out of its brackets, you must move the brackets closer together. If the brackets are mounted inside the window casing, you must add a shim behind the brackets. Usually, a cardboard shim will do. If the brackets are mounted outside the window casing, you can either reposition them or bend them slightly toward each other.
6. The shade that binds is the victim of brackets which are too close together. You can move outside brackets farther apart, but you must resort to other techniques for those mounted inside the window casing. First, try to tap the brackets lightly with a hammer. If that does not move them enough, take the metal cap and fixed round pin off the roller, and sand down the wood a bit.

21. Unsticking Windows

So YOU HAVE a window that refuses to budge. Have you checked to make sure that the window's lock is unfastened? The next most common cause of sticking is that windows often mistake a paint job for a glue job. The simple steps for getting your stuck window moving again are as follows.

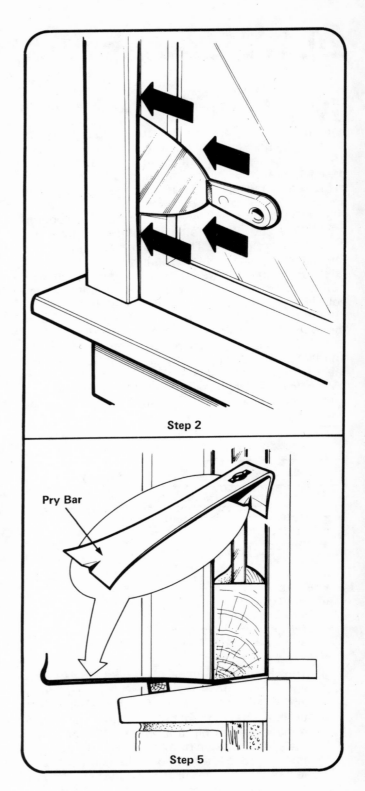

Step 2

Step 5

Here Is What You Will Need

Materials

- A candle, bar of soap, or silicone spray
- A block of wood

Tools

• Putty knife	• Sanding stick, rasp,
• Hammer	chisel, or hobby-size
• Pry bar	power tool

---

1. Examine all around the frame to see where the paint has sealed the sash to the stop. Usually the seal is complete all the way around.
2. Insert a sharp knife — a medium wide putty knife is good — in where the crack should be. If you cannot get the knife in the crack, tap the knife's handle with a hammer. If the window was painted both inside and out, cut the seals on both sides.
3. With the seal cut all around and the window still not moving, check the tracks above. If the paint is too thick in the track — preventing the window from sliding — remove the excess with a sanding stick, rasp, chisel, or a hobby-size power tool.
4. Lubricate the track. Rub a candle or a bar of soap along the track, or shoot some silicone spray on it.
5. If the window still refuses to budge, use a small flat pry bar on it. Pry from the outside if possible, and place a scrap block of wood under the bar.
6. Next, tap the frame away from window with a hammer and a 2x4. Even the slightest movement may be enough to free the sash.
7. If at first you fail, pry, pry again.

When you finally get it open, give some thought as to how you can paint it the next time without gluing it shut. Here is one easy way to prevent future window misery.

1. Raise the window about four inches.
2. Paint.
3. When you finish painting — but before the paint hardens — move the window up and down. The seal will not form, the window will not stick, and your temper will not flare.

22. Replacing A Sash Cord In A Window

MOST WOOD WINDOWS are operated by a system of ropes, pulleys, and weights hidden inside the wall. The ropes are attached to the sash — a fancy name for a frame that moves up and down — and then go along the tracks in which the window moves, finally extending up to a pulley at the top of the track. The rope passes over the pulley and then is tied to the weight, which acts as a counterbalance so that the window stays at the level to which you raise it. Ropes being what they are, though, they become frayed and then break after many years of service. When a rope breaks, of course, the weight falls down to the bottom inside the window frame. It also means that the window no longer stays where you want it to. Here is the step-by-step cure.

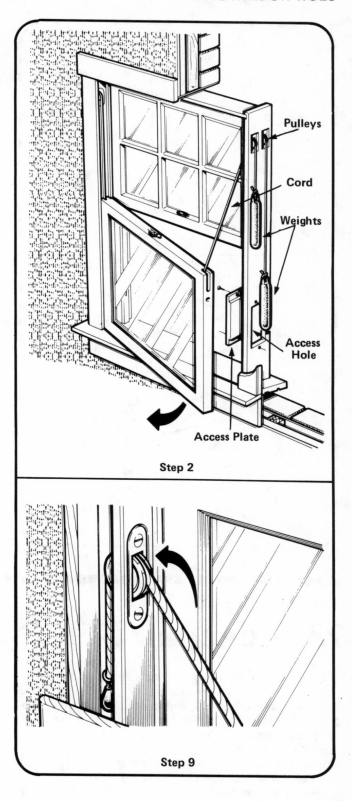

Step 2

Step 9

Here Is What You Will Need
Materials
• Replacement cord or sash chain
Tools
• Razor blade   • Hammer
• Putty knife or flat bar   • Screwdriver

1. Remove the stop molding from the side where the broken cord is, but do it carefully or the molding might break. If there is a paint seal along the molding strip, cut it with a sharp razor blade. Then use a wide putty knife blade or a flat bar to pry the stop molding out.
2. With the stop strip out of the way, angle the sash out of the frame to expose the pocket in which the rope is knotted.
3. Untie the knot and remove the rope from the sash frame.
4. Ease the sash out of its track on the other side, and untie the rope there. Knot this rope to prevent it from disappearing inside the wall.
5. Set the entire sash out of the way.
6. Look for the access plate. You should be able to locate it in the lower part of the track, but it may have been painted over several times. If it is hidden by the paint, tap the track with a hammer until you reveal the outline. Then cut along the line with a sharp razor blade. Once

you locate the access plate, find the screws holding it in place and remove them. (Some older windows do not have access plates; if that is what you find, you must pry the entire frame out to get at the weight inside.)

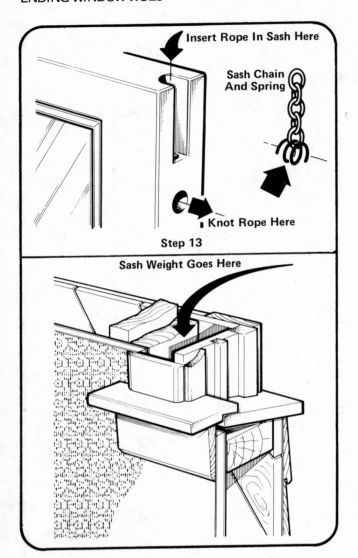

Insert Rope In Sash Here

Sash Chain And Spring

Knot Rope Here

Step 13

Sash Weight Goes Here

7. With the access plate removed, you will see the weight. Lift it out.
8. Untie the old cord and use the two broken pieces to measure the replacement cord.
9. Weight the new cord with something small enough to be fed in over the pulley, and feed the cord in.
10. When the cord reaches the access plate opening, pull the cord through the opening.
11. Remove the small weight you had put on earlier, and knot the cord to the regular window weight. Put the weight back into the access hole.
12. Tie the cord opposite the one you have been working with to the sash, and reinsert the sash in the track.
13. Tie the new cord to the sash, and then hold the sash against the parting strip as you raise it to the top.
14. Inspect the weight at the access hole. It should be about three inches above the sill as you hold the sash at the top. If it is not, adjust the rope at the sash.
15. When you get the weight properly adjusted, replace the access plate and the stop strip.

If the broken cord is in the upper sash of a double hung window, you follow the same procedure except that you must remove the parting strip after removing the lower sash in order to be able to get at the upper sash.

That is all there is to it. As long as you are replacing the cord, though, you should think about replacing it with a sash chain that will not wear out or break or stretch as rope does. The chain comes with a hook that you fasten to the weight and with a spring that you attach to the sash.

23. Venetian Blinds

EVEN IF YOU have trouble adjusting Venetian blinds, you will be pleasantly surprised to find that repairing them is a relatively simple task. The two major Venetian blind problems involve the webbing and cords getting broken or frayed. Since replacements are readily available at hardware stores and are easy to install, most Venetian blind problems are really not major ones at all.

First, consider the cords. As you can see, there are two sets of cords. One set, called the "lift cord system," raises and lowers the blinds. The other, called the "tilt cord system," changes the amount of light coming in by altering the angle at which the blinds tilt. Most replacement kits come with both sets of cords, and it is a good idea to change both cord sets.

Here Is What You Will Need
Materials
• Replacement webbing
• Replacement cord
• Silicone spray
Tools
• Scissors
• Pliers

1. Make a sketch of your own Venetian blinds to help you get the cords back in their proper places.
2. Open the blinds.
3. Start with the lift cord, and examine the knots under the tape at the bottom of the bottom rail.

The tape may be stapled on, or — if the rail is metal — it may be held in place by a clamp. Untie the knots and remove the cord by pulling on the loop as if you were going to raise the blinds.

4. Now, starting at the side next to the tilt cord, feed the new cord through from the bottom up through the openings in the slats. Be sure that the cord goes on alternate sides of the ladder tapes (webbing) as you feed it in.
5. Go up to and over the pulley at the top.
6. Then, run the cord along the top until you reach the mechanism at the other side. Thread the cord under the first and over the second pulley.
7. Bring the cord down through the lift cord locking device.
8. Now, go back and knot the other end, and then pull the cord until the knot is nearly against the bottom rail.
9. Feed the unknotted end back into the top rail, over the other pulley (or pulleys), and down through the slats in the same manner as you did on the other side.
10. When you get the cord all the way through, adjust it to set the size of the loop. Then snip off the excess from the unknotted end before tying the knot.
11. Install the equalizer and adjust it.
12. Now you are ready to replace the tilt cord. Just run it over the pulley and back down. When you get it positioned, add the pulls and knot the cord.

To replace the ladder tapes (webbing), just follow these steps.

1. Remove the blinds from the window and move them to the floor or a large table.
2. Remove the bottom rail clamp (or staples) to expose the knots on the two ends of cord under each tape.
3. Untie the knots and pull the cords up through the slots all the way up to the top of the blinds.
4. The slats will now come out of the tapes. Remove them.
5. Unhook the top of the tape from the tilt tube by removing the hook.
6. Hook in the new tape at the tilt tube.
7. Insert the slats in the new tapes.
8. Weave the cord back down through the slots, making sure that the cord goes on alternate sides of the ladder tapes.
9. Knot the cord under the bottom rail.
10. Reattach either the clamp or staples.

About the only other thing that you can do to Venetian blinds is keep the gears and pulleys — which can pick up lint and fail to work as they should — clean and well lubricated. If you think that the gears and pulleys need lubrication, apply a silicone spray.

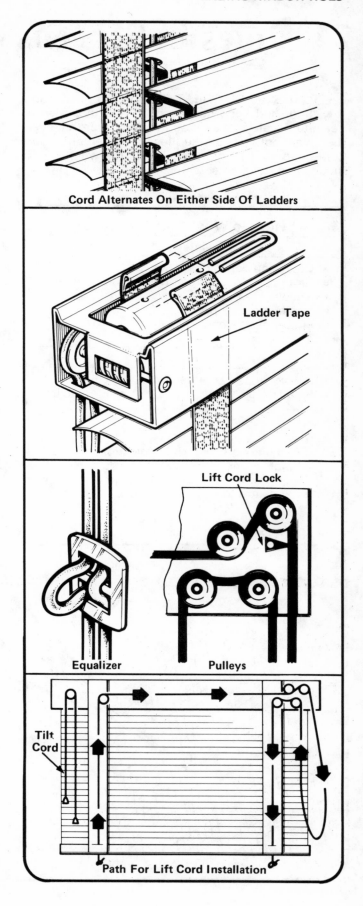

Cord Alternates On Either Side Of Ladders

Ladder Tape

Lift Cord Lock

Equalizer   Pulleys

Tilt Cord

Path For Lift Cord Installation

24. Holes In Screens

SCREENS ARE GREAT when they let in air and light and keep out the bugs, but they always seem to develop holes. You then discover that even the tiniest hole lets all the flies in the neighborhood come into your home. Patching is the way to cure most small holes in screens.

Here Is What You Will Need

Materials

- Clear nail polish or shellac
- Strand of wire or strong nylon thread
- Needle
- Screening material
- Fiberglass patch
- Aluminum foil

Tools

- Ice pick (or any pointed tool)
- Small brush
- Scissors
- Electric iron

---

1. For a tiny hole, use an ice pick (or any pointed object) to move as many strands as possible back toward the hole. If none of the wire strands are torn, you can close the hole back up and make the screen as good as new.

2. Unfortunately, there generally are a few torn strands. If that is the case, you can close up the hole by painting over it with either clear nail polish or shellac. Brush on a coat and let it dry; then keep applying more coats until the hole is sealed over.

3. If the hole is a long rip, you may need to stitch it back together. Once again, close the gap with your sharp pointed tool, and then use a strand of wire or a strong nylon thread to bind up the wound. A needle will make the sewing go quicker, and a few coats of clear polish or shellac will prevent the stitching from unravelling.

4. For a bigger hole, cut a square — at least two inches bigger than the hole all the way around — from a separate piece of screening.

5. Pick away at the strands of wire on all four sides to leave about a half inch of unwoven strands sticking out.

6. Fold the unwoven edges forward, and insert these wires into the screen over the hole.

7. Fold the unwoven strands toward the center of the patch on the other side, and stitch around the patch with a needle and nylon thread. Once again, a few coats of polish or shellac will seal the patch and stitching in place.

8. Repair fiberglass screening by laying a patch of the material over the hole and running a hot iron around the edges. The heat melts and fuses the patch in place. Be sure to place a scrap of foil over the screen itself to prevent the iron from touching it.

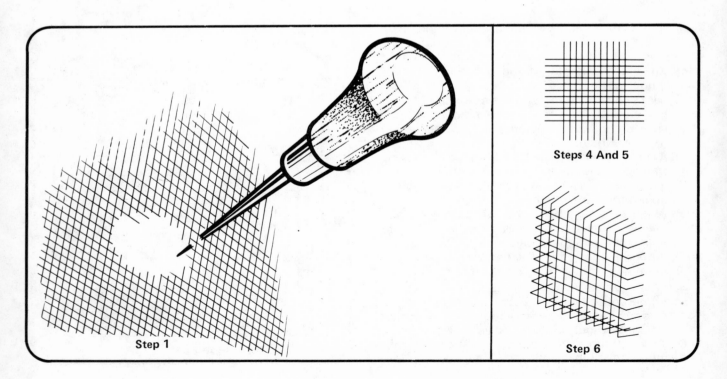

Step 1

Steps 4 And 5

Step 6

25. Screen Replacement

WHEN YOU SPOT a hole in your screen door or window screen that is too large to patch, you should start thinking about replacing the entire screen. In most cases you can buy screen cut to the proper width for standard doors or windows, and the actual installation of the new screen is not difficult — provided, of course, that the frame is still in good shape. The secret to any good rescreening job is knowing how to get the screen taut.

First, consider replacing a screen in a wooden frame.

Here Is What You Will Need

Materials
- Replacement screening
- Staples

Tools
- Putty knife
- Pliers
- C-clamps or metal weight
- 2x4's
- Work table or saw horses
- Staple gun
- Scissors or wire cutters
- Splining tool

---

1. Remove the molding from around the edges of the screen, but be sure to pry carefully so as not to damage the molding. Leave the brads in the molding.
2. Remove the old screen which is either tacked or stapled in place. Be sure to remove all the old tacks or staples.
3. Now you need to bow or arch the frame. Use either the weighted method or the clamp method.
4. With the frame arched, use a staple gun to attach the screen at each end; stapling is much quicker than tacking. Staple every two or three inches all along the top and bottom of the frame.
5. When the screen is fastened securely to the frame, release the weights or clamps. The screen should be very taut as the frame straightens out.
6. Trim off any excess screening, reinstall the molding, and the job is done.

With aluminum frames, you must examine the spline to see that it is still in good shape. The spline is a sort of rubber rope that holds the screening in the track all around the frame.

1. Remove the old screen and spline.
2. Position the new screen (about as wide as the entire frame) over the frame, aligning one end and one side of the screen with the corresponding edges of the frame.
3. For best results, you should have a splining wheel to insert the new screen in the frame. Use the end with the convex roller to push the screening down into the groove, working on the end and side you just aligned with the frame. Then do the remaining two sides. The screen should be quite taut.
4. Now you are ready to reinstall the spline. Use the other end of the tool — the concave wheel — to work the spline into the track all the way around the frame.
5. Trim off any excess screening, and your aluminum screen is as good as new.

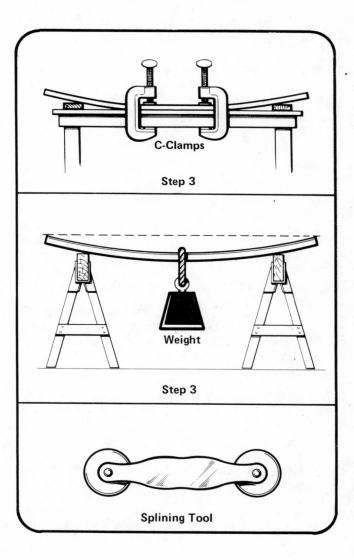

C-Clamps

Step 3

Weight

Step 3

Splining Tool

26. Weather~ stripping Windows

IF YOUR WINDOWS are letting cold air in during the winter and cold air out during the summer, you are losing a great deal of money to the utility companies. It will pay you to check your windows' weatherstripping for air tightness. If you can reach the windows from the outside, direct the air flow from a hand-held hair dryer all around the frame as someone inside follows your movements and marks the bad spots.

If your windows have no weatherstipping at all, you can install it without much trouble. You can use the spring metal type or the pressure sensitive adhesive backed type or the vinyl tubular type. All are easy to install. The following instructions are for the vinyl tubular type of weatherstripping.

Here Is What You Will Need
Materials
• Vinyl tubular weatherstripping
• Brads
Tools
• Hand-held hair dryer
• Ladder
• Hammer

1. Measure all cracks that could allow the passage of air to determine how much material you need. If you have a number of windows, it is often less expensive to buy weatherstripping in bulk than to buy individual rolls for each window.
2. Since you attach vinyl tubular weatherstripping from the outside of each window, you can save yourself several trips up and down the ladder by cutting the strips before you start climbing.
3. Nail the strips in place with brads placed about every two inches.
4. Install the vertical strips first, attaching them to the parting strips of the lower sash. The tubular portion should press lightly against the sash.
5. Next, attach a strip to the outside of the lower sash bottom rail in such a way that the tubular portion will rest snugly against the outside sill when the window is down.
6. Attach the strip for the upper sash bottom rail

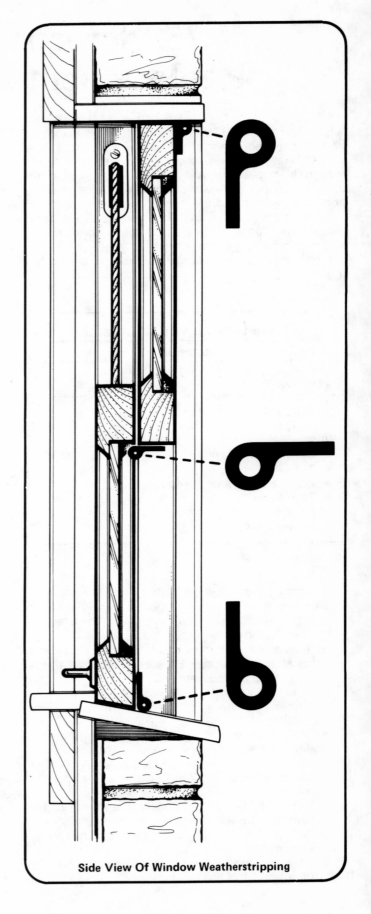

Side View Of Window Weatherstripping

Step 3

Steps 4-7

with the tubular part facing in toward the lower sash and positioned so that it will press lightly against the lower sash when it is down.

7. If the upper sash is movable, you must attach strips to the blind stop and a strip across the top of the yoke.

Vinyl tubular weatherstripping is very easy to install if the windows are easily accessible from the outside. It is also very effective when installed properly, and it will last a long time. The big disadvantage to such weatherstripping is the fact that it cannot be painted; paint often makes vinyl tubular weatherstripping stiff and reduces its effectiveness. In addition, the vinyl tubular type is probably the least attractive kind of weatherstripping.

27. Installing And Adjusting Drapery Hardware

ALL TOO OFTEN, when you try to hang curtain or drapery rods yourself, they wind up sagging at one end. Then, if you fail to remedy the situation, the whole unit falls off when you open the drapes. This sad scene need not occur, though, if you learn how to hang drapery rods properly.

1. If you plan to attach the rods to a wooden window frame, use the frame as a guide for getting the curtain rods up straight. You can position the end brackets at the outside corners of the frame and install a center brace (if needed) at the frame's center. Make sure that

Here Is What You Will Need
Materials
• Drapery or curtain rods
• Cardboard
• Plastic wall anchors or expansion bolts
Tools
• Screwdriver
• Measuring tape
• Drill

the screws you use to hang your drapery or curtain rods are at least 3/4 of an inch long.

2. If there is no window frame to use as a guide or if you want the drapes out away from the actual opening, you must measure out laterally from the top of the opening and up toward the ceiling from the corners of the window opening. Make a cardboard template that fits against the corner of the window opening to indicate where the bracket goes. Place the

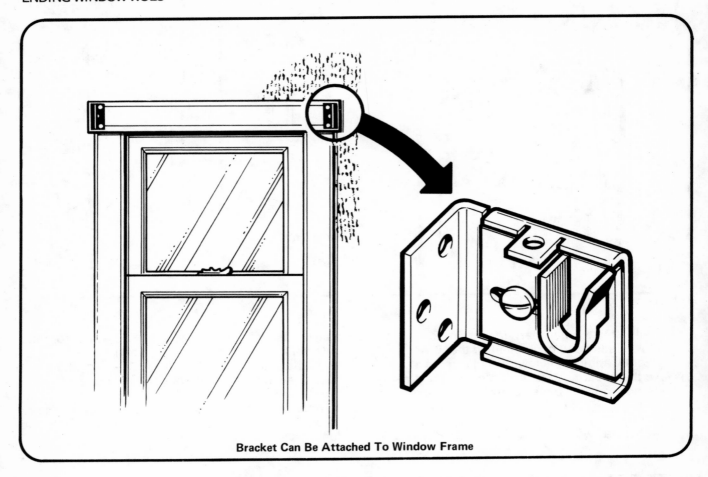

Bracket Can Be Attached To Window Frame

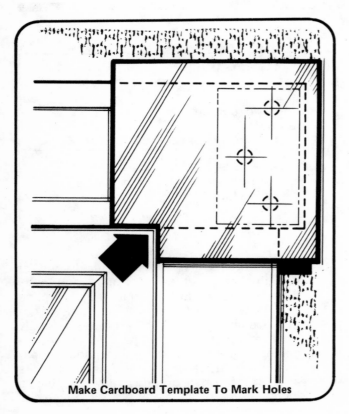

Make Cardboard Template To Mark Holes

bracket over the cardboard, make dots where the screws will go, and punch out the holes where you marked the dots. Then just reverse the template and you are all set to mark the holes on the other side of the window.

3. Drill pilot holes at the spots you marked on the wall. If you have hollow wall construction, use either plastic wall anchors or expansion bolts. If there are studs where you want to hang the brackets, use screws that are long enough to go through the sheetrock and into the studs.

4. Attach as many center support brackets as are needed to prevent the rods from ever sagging.

5. Adjust the end brackets and center supports so that they are as far out from the wall as you desire. When all the brackets are in place, place the rod in the brackets and adjust it to the proper length.

Naturally, you want to rig up the traverse rod so that when you hang the drapes and pull them, both panels will open at the same time and go all the way to the ends. Similarly, when you close them, you want the rod to carry both drapery panels back to the center and not leave a six-inch gap in the middle. Here is how to adjust a traverse rod to draw your drapes properly.

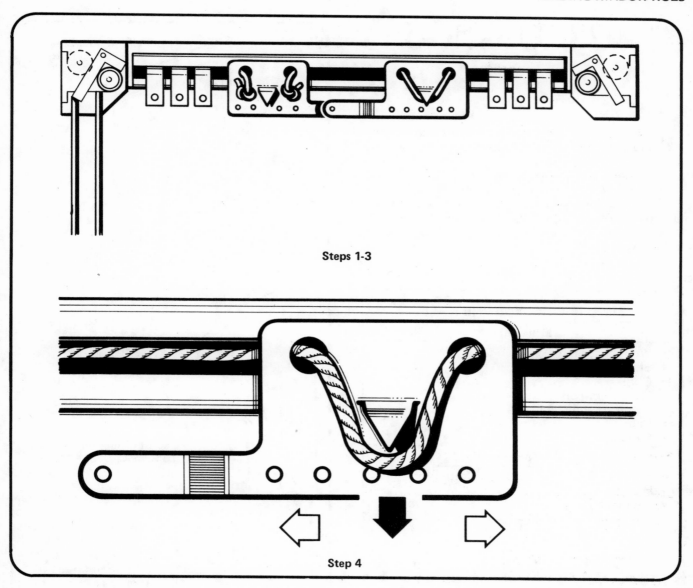

Steps 1-3

Step 4

1. Lift the rod out of the brackets and lay it on the floor face down.
2. Pull the outer cord at the side to bring the master slide on that side all the way over as far as it will go toward the cord.
3. While holding the cord tight, manually slide the other master slide over as far as it will go.
4. On this second slide you will notice a loop of cord running through two holes. Lift up the loop and hook it over the lug just below it.
5. Now replace the rod back in the brackets and lock it in place. Insert drapery hooks through the plastic slides, and remove any extra slides at the end gate.
6. When you pull the drapes open and closed, you will see both sides moving at the same time and at the same rate and hanging from drapery rods that are not going to fall down.

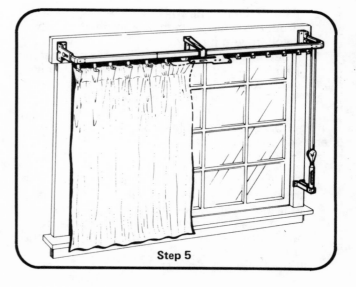

Step 5

28. Unsticking A Door

FEW THINGS ARE more annoying than a sticking door. When you finally do get it open, you cannot get it closed again. Unfortunately, most homeowners grab a plane and start shaving away some wood. Although frequently there is no alternative, planing down your door should be a measure of last resort. The first thing to do is to inspect the door to see what is causing it to stick. Here are the steps to follow.

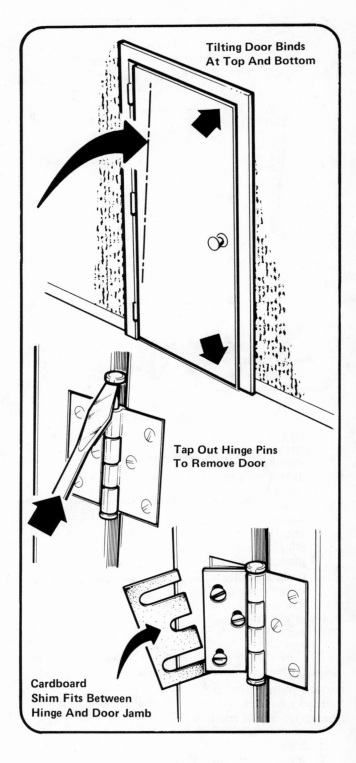

Tilting Door Binds At Top And Bottom

Tap Out Hinge Pins To Remove Door

Cardboard Shim Fits Between Hinge And Door Jamb

Here Is What You Will Need

Materials

- Wooden toothpicks
- Shim (shirtboard)
- Chalk
- Penetrating oil
- Large wooden box
- Paint
- Padded 2x4

Tools

- Plane
- Hammer
- C-clamp
- Carpenter's square
- Screwdriver

1. Close the door, if possible, and examine the edge opposite the sticking place. If you see a large gap there, the problem may well be in the hinges.
2. If there are no gaps — or very few — anywhere around the door, then the wood probably is swollen with moisture.
3. Open the door and place a square against the frame to see whether it is out of line. If that is what you find, then the house has probably settled and forced the frame out of shape.

If your diagnosis is a hinge problem, here are the steps you should follow.

1. Check all the screws in the hinges to see that they are tight. If any continue to turn, it means that the screw holes have become enlarged. Insert pieces of toothpick into the hole, reinsert the screw, and you should find that the screw bites securely.
2. If the hinges are not loose, they may need to be shimmed up or recessed to relieve the sticking problem. Look at the door to see where it is rubbing. A door that sticks toward the top of the latch side and down at the bottom against the floor is a door that is tilted out at the top. Bring the bottom hinge out a bit, and you may solve the problem. Try cutting a piece of shirtboard to fit between the bottom

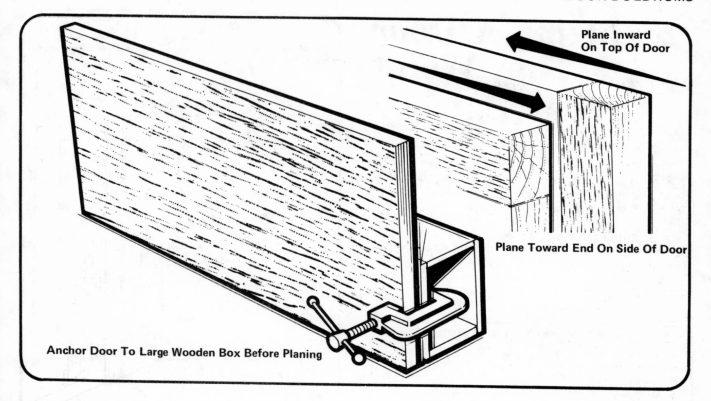

Plane Inward On Top Of Door

Plane Toward End On Side Of Door

Anchor Door To Large Wooden Box Before Planing

hinge and the door jamb; then slot the cardboard so that you only have to loosen the screws to insert the shim. Retighten and see if the shim cures the problem. If it helps but does not eliminate the problem, add another thickness of shim. Naturally, if the door sticks toward the bottom of the latch side, you should shim out the top hinge. If the door sticks along the latch side and there is no gap along the hinge side, you can sometimes cut a deeper mortice in the jamb to set the hinge deeper and move the door away from the frame on the latch side. Similarly, if the door sticks at the top and there is more than 1/4-inch space at the bottom, you could consider moving the hinges down a bit.

When you determine that the door is swollen with excess moisture and is just too big for the frame, then you have to remove some of the wood. Here is how to go about planing down your door.

1. Mark the sticking places with a piece of chalk.
2. If the door binds along the top, you can plane without first removing the door from its hinges. Just make sure that when planing the top (or bottom) you cut from the edge toward the center; otherwise, the plane could catch the side rail and rip off a piece of the door.
3. If the door sticks along the side, remove the door by tapping out the hinge pins. Always remove the bottom pin first. Place the tip of a

screwdriver under the pin, and tap the screwdriver handle with a hammer. If the pin refuses to budge, insert a nail into the bottom of the hinge and tap upward. Penetrating oil can also help loosen stubborn pins.
4. Once the pins are out, the door is free.
5. Anchor the door to a large wooden box with a C-clamp to help keep the door upright during planing.
6. When planing the side, always cut toward the edges. Keep in mind that the latch side is slightly beveled to prevent the edge from striking the frame when you close the door. Therefore, try to plane the hinge side instead; but if you must plane the latch side, make sure your planing retains this bevel.
7. After you plane all the chalked spots, put the door back on the hinges and give it a trial run. If it still sticks, plane off some more wood.
8. Once you get the door to open and close easily, paint the newly planed areas and any other bare wood to prevent future moisture problems.

If the door frame is out of line from the house having settled, there is little you can do. Try placing a padded 2x 4 against the frame, and then hitting the padded board several times with a hammer. Sometimes you can reset the frame just enough to allow the door to pass without sticking. If that does not work, try moving the hinges or planing off enough wood to make the door fit the misaligned frame.

29. Fixing A Door That Won't Stay Latched

I F YOU HAVE ever been in a room when all of a sudden, "Surprise!" the door swings open of its own accord, you know how embarrassing this can be. And if your front door has a similar latch problem, you might sometime find that all your valuables have departed for regions unknown. Assuming that the latch difficulty is not symptomatic of a serious door problem, you can fix it easily. Here are the steps to take.

Here Is What You Will Need
Materials
• Shim (shirtboard)
• Chalk
• Wooden toothpicks
• Wood glue
• Wood putty
• Lubricant
Tools
• Screwdriver
• File
• Utility knife
• Wood chisel
• Drill

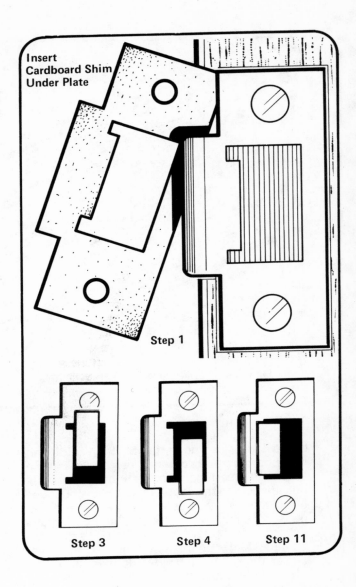

Insert Cardboard Shim Under Plate

Step 1

Step 3   Step 4   Step 11

1. Close the door and examine it carefully. See if the bolt comes far enough out of the door to press against the striker plate. If not, you must remove the striker plate and insert a shim behind it. One or two thicknesses of shirtboard should move the plate close enough to the door for the bolt to catch.

2. If the bolt and the striker plate are sufficiently close, then there must be a misalignment. To see where the trouble is, open the door and rub chalk over the bolt's edge. Now close the door, and then reopen it and note where the chalk has rubbed against the striker plate.

3. If there is chalk above the opening in the striker plate, you must move the striker plate up. When the misalignment is only slight, however, you may be able to correct the problem by merely filing off the corner of the latch bolt.

4. If there is chalk below the hole, you must lower the striker plate or file off the bolt.

5. To move the striker plate, remove the screws and pry the plate out of its mortice.

6. Move the plate to its new location and draw a line around it. Cut along the line with a utility knife to the depth of the rest of the mortice.

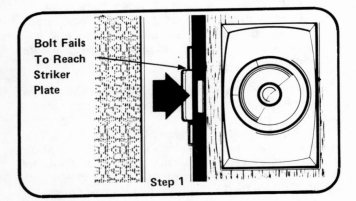

Bolt Fails To Reach Striker Plate

Step 1

7. Use a wood chisel to cut the mortice down to that line.
8. Fill the old screw holes with pieces of wooden toothpicks dipped into wood glue, and cut them off even with the surface.
9. Drill pilot holes for screws in the new mortice, and replace the striker plate.
10. Fill in the gap, if noticeable, with wood putty.
11. If the chalk mark goes right toward the middle of the hole, then the plate is either too deep or too shallow in the mortice to engage the bolt.

If you have a spring-catch type latch on the door, then the striker plate must be too deep. If you have a deadbolt, the chalk line will show which side of the hole the bolt is hitting. Move the striker plate accordingly; then remortice and fill as before.

12. If the problem is in the lockset, meaning that the latch does not come out of the door as far as it was intended to do, try lubricating the latch. If that is no help, you probably will have to replace the lock.

30. Making Your Home More Secure

A RESIDENTIAL burglary occurs somewhere in the United States every thirteen seconds. By making your home more secure, you might cause the local thief to try another house down the block. While there is no way to make your home absolutely burglar-proof, you can make it somewhat less vulnerable. Here are some steps you can take to deter a burglar from your home.

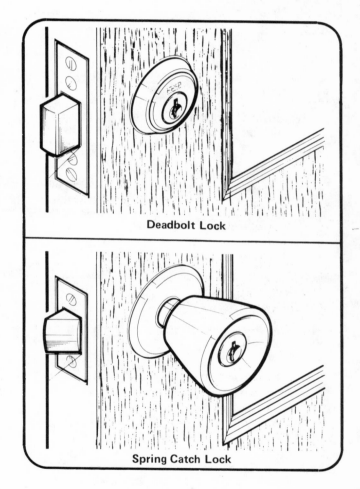

Deadbolt Lock

Spring Catch Lock

Here Is What You Will Need
Materials
• Deadbolt locks
• Wide-angle viewer
• Nails
• Rods or pipes
• Extra window locks
• Exterior lighting
Tools
• Screwdriver
• Hammer

1. Install a deadbolt lock on every outside door. Many doors have the convenient spring-catch locks, but these locks are also convenient for the burglar. Anyone can open a spring-catch lock with nothing more than a plastic credit card. Your lock dealer will be happy to show you how to install deadbolts, and the job itself is usually a snap.
2. Install a wide-angle viewer on each outside door to permit members of your family to see who is calling without opening the door.
3. Prepare a rod or pipe to fit in the track of every sliding glass door. In addition, if the sliding door is of the type that can be lifted out of its track for repair, install three sheet metal screws in the track above the door at its closed position. If you should ever need to lift the door out, slide it open and remove the screws.
4. Provide an auxiliary lock or pin on windows so

Step 3

Step 4

that no one can merely break the glass, reach in, and open the window.

5. Check to see if shrubbery hides doors and windows from view. Such shrubs might allow an intruder to break in without being seen.

6. When you leave — even for just a few moments — lock up.

7. Always keep your garage locked.

8. Avoid leaving tools and ladders outside where a burglar could use them to his advantage.

9. When you are outside doing yard work, keep all doors locked.

10. Keep all gates to your yard locked.

11. Provide good lighting all around your home, and keep it on all night long. Burglars seldom like to be seen on the job.

12. Check the Crime Prevention Department of your local police department and ask about a property identification program. This program enables you to borrow an electric engraver to mark your valuables. You should, of course, always maintain a record of the serial numbers from your appliances, guns, TV sets, and stereos.

31. How To Install A New Lock

MANY PEOPLE are upgrading the locks around their homes. One of the best moves you can make is to put a deadbolt cylinder lock above the present knob. This additional lock may increase the amount of time it takes you to get into your house, but it provides important extra protection. Installation is not complicated. Here is how you can put in a new lock in very little time.

1. The new lock will come with a paper template that fits around the door's edge to permit you to mark the two holes. One hole goes through the side of the door for the cylinder, while the other goes into the edge of the door for the bolt.

2. Use a hand brace and an expansion bit to drill

Here Is What You Will Need
Materials
• New lock
• Large escutcheon plate
Tools
• Drill
• Wood chisel
• Screwdriver

a hole of the size specified for your lock, but be careful not to damage the veneer on the sides of the door. When you see the point of the drill coming through, stop and go around to the other side to finish the hole. You avoid splintering the door that way.

3. Drill a hole of the appropriate size for the bolt into the edge of the door. Be sure to drill at a right angle to the door, and keep drilling until

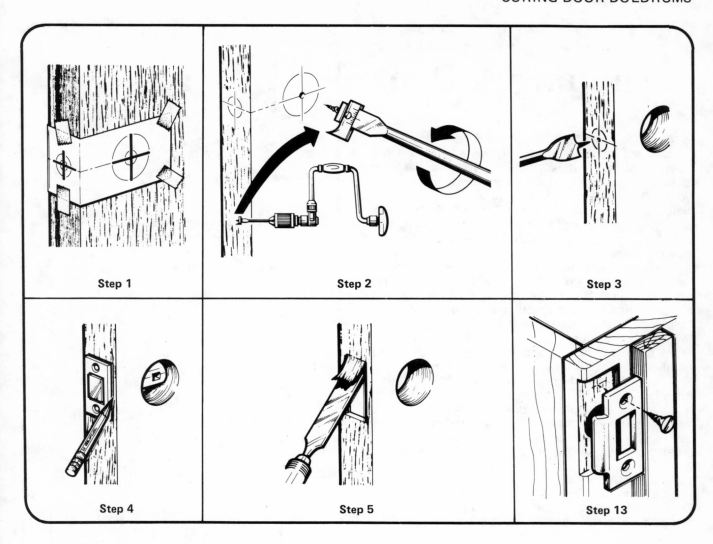

Step 1   Step 2   Step 3

Step 4   Step 5   Step 13

you reach the cylinder hole.

4. Insert the bolt into its hole, and mark the area for the plate.
5. Remove the bolt, and mortice out for the plate to make it fit flush. Use a wood chisel to cut the mortice.

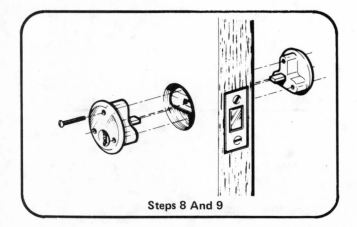

Steps 8 And 9

6. Insert the plate in the mortice, and drill pilot holes for the screws.
7. Install the screws to secure the bolt in place.
8. Insert the outside cylinder so that the stems or the connecting bar fits into the bolt assembly.
9. Attach the interior cylinder and secure it with screws.
10. Locate the proper spot for the strike plate on the jamb.
11. Drill the required size hole.
12. Use the plate as a pattern, mark the jamb for morticing, and cut the mortice.
13. Install the plate with screws so that it fits flush with the jamb.

If you just want to replace an existing lock with a better one, look for a new lock that will fit in the existing holes. Sometimes you will not be able to cover the old holes with the new lock, but you can generally cover them with a large decorative escutcheon plate. If need be, you can usually enlarge mortices and holes to accommodate the new lock.

32. Weather-stripping A Door

I F YOU CAN feel little gusts of cold air coming in around the door during the winter, or if you have a door that hums a note or two when the wind blows, you better check your weatherstripping. All of your outside doors should be airtight, and the same holds true for doors to unheated basements, garages, and attics. Proper weatherstripping will save you money during both heating and air conditioning seasons.

There is really only one way to check a door's weatherstripping. You must direct a strong wind against it to see if air comes through. The best way is to use a hand-held hair dryer outside and have a helper inside. As you move the stream of air along the door, have your helper hold his hand against the crack between the door and the frame and mark with chalk any places where he feels air coming through. Take your time and make a thorough check. If you have just a few minor air leaks, you may be able to fix your present weatherstripping. Most doors have a springy metal strip that fits against the door jamb all the way around except at the bottom. See if you can bend the metal flange out a little more to stop any leaks.

If the existing weatherstripping is not doing its job, you can add additional protection outside the jamb. The easiest type to install is the foam rubber strip that has a pressure sensitive adhesive backing.

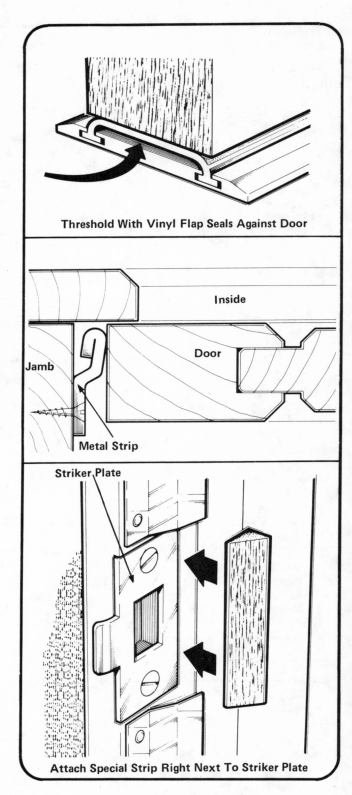

Threshold With Vinyl Flap Seals Against Door

Inside

Jamb

Door

Metal Strip

Striker Plate

Attach Special Strip Right Next To Striker Plate

Here Is What You Will Need
Materials

- Chalk
- Foam rubber weatherstripping
- Cleaning solvent
- Nails
- Replacement threshold
- Metal strip weatherstripping
- Brads

Tools

- Hand-held hair dryer
- Scissors
- Hammer
- Screwdriver
- Hacksaw
- Tin snips

1. Unroll enough of the stripping to go around the top and both sides of the door.
2. Cut the strip into pieces to fit each of these three sections.
3. Open the door and clean the face of the jamb.
4. Let the wood dry.
5. Peel the backing off of the strip and apply the foam rubber to the face of the jamb so that the door closes against it.
6. Recheck the door for leaks.

If the leak is at the bottom of the door, you may need a new threshold. If the threshold is the problem, you can put a new one in easily.

Aluminum thresholds with vinyl flaps that seal against the door come packed with all the screws and instructions. You can cut the aluminum to size with a hacksaw.

There are also strips of both wood and metal that you attach to the jamb with nails. You fit these strips so that they will be snug against the closed door, and then you nail them in place.

1. Unroll enough of the thin metal weatherstripping for the hinge side of the door. Use tin snips to cut the strip to the exact size required.

2. Place the strip against the jamb so that the springy part that flares out faces to the outside and is almost against the stop.
3. Nail the strip in place by driving tiny brads in about every two inches. Tack the strip at top and bottom first to make sure that it goes on straight.
4. For the latch side, attach the folded strip that comes with the roll right next to the striker plate. If there is no such strip with the roll, you can purchase one separately.
5. Cut the strips to fit above and below, and nail them in place.
6. Cut the strip for the top, miter it at each end, and then nail it in place.

33. Garage Doors

MOST GARAGES built during the past twenty years have overhead doors. There are two basic types of overhead garage doors, the roll-up and the swing-up. Both types rely on a heavy spring (or springs) for their ease of operation. When the door slows down or becomes difficult to raise or lower, most people try to remedy the problem by adjusting the spring. In most cases, however, the spring is not the culprit. Here are the steps to a smoother upswing in your garage door.

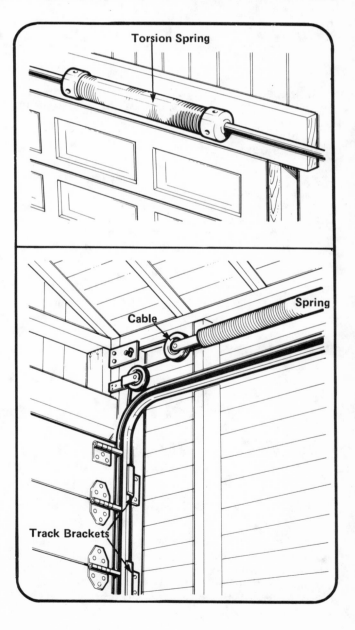
Torsion Spring

Cable   Spring

Track Brackets

Here Is What You Will Need

Materials

- Cleaning solvent
- Machine oil or spray lubricant
- Grease
- Paint

Tools

- Carpenter's level
- Adjustable wrench
- Hammer
- Screwdriver

1. Check the vertical tracks with a level to be sure they are plumb. If they are not, adjust the tracks by loosening the brackets which hold the tracks to the wall, and then tap them back in alignment.
2. Check all tracks for any crimps. If you find any, straighten them out.
3. Be sure the tracks are positioned so that the rollers do not bind in the track.

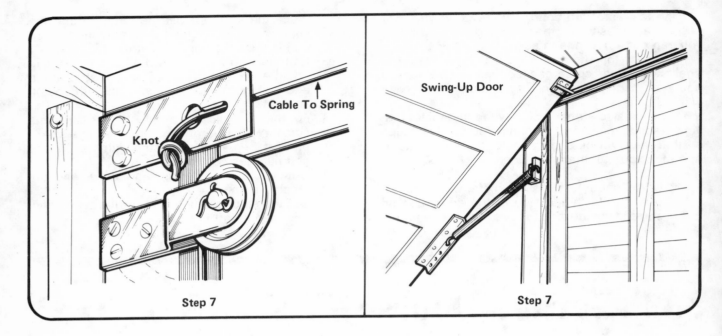

Step 7

Step 7

Cable To Spring

Knot

Swing-Up Door

4. Inspect the tracks for dirt. Old grease can collect dust and dirt, and you might need to swab out the track with a solvent to dissolve the old grease and remove the dirt.
5. Lubricate the track, the rollers, and the pulleys (if any). Use machine oil or spray lubricant on the rollers and pulleys; use grease in the tracks.
6. Look for any loose hardware such as hinges, tracks, or brackets. Any of these can cause balky operation when they loosen.
7. After you have checked everything else, you can go to work on the spring. If you have the type of roll-up door with a spring on either side, try shortening the spring cable while the door is up. This cable is held in a hole in a

plate above the door. To shorten the cable, move the knot (or stay) inward. The other type of roll-up door has a torsion spring in the center. If you have this type, seek the help of a pro who has the proper tools and experience; the torsion is so great that you could easily be hurt. The swing-up type doors have springs that hook into holes or notches; you can adjust them by moving the spring hook from one hole or notch to another.
8. Another reason for doors not working properly is that they become too heavy. A wooden door can absorb a great deal of moisture. You can prevent serious moisture problems by painting the garage door; just make sure to paint both sides and to seal the top, bottom, and sides.

34. Installing An Automatic Garage Door Opener

CONVENIENCE AND safety are the two major reasons for having an automatic opener on your garage door. If you have decided to get one, you can save up to $50 by installing it yourself. Before you buy your opener unit, though, make certain that it will be

Here Is What You Will Need

Materials

- Automatic opener unit
- Oil and grease
- Lag screws

Tools

- Screwdriver
- Measuring tape
- Adjustable wrench

adequate for the size and type of garage door you have. Then check to make sure that there is adequate clearance between the arc of the door and the garage ceiling to accommodate the unit. Once you have the right unit, here is what to do.

1. Oil the garage door's rollers and pulleys — if any — and grease the tracks. Also make certain that the current mechanism is adjusted and working properly.
2. Remove the present lock or make it inoperable.
3. Find the exact center of the door and of the header beam above the door.
4. Attach the header bracket to the header beam, centering the bracket exactly. These parts may be called something else in your unit; use the unit's parts list and diagram to identify them.
5. Install hanger straps (some units may have two sets of hanger straps) in the ceiling with lag screws. If your garage does not have exposed beams, locate the beams behind the ceiling, and then use additional lag screws to attach a 2x4 centered on the door and about three-quarters of the way back to where the motor unit will go.
6. Now you are ready to attach the track assembly to the header bracket and the hanger strap. In most cases the track and motor unit will be attached, but if not, you must fasten them together. You will need help in holding the parts together while you attach them.
7. Next, put the connector arm plate on the garage door. Position it right at the top and in the exact center of the door.
8. Attach the connecting arm to this plate, and then to the carrier in the track. Move the carrier all the way toward the door by hand-turning the unit.
9. Hook up the wires from the push-button unit and from the automatic reversing control to the opener, and then plug the opener into a convenient outlet. Some units must be wired into a junction box.
10. Install batteries in the transmitter, a light bulb in the socket, and put the housing in place over the opener unit.

Now try it out, but take it easy if the opener fails to work just right. Most units must be adjusted. There is a plate attached to the unit itself telling you how to adjust the opener. All adjustments are simple; just turn a nut to change the unit's opening or closing. To adjust the automatic reverse, merely turn a nut at the header bracket.

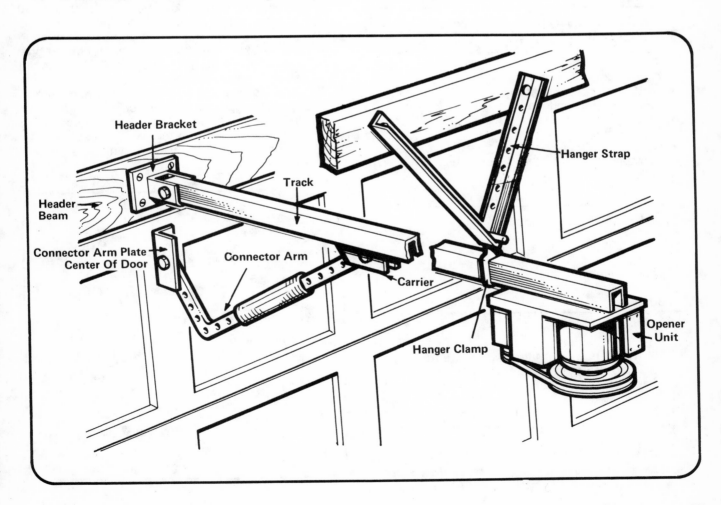

35. Refinishing Hardwood Floors

DESPITE ALL OF the fantastic new easy-to-apply flooring materials, there are few that can beat the beauty of hardwood floors — when they are in good condition, that is. By the same token, a hardwood floor in bad condition can look terrible. If you now have ugly hardwood floors, you can either cover them with carpet or you can restore their beauty.

The best way to remove the old worn-out finish is to sand it off. When you look at an average-size room, though, and think about how long it will take to sand, you may wish to give up and forget about refinishing. Fortunately, you can rent a large drum sander that does the job quickly. When you go to the rental company, have the dealer show you how to operate the unit properly. The same holds true for the other sander you will need for the edges. This tool is a disc sander, commonly called a floor edger.

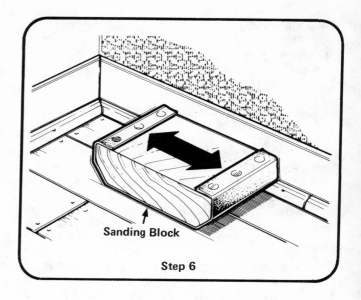

Sanding Block

Step 6

Here Is What You Will Need

Materials

- Tape
- Coarse (20 grit) open coat sandpaper
- Medium (40 grit) sandpaper
- Fine (100 grit) sandpaper
- Wood stain
- Turpentine
- Rags
- Synthetic varnish or other floor finish
- Wax

Tools

- Drum sander
- Disc sander
- Putty knife
- Nailset
- Vacuum cleaner
- Paintbrush
- Buffer

1. Move all of the furniture out of the room, and take down any wall hangings.
2. Tape over all heating and air conditioning ducts.
3. Carefully remove the shoe molding.
4. Check the entire floor for nail heads. If you find any, use a nailset to drive them below the surface.
5. When you finish all of the preparatory steps,

open all the windows and close the doors to adjoining rooms.

6. For the initial sanding, place coarse (20 grit) open coat sandpaper on the drum sander. Go over the entire floor with the sander, sanding with the grain. Since the sander works in both directions, you make one pass pushing and another pulling. You must tilt the unit to raise the drum at the beginning and ending of each pass. Lower it back slowly each time to prevent it from digging into the floor. Proceed slowly; never let the machine run away with you. Go over the edges with the disc sander, using the same grit abrasive. To get right up in the corners, however, you must use a sanding block equipped with the same grit sandpaper.
7. When you finish the first sanding, change to a

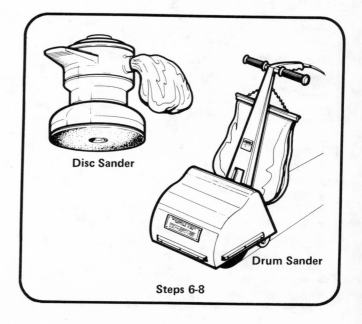

Disc Sander

Drum Sander

Steps 6-8

medium sandpaper, a 40 grit. Repeat the same sanding procedure.

8. Next comes the final sanding. Use a fine or 100 grit sandpaper.
9. Return the rented equipment.
10. Vacuum the room to get all of the dust out.
11. The next step is optional; it is a matter of personal taste whether to stain the floor or leave it natural. For a pretty good idea of how the natural wood will look without a stain but with a finish, take a rag and rub turpentine over a small section of the floor. What you see is quite close to the way the floor will look with just a finish on it. If you think it lacks character

or is too light, then staining is the answer.
12. After you stain the floor or decide against staining, you must apply the finish. The most popular finishes today are synthetic varnishes — such as polyurethane — but you should consult your paint dealer and let him show you samples of how each finish will look on your floor. Whatever type you decide to apply, be sure to follow the directions on the label. Put down at least two coats of the finish on your floor.
13. Most finishes wear better when given a periodic waxing. Wax the floor and then buff the new finish when it is completely dry.

36. Squeaking Floors

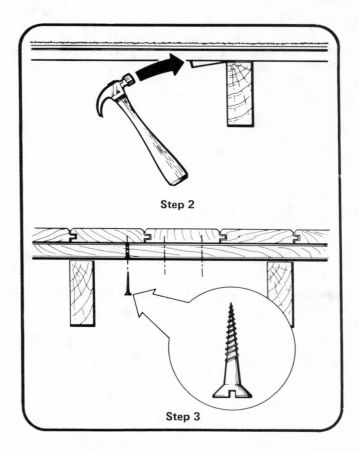

Step 2

Step 3

NEARLY ALL floor squeaks are the result of two pieces of wood rubbing against each other. If you know where the loose boards are, you can step over these spots; but if you want to stop the squeaks without having to resort to this broken field running, there are some simple remedies you can try.

If you have exposed hardwood floors and if the rubbing occurs between boards of this top flooring, an easy way to stop the noise is to sprinkle talcum powder over the area and sweep it back and forth until you get the powder to go down between the cracks. Talc acts as a dry lubricant, and even though the boards will still move, there will be no more squeaks. Liquid floor wax or glue will accomplish the same thing as the talc, but there are more permanent ways to stop squeaks — and they are almost as easy. The best way to attack floor squeaks is from underneath.

Here Is What You Will Need

Materials

- Talcum powder, liquid floor wax, or glue
- Chalk
- Wooden wedges
- Wood screws
- Finishing nails
- Wood filler
- Padded wood block

Tools

- Hammer
- Screwdriver
- Drill
- Nailset

1. Go to the basement or crawl space under the floor, and have someone on the floor above step on the squeaky spot. If you can see any movement in the subfloor, mark the spots with chalk.
2. Drive wedges in between the joists and the subflooring to stop the boards from moving. You can fashion wedges from scrap shingles or other scrap lumber.
3. If the wedges are no help, use wood screws to

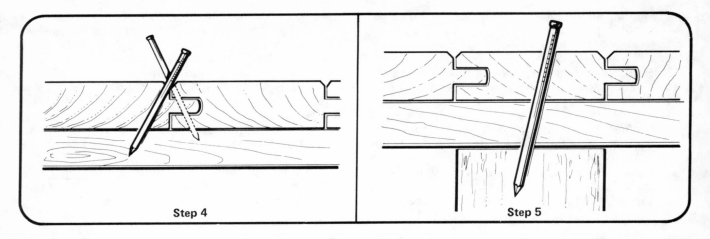

Step 4   Step 5

pull the subflooring and surface flooring together. Make sure, however, that the screws
are not so long as to go all the way through
the floor and stick up into the room above.

4. If you cannot reach the floor from underneath,
drive six penny finishing nails through the
cracks of the hardwood flooring at points
around the squeaking boards. Drive the nails
in at an angle so that each nail goes through
both of the two adjoining boards. Be sure to
drill a pilot hole first, before you drive a nail
into hardwood. Then, after the nails are in,
drive them below the surface with a nailset
and hide them with wood filler.

5. You also attack from above if the movement is
between the top flooring and the subfloor.
Drive ten penny finishing nails through the
center of hardwood planks and on into the

subfloor below. Again, drive the nails at a
slight angle, and then countersink and hide
them as mentioned above.

6. If the floors are covered with carpet, vinyl, or
some other such covering — and if there is no
way to work from underneath — you may have
to tolerate the squeaks or else learn how to
dodge the bad spots. Nevertheless, there is
one thing you can try: Put padding over the
floor, and then pound a block of wood with a
hammer to reseat the loose nails. Move the
block in an area about two or three feet all
around the squeak, tapping sharply with the
hammer. If the floor still squeaks, then wait
until it is time to recover the floors. With the
old flooring out of the way, you can drive wood
screws in to pull the subflooring tight against
the joists.

37. Laying A Tile Floor

IF YOU REALLY want to amaze your friends —
and maybe even yourself — with the professional appearance of a do-it-yourself project, put
down a resilient tile floor. In a matter of only a few
hours, you can change a drab floor into one that will
perk up the entire room. You will be amazed at how
easily and quickly the work goes.

Floor tiles now come in a wide range of prices and
materials. The two most popular types are asphalt
tiles and vinyl tiles. The use to which you put the
room, the type of subflooring that is already down,
and the availability of patterns will have much to do
with your selection of tile. Spend some time in

Here Is What You Will Need
Materials

- Sandpaper
- Chalk
- Asphalt or vinyl tiles
- Adhesive

Tools

- Heavy-duty scissors
- Rolling pin
- Paintbrush or roller or thin-notched flooring trowel

choosing; you might as well get it right the first time.
Purchasing right adhesive is important too. Different
materials and different subfloors require different
mastics. No matter what type of tiles you choose,
however, the procedures for installation are about
the same. Here are the steps to follow.

1. The first step — preparation — is the most important one of all. Pry up the moldings; remove all wax and dirt from the floor surface; search for and sand down any high spots; and make sure there are no nails sticking up. Since resilient tiles are flexible and will conform to whatever is under them, any irregularities in the sub-floor will eventually show through. And unless the sub-flooring is solid, the tiles will loosen.

2. Next, find the exact center of each wall and draw chalk lines from these points across the floor. Where the two lines intersect is the center of the room.

3. Lay a full run of loose (uncemented) tiles from the center of each wall within one quarter of the room. If the last tile in either direction is less than half the width of a full tile, draw a new chalk line beside the actual center line, moving the original line half a tile in either direction. This technique will give you even-sized end tiles at both ends of the room.

4. Now you are ready to start cementing the tiles down. Work on a quarter of the room at a time. Be sure that you check the back of each tile to see that all of the arrows are aimed in the same direction. This keeps the pattern, if any, aligned. If you are using a mixed tile pattern, you should lay it out without mastic before putting the tiles in place. If you have tiles with the adhesive already on the backing, peel off the release paper. Start at the center point, and place the tile down precisely on both lines. It will not slide into place; once down, it is down for good. If you have tiles without mastic, spread the cement over the first quarter only, bringing it right up to the lines. Be sure to use the proper mastic, and follow

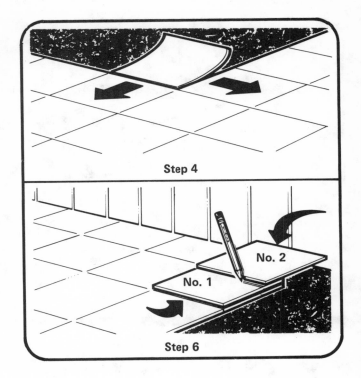

Step 4

Step 6

the directions regarding how long to wait before setting the tiles in place. Usually, you are instructed to wait until the adhesive is tacky.

5. After you get the first center tile in place, lay tiles alternately toward each wall, building a sort of pyramid until the entire quarter is covered except for the tiles along the edges.

6. To cut and fit the border tiles, first place a loose tile (#1) on the last tile in the row. Then butt another loose tile (#2) against the wall,

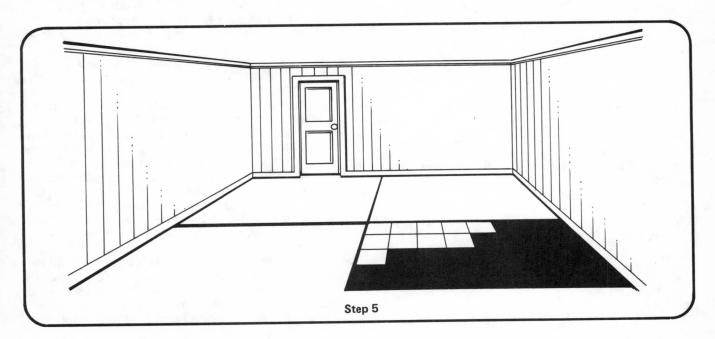

Step 5

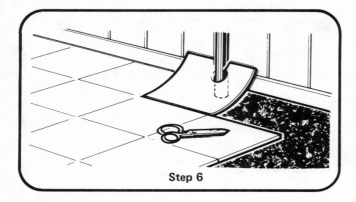

Step 6

with its sides aligned with those of the #1 tile. Now, make a mark on the #1 tile, along the edge of #2 where the two tiles overlap. If you then cut the #1 tile along the line, you will

have an exact fit for the borger tile. If you have any irregularities (such as pipes) to fit tiles around, make a paper pattern of the obstacle, trace it onto the tile, and then cut along the line. You should be able to cut most tiles with ordinary heavy-duty scissors.

7. Go over the tiles with a rolling pin.
8. Follow the same procedures for the other three quarters, and then be prepared to receive pats on the back for doing such professional-looking work.

Here are some tips that will make the job easier. Make sure that the temperature of the room is at least 70 degrees before you start, put all the boxes of tile in this room for at least 24 hours prior to putting them down, and keep the temperature at that level for about a week afterward. Then wait at least a week after installation before washing the floor.

38. Fixing A Loose Floor Tile

PERHAPS YOU HAVE seen the commercials that show how easy it is to lay floor tiles yourself. Although it really is easy to lay new tiles, it is something else again to fix loose ones. If for some reason a tile should get loose and start to curl up at the ends — or if you happen to drop something sharp on the floor and gouge out a chunk — you could find yourself with one heck of a job removing that one tile and either regluing it or replacing it . . . unless you know the secrets.

Here Is What You Will Need

Materials

- Aluminum foil
- Dry ice or metal pot filled with ice, water, and ice cream salt
- Sandpaper
- Floor tile mastic
- Replacement tile
- Weights (i.e., heavy books)

Tools

- Propane torch or electric iron
- Putty knife

1. If the tile is loose just around the edges, try to heat the mastic; sometimes you can then press the tile back down for keeps. The best way to heat the mastic is to play the flame of a propane torch across the tile. You must be careful, of course, not to leave the flame in any one spot, and you must not overheat. If you want a less hazardous method, you can place aluminum foil over the square and use a warm iron. Press the edges of the loose tile with the iron, and then place weights over the tile to clamp it in place until the mastic sets up fully.

2. If there seems to be insufficient mastic to glue the tile back down, apply heat again and peel back the edges. Then clean out the old mastic as completely as you can. Apply new floor tile mastic, but be careful not to put so much down that mastic will squeeze out when you press down on the tile. Replace the tile and weight it down until the mastic has cured. Check the label for the prescribed drying time.

3. If the tile is botched up and needs to be replaced, you can use either heat or cold to remove the bad tile. If you do not have a propane torch, try placing dry ice or a metal pot filled with ice, water, and ice cream salt over the tile. After about five to ten minutes, the cold will make both the tile and the mastic very brittle, allowing you to flip the tile out in chips with a putty knife. Tap the putty knife with a hammer as you go, and the tile will shatter.

4. Once you remove the tile, clean away all the old mastic. Scraping with a wide putty knife is probably the best way to clean the entire area.

5. Now you are ready to lay the new tile. Place it down in the opening before you apply any

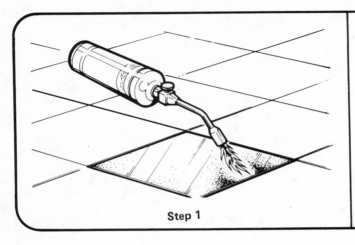

Step 1

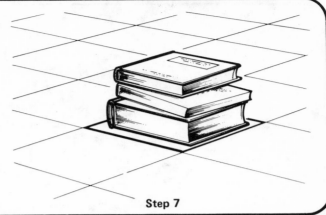

Step 7

mastic. This enables you to match up the pattern. You may find that the new tile does not fit exactly. If such is the case, sand down the new tile until it fits.

6. Apply the floor tile mastic (be sure it is the kind made for your type of tile) directly to the floor, following the instructions on the label. Now warm the new tile, using either the propane torch or the electric iron, and press the tile firmly in place.

7. Put weights on the tile, and leave them there for the prescribed drying time. Volumes A through L of the encyclopedia should do the job nicely.

39. Removing Spots From Resilient Floors

THOSE STURDY and beautiful resilient floors that are so popular in modern kitchens receive a great deal of punishment. Although you can usually just mop them clean, there are some stains that will not respond to the mop. Rather than letting such a floor become so unattractive that you must replace it, follow these tips for removing spots from your resilient floor.

1. Remember, you can prevent spills from turning into stains by treating them immediately. In many cases, a damp cloth removes the spill and the possibility of a stain.
2. Know the material the flooring is made of; it could be vinyl, asphalt, rubber, or linoleum.
3. Treat heel marks, probably the most common problem, with an all-purpose spray cleaner. If the cleaner fails to get rid of the marks, use 0000 steel wool dipped into liquid wax. Then go over the area with a damp cloth. When dry, wax the floor.

Here Is What You Will Need
Materials
• All-purpose spray cleaner
• 0000 steel wool
• Liquid wax
• Ice
• Dry cleaner
• Rubbing alcohol
• Ammonia
• Oxalic acid
• Hydrogen peroxide
• White vinegar
Tools
• Metal spatula
• Mop

4. Tar, chewing gum, or candle wax will get brittle if you hold an ice cube against the substance. Then use a metal spatula or some other such dull tool to scrape away the brittle matter. If there is residue left, try a dry cleaner and 0000 steel wool. Wash the area, and wax it when dry.
5. Ink stains should be covered for a few minutes with a rubbing alcohol compress. Then — unless the floor is linoleum — wipe the area

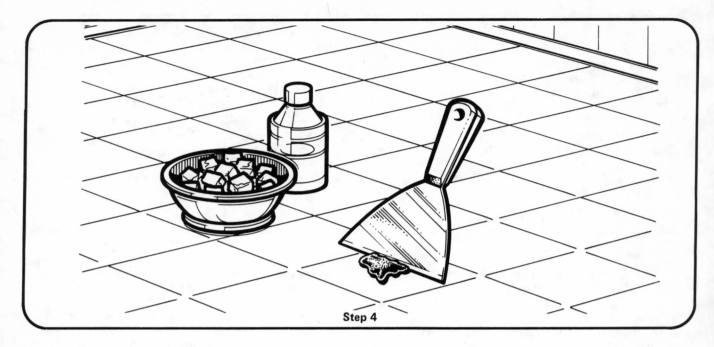

Step 4

with an ammonia dampened rag.

6. You can often scrape up paint spots with a spatula. If not, try wearing them away with 0000 steel wool and liquid wax.

7. Rust stains should be treated by rubbing on a dilute solution of oxalic acid with 0000 steel wool. Oxalic acid is available at paint stores, but you must observe all the caution notices when using it on your floors.

8. Mustard will sometimes leave a stain if allowed to dry. After removing all the dried matter with a spatula or damp cloth, make a

compress soaked with hydrogen peroxide and leave it on the stain for several minutes. Then wash, let dry, and wax.

9. Drain cleaners are caustics and should be neutralized with white vinegar as soon as possible. Wash, let dry, and wax.

10. Fruit stains and coffee stains that you cannot wipe up should first be rubbed with 0000 steel wool and liquid wax. Then, remove all the wax and make a compress soaked with hydrogen peroxide. Leave the compress on for several minutes. Wash, let dry, and wax.

40. Clean Your Own Carpets

PROBABLY NOTHING in your home is subjected to as much abuse as your carpeting. And when the carpeting gets dirty or stained it detracts from the appearance of the whole room. Of course, there is no way to prevent carpeting from getting dirty, but you can clean it yourself and keep your floors looking great. Here is what to do.

1. Treat spots and stains as soon as you see them, but before you use any spot remover formula, pretest it on some inconspicuous area

Here Is What You Will Need

Materials

- Spot remover
- Cleansing tissues
- Carpet shampoo
- Aluminum foil
- White vinegar
- Dry carpet cleaner
- Ammonia

Tools

- Nonpowered sweeper
- Vacuum cleaner
- Electric shampooer
- Stiff brush

of the carpet. Apply the spot remover to the carpet and let it remain there for a few moments; then dab at the area with a white cleansing tissue. If the formula is harmful to the dye in the carpet, you will know it now.

2. Go over the carpet daily with a nonpowered sweeper.

3. Vacuum once or twice a week, depending on the traffic over your carpets. Make seven to eight passes over each section to remove imbedded dirt as well as to pick up surface particles.

4. If your carpets are not tacked down, turn them annually to spread the effects of wear. If you have wall-to-wall carpeting, rearrange the furniture from time to time, and place throw rugs over high traffic areas.

5. Shampoo your carpets at least once a year, before they get really dirty. You can rent an electric shampooer, and there are several good shampoos on the market. Vacuum thoroughly before shampooing, and be sure to avoid soaking the carpet or using too much shampoo. Move all of the furniture out of the way, and if you have to put it back before the carpet is completely dry, place squares of aluminum foil under the furniture legs. Vacuum again after shampooing.

6. Never pull loose carpet threads. Always snip them off even with the rest of the carpet.

Here are the best ways to get rid of various spots and stains. Once again, remember to treat the spot immediately and to pretest any solution on an inconspicuous area of the carpet before you apply it in the middle of the room.

1. Blot all spilled liquids with a white paper towel or cleansing tissue.

2. Scrape up all semi-solids which fall on the carpet.

3. Always work from the outer edge of the stain toward the center.

4. Take care not to overmoisten. Use small amounts of spot remover and blot.

5. After removing the excess, treat any greasy or oily stain with a dry cleaning solution. Be sure to read the caution notice on the label and to provide adequate ventilation. Follow with shampoo, but if you do not have any carpet shampoo in the house, you can use a detergent that is mild enough for lingerie.

6. Coffee and tea stains require carpet shampoo. If the stains are still visible after you shampoo them, blot with a white vinegar solution — one part vinegar to two parts water — or apply a dry cleaner.

7. Dampen blood stains with cold water, and then use a concentrated solution of carpet shampoo. When dry, apply a dry cleaner and then shampoo once again.

8. Treat milk, gravy, or ice cream stains as you

Carpet Sweeper

Electric Shampooer

would blood stains, following the procedure in step 7.

9. Ink stains fall in three categories: ball point pen marks respond to a dry cleaner; washable ink should come up with a concentrated solution of carpet shampoo; but indelible ink is a lost cause. Try to minimize the damage with carpet shampoo.

10. Usually, alcoholic beverages respond well to

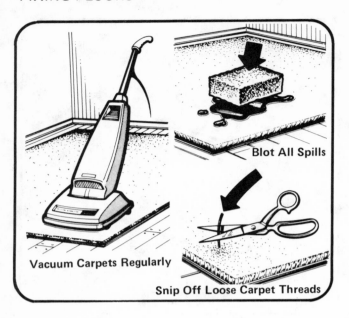

Vacuum Carpets Regularly

Blot All Spills

Snip Off Loose Carpet Threads

blotting, but it is best to play it safe and apply carpet shampoo. Red wines must be shampooed.

11. Hold an ice cube against chewing gum and candle wax until they become brittle enough to be chipped off. A dry cleaner can soften them and allow you to scrape them away.

12. Chocolate responds to a concentrated solution of carpet shampoo or to a very mild ammonia solution (one tablespoon per cup of water).

13. Crayon marks can be removed with a dry cleaner followed by shampooing.

14. Fingernail polish could be removed with polish remover, but this procedure often removes carpet dye and damages some fibers. Try a dry cleaner.

15. Mud should be allowed to dry, and then loosened with a stiff brush and vacuumed away.

41. How To Remove Cigarette Burns From A Carpet

AFTER EVERY party you find some evidence of totally careless people, but one of the worst sights you can spot is the cigarette burn in the living room carpet. Although you cannot repair the damage completely without having the carpet rewoven, there are several ways to hide the burned spot very effectively. Here are the steps to take.

Here Is What You Will Need
Materials
• Carpet scrap
• Glue
• Carpet tape
Tools
• Fingernail scissors

1. Use a pair of fingernail scissors to clip away all the blackened fibers. If the burn failed to go down all the way to the backing, you may not have to do anything else; the one low spot

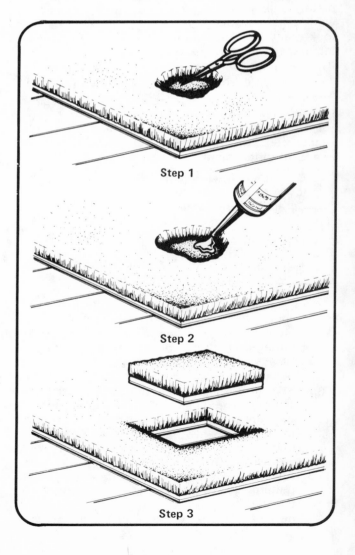

Step 1

Step 2

Step 3

generally is not noticeable. If the burn did go to the backing, however, scrape the charred matter away.

2. If the backing shows, clip new fibers from a carpet scrap and glue them in place over the hole. First put glue on the hole, and then as the glue gets tacky enough to support the fibers, carefully place a few of them at a time upright in the glue.

3. If the damage is even more severe, cut an entire square out of the carpet and replace it with a scrap piece. Use carpet tape that is sticky on both sides to hold the patch in place, and make sure that the nap of the new carpet scrap lays the same way as the nap of the carpet already down.

42. Installing A Bathroom Carpet

ONLY A FEW years ago, laying a carpet in the bathroom was strictly a job for the professional — and that cost money. Now the situation is completely different. In a single afternoon you can lay wall-to-wall carpeting in your bathroom that will look great, feel great, and leave your budget in better shape than you probably think. Here is how to do it.

Here Is What You Will Need
Materials
• Bathroom carpet
• Brown paper or newspaper
• Tape
• Carpet tape
Tools
• Measuring tape
• Heavy-duty scissors
• Ball point pen

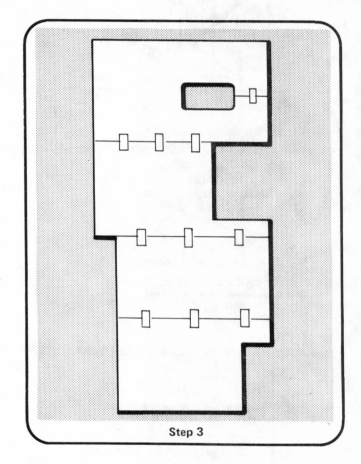

Step 3

1. Measure the bathroom to figure out the square footage. Then draw a floor plan.
2. Now you are ready to shop. You will find packaged bathroom carpets that come in several sizes with a paper pattern included. They make installation easy. You can also buy carpet remnants on sale, but just remember that the carpet will get wet; therefore, be sure to buy a synthetic material that will stand up to the use it will receive.
3. After you buy your carpet, you must make a pattern. You can buy rolls of brown paper at the variety store, or you can tape sheets of newspaper together. The pattern is easier to handle if you use several small sections at first, and then put them all together when you finish the entire bathroom.
4. To make the pattern for around the toilet, fold the paper in half and place it beside the toilet. Press the pattern against the toilet with your hand to give you an outline, and then use a scissors to cut along the line.
5. Now cut a straight line in the paper from the part that goes against the back wall to the opening for the toilet.
6. Fit the pattern around the toilet and trim.
7. Use the same technique around any other immovable objects.

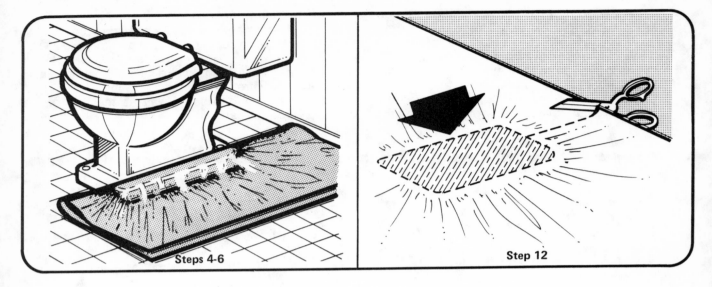

Steps 4-6   Step 12

8. When you get all the sections cut out, piece them together on the floor to make sure they fit the room precisely. Then add extra tape to prevent the separate pieces from pulling loose. Mark the pattern "TOP."
9. In another room, lay the carpet face down on the floor.
10. Turn the pattern face down on the carpet and tape it to the backing. Mentally check the pattern as it rests on the carpet to be sure that the cutouts will be in the right parts of the room for the toilet, etc.

11. Carefully trace the pattern onto the backing with a ball point pen.
12. Use a heavy-duty pair of scissors to cut along the lines.
13. Place carpet tape (sticky on both sides) around the perimeter of the room and around any cutouts. If you must have seams in the carpet, use tape to keep joints together.
14. Place the carpet down in place and press it against the carpet tape. If later you need to move the carpet, you can peel it up from the tape and then stick it back down again.

43. Getting The Squeaks Out Of Stairs

Here Is What You Will Need
Materials
• Wooden wedges or blocks
• White polyvinyl or any wood glue
• Finishing nails
• Graphite powder or talcum powder
• Wood putty
Tools
• Hammer
• Nailset

THE STAIRWAY that squeaks when you walk up or down is caused by the same thing that causes your floor to squeak; two pieces of wood rubbing together. It is usually the tread rubbing against either the riser or the stringer because these boards are not fastened down securely. Stop their movement, and you stop the squeak. If you can work from under the stairs, here is how to cure the problem.

1. Have someone walk on the stairs, going back and forth on the step that squeaks, while you

try to spot movement from below. Look especially for loose nails, split boards, or anything else that could cause the movement.
2. The best way to stop the movement is to drive wedges between the rubbing members. Cut

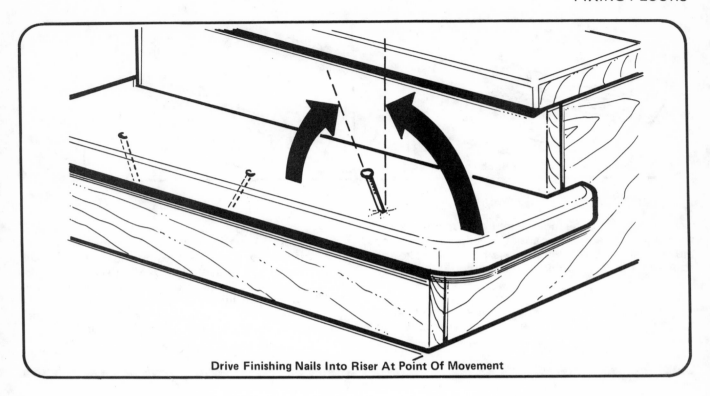

Drive Finishing Nails Into Riser At Point Of Movement

the wedges from scrap shingles.

3. Coat the wedges with glue (white polyvinyl or any wood glue) on the side that will press against a flat surface.
4. Drive the wedges into the seam, making them go in as tight as possible.
5. When you get them in place, secure the wedges with nails. Use small nails, and blunt the points to avoid splitting the wedges.

6. If the seams are too small to admit wedges, cut wood blocks (1x2's) to fit into the joints under the stairs. Put a coat of glue on the sides that will touch the stairs, and then — as you hold the blocks in place — secure them with nails. Be sure your nails do not go through the stairs and protrude from the top.

If there is no way to work from under the stairs, you

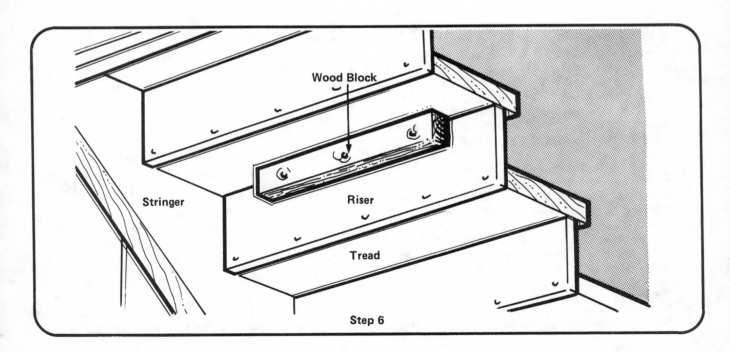

Wood Block

Stringer

Riser

Tread

Step 6

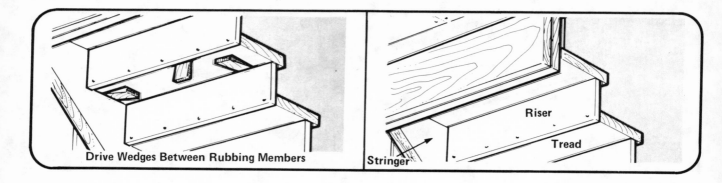

Drive Wedges Between Rubbing Members

Riser

Tread

Stringer

have to try to find the movement from topside. Unfortunately, you frequently cannot spot the problem and must guess where the trouble is by listening to the squeak. After you track down the squeak, here is what to do.

1. Buy a tube of graphite powder and squeeze the graphite into the joints all around the

squeak. You can also use talcum powder in a plastic squeeze bottle with a spout.

2. If the powder fails to stop the squeak, drive finishing nails into the tread at such an angle that they will go into the riser or the stringer where you think the movement is. Use a nailset to sink the heads below the surface, and then cover the holes with wood putty.

44. Sagging Support Beams

MANY TIMES, a cracked wall or a sticking door upstairs — or even a roof leak — is actually caused by a problem in the basement. The problem is that the joists under the first floor are sagging. Once the joists give a little, the sag continues on up the line. Before you start trying to remedy the results upstairs, therefore, you need to take care of the cause in the basement. Although the cure is simple, you first must check your local building code to see that what you do conforms to the law. Once you get that aspect of the problem cleared up, just follow these steps to remedy your sagging supports.

1. Buy or rent a screw-type house jack (commonly called a screw jack).
2. Place a 4x4 timber directly under the center of the sag to serve as a support base for the screw jack.
3. Cut another 4x4 timber to run across the sagging joists and beyond to several non-sagging joists on each side. Nail this beam in place across the joists.
4. Place the screw jack on the support base.
5. Measure from the top of the lowered screw jack to the bottom of the beam you nailed up

Here Is What You Will Need

Materials

- Nails
- 4x4's
- Steel columns or adjustable jack posts
- Concrete mix

Tools

- Screw jack
- Saw
- Hammer
- Measuring tape
- Carpenter's level
- Chisel
- Trowel

and cut a third 4x4 to this length.

6. Install this third piece as a vertical between the jack and the beam. Since it must be plumb, use a level to set it.
7. Turn the handle of the screw jack until you feel resistance, and **STOP.** The leveling process must be very gradual; otherwise, you can crack your walls and do great damage to the house.
8. Wait a full 24 hours, and then turn the screw jack handle only one quarter of a turn. The handle will probably be very easy to turn, and you will be tempted to turn more, but be pa-

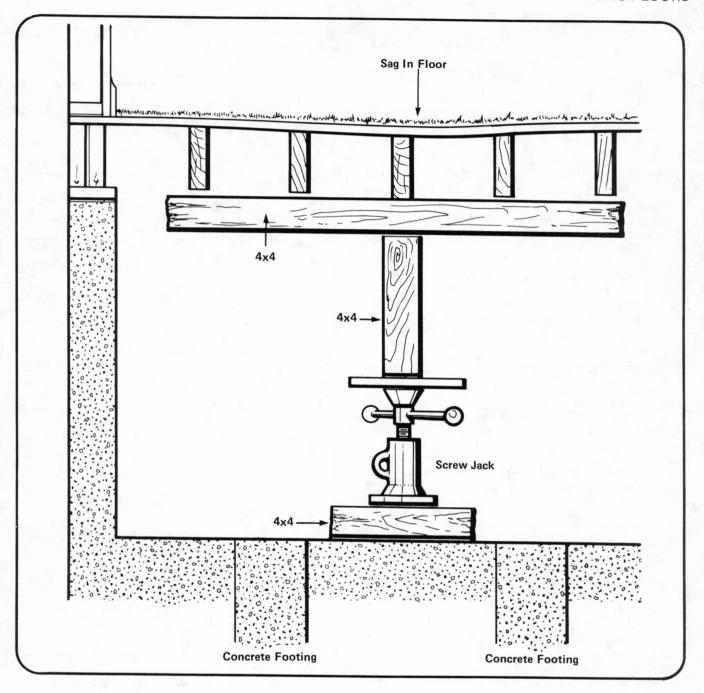

Sag In Floor

4x4

4x4

Screw Jack

4x4

Concrete Footing   Concrete Footing

tient. Continue to make no more than a quarter turn every 24 hours. If you miss a day, do not compensate for it with additional turning.

9. When the sagging beams begin to straighten out, start checking them with your level every day.

10. When they are all level, install columns at each end of each beam to secure them. You can buy steel lally columns or you can cut 4x4's; there are also adjustable jack posts that work like the screw jack and are the easiest

supports to set.

11. No matter what kind of supports you decide to install, you must make sure that the footing below is sound. The common concrete basement floor is not reliable enough. You should remove a two-foot section of the old floor where each support post will go, pour a concrete footing that is at least a foot thick, and make it level with the rest of the floor. When it has cured, you can put the support posts on the footing and know that the floor will not give way.

45. First Aid For The Damp Basement

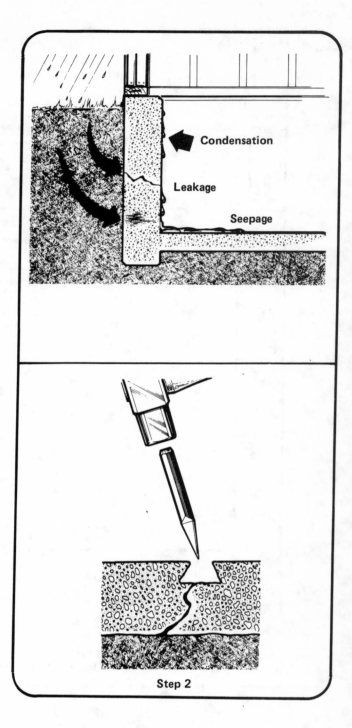

Step 2

THERE IS A tremendous amount of wasted floor space in this country; it is not being used because it happens to be in basements that suffer from a dampness problem. In some cases, the usable floor space in a home could almost be doubled if the basement were dry.

The first step toward solving the dampness problem is to ascertain where the moisture is coming from. Assuming that there is no plumbing problem, the dampness must result from leakage, seepage, or condensation. Leakage is outside water that comes in through cracks. Seepage is also outside water, but it is in such abundance that it makes its way through pores in the concrete. Condensation is inside water that exists as humidity in the air until it condenses on the cool masonry walls or cold water pipes.

You should be able to tell when the problem is leakage because the moisture will only be around cracks. Seepage and condensation may appear much alike, however. To find out which one it is, tape a hand mirror against the wall in the middle of a damp spot, and leave it there overnight. If the mirror is fogged over the next day, you have condensation. If not, you have seepage.

Here Is What You Will Need	
Materials	

Materials
- Hand mirror
- Hydraulic cement
- Patching compound
- Concrete mix
- Clay tile pipe drains
- Waterproofing compound
- Pipe insulation
- Dehumidifier
- Exhaust fan

Tools
- Hammer
- Chisel
- Garden hose
- Trowel
- Shovel
- Stiff brush

1. The first step to take for leakage is to patch the crack. Buy a special hydraulic cement, the kind that is quick setting and can actually set up with water coming in through the crack.
2. Anything other than a hairline crack should be undercut. That means taking a hammer and chisel and making the crack wider beneath than the crack is on the surface. Undercutting lets the cement lock itself in place.
3. Clean away all the loose debris, and then hose out the cavity.
4. Mix the patching compound according to directions.
5. Push the mixture into the crack with your

trowel, making sure to fill all cavities.

6. Smooth the surface and let it cure according to directions.

That takes care of the cracks, but you are not through yet. You should try to divert the outside water that has been attacking your foundation. Here is what to look for and what to do about the water outside.

1. Check your gutters and downspouts. They must be free of debris, pitched properly to carry the water off, and the ground on which the downspouts spill should be sloped to carry the water away from the house. If it is not, pour concrete splash blocks.

2. Inspect the ground around the house to be sure it slopes away all the way around. If not, fill it in until there is good run off, and then roll and seed (or sod) to prevent the soil from washing away.

3. Examine the flower beds to be sure they are not trapping the water that should be running off.

4. Be sure patios and walks butting against the house are sloped away, and check the joints to see that they are sealed and curved properly. If they are not, use a chisel and hammer to undercut the joints, and then fill them with a mortar mix.

Some outside conditions can be cured only by digging down around the foundation and laying drains. This is not a do-it-yourself project for someone lacking experience in such work. If you want to tackle it, though, you must dig down to a level below the basement floor (but not below the footing), set a drain alongside each wall, and extend the drain out to carry the water away. The drain is made of sections of clay tile pipe covered with about two feet of gravel. While you have the outside wall exposed, coat it with a waterproofing compound. There are several good ones on the market.

There are also companies that have a process for pumping a special sealing compound into the ground under pressure. The compound flows along the same paths that the water takes and then seals the wall. Be sure to check with your Better Business Bureau, though, before contracting for such a treatment because there are some dishonest companies in this field.

Another way to deal with the seepage problem is to coat the inside of your basement with a waterproofing compound. There are many good ones on the market. Such compounds will not eliminate your seepage problem, however, unless you reduce the amount of water outside your house. Once you take care of the outside problem, follow these directions to waterproof your basement walls.

1. Clean the walls.
2. Wet the surface.

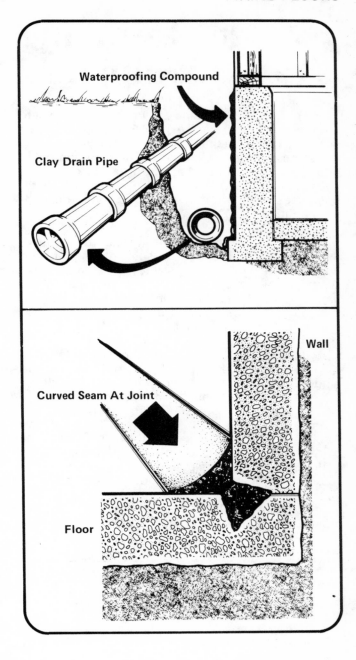

3. Mix the waterproofing compound according to directions.

4. Apply the mixture with a stiff brush to cover the walls completely.

5. Apply a second coat if necessary; usually it is.

Condensation results from too much moisture in the air combining with a cold surface. A dehumidifier can take much of the excess moisture out of the air, and you should also try to provide better ventilation in the basement. If you cannot air it out regularly, you might consider installing an exhaust fan. In addition, be sure to wrap exposed cold water pipes with the type of insulation made especially to stop pipes from sweating.

46. Installing Wallboard

IF YOU EVER decide to finish a room where presently there are exposed studs, the easiest way to accomplish the task is to attach wallboard to the studs. After the wallboard is up, you can paint, paper, or texture it. Wallboard (also known as sheetrock, plasterboard, and gypsum board) possesses excellent insulating and sound deadening qualities.

Although it is a snap to figure how much wallboard to buy (just compute the square footage of the walls and ceiling), it takes some planning to end up with as few joints as possible. The standard size sheets for walls are 4x8 feet. You normally place them with the long side running from floor to ceiling, but you can place them horizontally if by doing so you eliminate a joint. You can buy longer sized sheets for the ceiling. All wallboard sheets are four feet wide, but most lumberyards offer 12 foot lengths.

As to the number of nails, rolls of tape, and the amount of joint compound you will need, consult the table at your local lumberyard to learn how much of each is required for the square footage involved. For example, 1000 square feet of 1/2-inch thick wallboard (the most popular home thickness) requires about 5¼ pounds of coated nails, a five-gallon pail of joint compound in mixed form, and a 500-foot roll of tape. Each outside corner requires a metal cornerbead.

Once you buy all the materials you need for the project, just follow these steps to install your new wallboard walls.

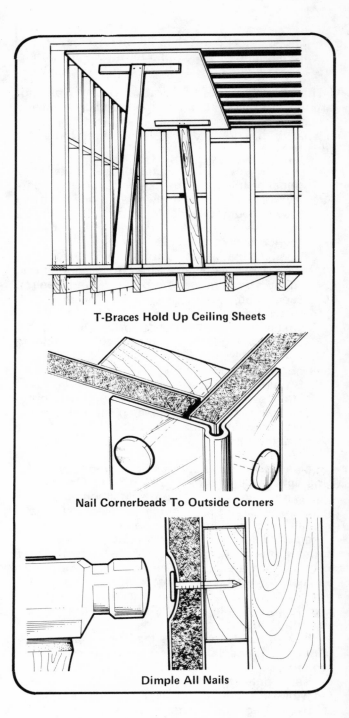

T-Braces Hold Up Ceiling Sheets

Nail Cornerbeads To Outside Corners

Dimple All Nails

Here Is What You Will Need

Materials

- Wallboard sheets
- Coated nails
- Joint tape
- Joint compound
- Metal cornerbeads
- 2x4's
- Wooden boards
- Sandpaper
- Molding and baseboards
- Sealer or primer
- Paint

Tools

- Measuring tape
- Hammer
- Wallboard knife
- Straightedge
- Sawhorse or other support
- Sanding block
- Drill
- Keyhole saw
- Putty knife
- Metal Float
- Paintbrush

1. Install the ceilings first. If possible, try to span the entire width with a single sheet of wallboard to reduce the number of joints. Before you can work on the ceilings, though, you need to construct a pair of T-braces from 2x4's about an inch longer than the distance from floor to ceiling. Nail lighter boards about three feet long to the 2x4's to form the T's, and then position and wedge the braces against the wallboard sheet to hold it in place until you finish nailing.
2. Drive nails at seven-inch intervals into all the

joints covered by the sheet. Start in the center of the wallboard panel and work out.

3. After you drive each nail in, give it one extra hammer blow to dimple the surface slightly. Take care, though, not to break the face paper.

4. When you need to cut panels to complete the coverage, use a wallboard knife along a straightedge. All you want to do with the knife is cut the face paper. After you make the cut, place the board over the edge of a sawhorse (or some other type of support) and bend it down. The gypsum core will snap along the line you cut. Then turn the panel over, cut the paper on the other side, and smooth the rough edges with a very coarse sanding block.

5. When the ceiling is finished, put up the walls. Again space the nails seven inches apart, but start nailing seven inches from the ceiling. Butt the wall panels against the ceiling sheets.

6. Dimple all nails.

7. If outside corners are involved, nail the cornerbeads in place.

8. Be sure to measure carefully for any cutouts such as electrical outlets, switches, or light fixtures. To make cutouts in the wallboard, first draw a pattern of the cutout, drill a hole, and then use a keyhole saw to follow the pattern around.

Once you are through applying the board to the walls, you face the problem of covering up all the nails and joints. This is where you use the joint compound and the tape in a technique called taping and bedding.

1. Use a wide putty knife to spread joint compound into the slight recess created by the tapered edges of the wallboard sheets. Smooth the compound until it is even with the rest of the surface.

2. Next, center the wallboard tape over the joint and press it firmly into the compound. Since some compound will squeeze out, you should make sure that there is still a good bed underneath.

3. When you get the tape imbedded into the compound all along the joint, smooth it with your putty knife.

4. When the compound is completely dry (usually 24 hours later), apply a second very thin coat of compound which extends out a few inches to either side of the first coat.

5. After the second coat dries completely, apply a third coat, extending it out to about six inches to either side. A metal float will do better than the putty knife at this stage.

6. When the third coat is dry, feather all the edges with a sanding block covered with medium grit paper.

7. Fill all the dimples with compound. They also

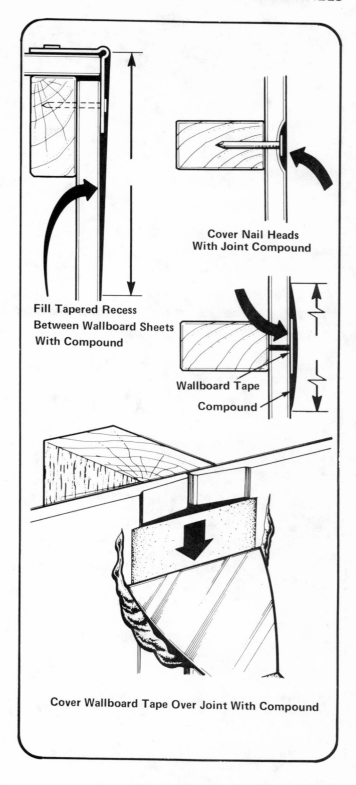

Fill Tapered Recess Between Wallboard Sheets With Compound

Cover Nail Heads With Joint Compound

Wallboard Tape

Compound

Cover Wallboard Tape Over Joint With Compound

require three coats as well as drying time in between. After the final coat, sand to feather and smooth the dimpled spots.

8. Inside corners, including spots where the walls and ceiling meet, must also be taped and bedded. Cut the tape to length and then fold it in half. After laying the bed of com-

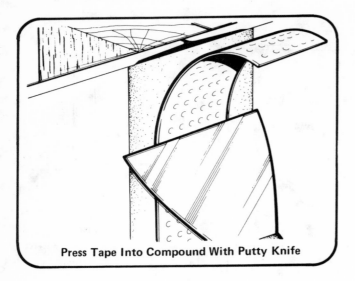

Press Tape Into Compound With Putty Knife

pound, press the folded tape into the compound and then feather the compound out at least 1½ inches to each side. The corners require three coats, and the last coat should extend out about eight inches to each side. Sanding is required here too.

9. If you have any outside corners, apply three coats that taper up to the bead. The last coat should extend the compound on each wall to about eight inches wide. Sand here too.

10. If there are cracks at the floor and ceiling, install moldings to hide them. Always attach baseboards at the floor.

After you are sure that the compound is completely dry, wait at least another couple of days before applying the sealer or primer coat and any subsequent decorative treatment.

47. Holes In Wallboard

THE EASE AND economy of dry wall construction are marred only by the fact that wallboard can develop holes the first time someone slams a door knob against it or gets mad and punches a fist through it. These holes may look like complete disasters, but you will be amazed at how easily you can patch them up. Small holes require one kind of backing, while larger ones may necessitate another. First, here is what to do for the smaller hole that needs a backing for a patch.

Here Is What You Will Need
Materials

- Tin can lid
- Wire
- Wooden stick
- Spackling compound
- Paint
- Scrap wallboard
- Wooden board
- Countersunk screws

Tools

- Keyhole saw
- Wire cutters or scissors
- Brush or trowel
- Screwdriver

1. Remove any loose material around the hole.
2. Select a tin can lid that is bigger than the hole and measure across the lid. Then use a keyhole saw to cut a slit extending out from both sides of the hole so that you can slip the lid into the hole sideways.
3. Punch two holes in the center of the lid and run a wire through them.
4. Now slip the lid through the slit, holding onto the wire. With the lid inside, pull the wire until the lid is flat against the inside of the wall.
5. Twist the wire around a stick which is long enough to span the hole. This technique will hold the lid in place.
6. You can now plaster over the hole with spackling compound (available at paint or hardware stores in either ready mixed or powered form). Cover all of the backing plate, the slit, and the edges, but resist trying to make the main body of the patch level with the rest of the wall.
7. When the first patch dries, remove the stick and snip the wire off flush with the patch.
18. Apply a second coat of spackling compound, bringing the surface up level with the rest of the wall. This coat will, of course, cover the remaining tip of wire.
9. Use a brush or trowel to texture the patch so that it matches the rest of the wall.
10. Let the patch dry overnight before applying the primer coat for repainting.

Now, here is how to take care of those bigger patches. Rather than applying many layers of the compound to patch, you should insert a scrap of wallboard into the hole.

1. Cut a scrap piece of wallboard into a square that is slightly larger than the hole.
2. Lay the wallboard over the hole and trace around it.

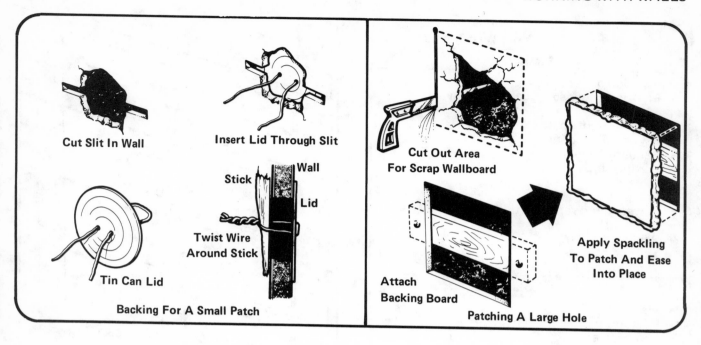

Cut Slit In Wall

Insert Lid Through Slit

Wall

Stick

Lid

Twist Wire
Around Stick

Tin Can Lid

Backing For A Small Patch

Cut Out Area
For Scrap Wallboard

Attach
Backing Board

Patching A Large Hole

Apply Spackling
To Patch And Ease
Into Place

3. Use a keyhole saw to cut along the pattern you just traced.
4. Now you need backing. Select a board about six inches longer than the widest span of the hole you just cut.
5. Slip the backing board into the hole, and hold it firmly against the inside of the wallboard.
6. Insert countersunk screws through the wall and into the backing on each side of the hole to hold the backing securely against the inside of the wall. Keep turning the screws until the flat heads dig down below the surface.

7. Now butter all four edges of the patch with spackling compound or joint compound, and spread compound over the back of the patch where it will rest against the backing board.
8. Ease the patch into place, and hold it there until the compound starts to set up.
9. When the compound is dry, fill up the slits around the patch. Then cover the entire patch — plus the screw heads — with spackling, using a brush or trowel to make the compound match the texture of the rest of the wall.
10. Let the entire area dry; then prime and repaint.

48. Panel A Wall

THE TREMENDOUS selection in wall paneling makes it possible to achieve almost any effect you want in a room. You can purchase actual plywood paneling either finished or unfinished, or you can buy hardboard panels in finishes ranging from barn siding to marble. The plastic-coated finishes on both hardboard and plywood panels are almost impervious to scratches and stains, and they are entirely washable as long as you do not drown them. Just go over the finish with a damp cloth and detergent.

The ease with which the panels go up makes paneling a wall a simple do-it-yourself project. Modern adhesives virtually eliminate nailing, and the preparation and basic installation steps are the same for both plywood panels and hardboard.

1. You could actually apply panels directly to the studs where you have new construction, but since the panels tend to give a little and are far from soundproof, it is best to provide either a plywood or gypsum board backing. Nevertheless, if you decide to apply paneling directly to the studs, make sure that the studs are free of high or low spots. Plane away high spots and attach shims to compensate for low spots.
2. Remove the molding and trim from existing walls and check for highs and lows by drawing a long straight board across the wall and watching for any gaps as it moves across. Build up the lows with drywall compound, and sand down the high spots. If the walls are badly cracked or extremely uneven, you should install furring strips.
3. Masonry walls must always be furred and waterproofed. Furring strips are actually slats

Here Is What You Will Need

Materials

- Plywood or hardboard paneling
- Plywood or gypsum board backing
- Shims
- Long straight board
- Drywall compound
- Sandpaper
- Furring strips
- Nails
- Shingles
- Polyethylene vapor barrier
- Moldings
- Panel adhesive
- Tape
- Wood putty

Tools

- Plane
- Putty knife
- Screwdriver
- Hammer
- Measuring tape
- Level
- Scribing compass
- Saber saw or coping saw
- Caulking gun
- Padded block
- Scissors
- Crosscut hand saw or power saw
- Drill
- Keyhole saw
- Miter box
- Nailset

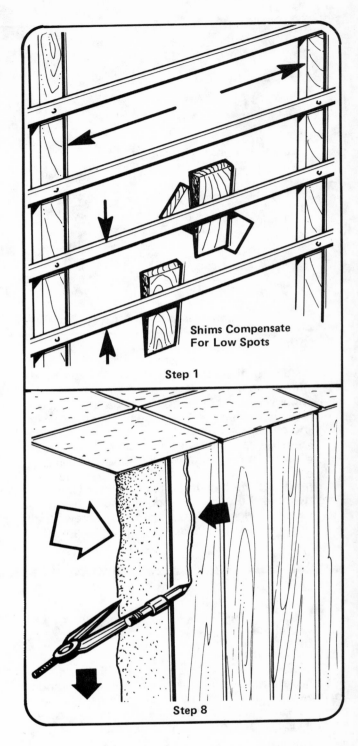

Shims Compensate For Low Spots

Step 1

Step 8

of wood (1x2's or 1x3's) nailed to the wall. Nail the furring horizontally on 16-inch centers, starting at the floor and finishing at the ceiling. Place short vertical strips between the horizontals, spacing them every four feet so that they will come under the joints between the panels. Nail furring strips to the wall with masonry nails, compensating for lows by wedging shingles under the strips. A four mil polyethylene vapor barrier should be placed over the furring of masonry walls and on any other type of walls where moisture might be a problem.

4. Remember that you must compensate for the increased thickness of the wall at electrical switches and wall outlets. Remove the plates and reset the boxes out the necessary distance.

5. Allow the paneling to stabilize to the moisture content of the room before you begin attaching it to the walls. Stack the panels with strips of boards between each one, and then leave

them there for at least two days. This step is very important for a successful paneling job.

6. When the panels are ready to go, lean them against the wall as you think they should be placed. This gives you a chance to match the wood graining in the most pleasing manner. When you have them the way you want them, be sure to number the panels.

7. Measure the distance from floor to ceiling at

several different points. If the panels have to be cut for height, you can cut all of them the same, provided that there is no more than a quarter inch variance. If there is more variance than a quarter of an inch, you should measure the height for each panel and cut it to fit. If you are not going to use a ceiling molding, each panel must be cut to conform to the ceiling line, but if you do use ceiling moldings — and you should — leave a quarter inch gap at the top. There also needs to be a quarter inch gap at the floor which will be covered by the floor molding.

8. Since very few corners are plumb, place the first panel which is to go in a corner next to the wall and check the plumb with a level. Get the panel plumb and close enough to the corner so that you can span the space with a scribing compass. Then run the compass down the corner, with the point in the corner and the pencil marking a line on the panel. Cut the panel along the line with a saber saw equipped with a fine-toothed blade or with a coping saw.

9. If instead of cementing the panels you plan to nail them, use the nails made by the paneling manufacturer. You can use 2d finishing nails to attach the panels to furring strips, but if you must go through a wall to reach the studs, be sure to use nails long enough to penetrate about an inch into the studs. Drive the nails every six inches along the edges and about every twelve inches through the center. Check frequently to make sure you are hitting the furring strips.

10. If you are using mastic to panel the wall, get the kind that you apply with a caulking gun. Run a ribbon across all furring strips or — if there are no strips — in about the same pattern as if there were furring strips. Place the panel against the wall and nail it in place at the top with a pair of nails. Then pull the bottom of the panel out from the wall and prop it with a scrap block of wood until the adhesive gets tacky. When this happens, remove the block and press the panel against the wall. Then secure the entire surface by pounding the panel with a padded block and hammer.

11. When you come to a door or window, take one of the large pieces of paper that came between the sheets of paneling and use it as a pattern. Tape the paper in place, press it against the door or window frame and then cut it with a scissors. Use this pattern to mark the panel, which you can then cut with a fine-toothed crosscut hand saw or with a power saw equipped with a fine-toothed blade. When using a hand saw or a table saw, cut the panel with the face up. When using a hand power saw, cut with the face down.

12. To make cutouts for electrical outlets or switches, drill pilot holes and then use a

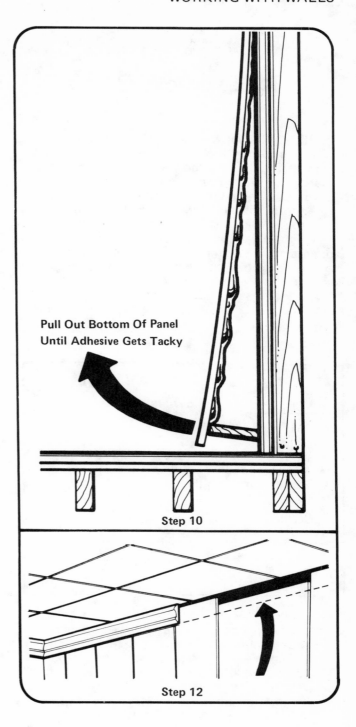

Pull Out Bottom Of Panel Until Adhesive Gets Tacky

Step 10

Step 12

keyhole saw.

13. Next comes the finishing touch that will hide any and all of your mistakes — the application of molding. Most panel manufacturers offer prefinished moldings to match. You can get floor moldings, ceiling moldings, inside or outside corner moldings, and just about anything else you need. Use a miter box and a fine-toothed saw to cut the moldings, and be sure to countersink the nails and fill the holes with matching wood putty.

49. Installing A Pegboard Wall

NO DOUBT you have seen pictures of workshops where every tool hangs neatly from the wall. Chances are the hanging was done with hooks and a perforated hardboard panel commonly called pegboard. Installing pegboard is an easy way to provide wall storage for a multitude of items. You can use it all through the house, not just in a garage or workshop. When painted, pegboard has a pleasing appearance that can blend in with nearly any decor. You can also buy pegboard with prefinished wood tones and patterns. The hanging devices now include special hangers to hold all sorts of items, including dishes, shelves, record albums — even lawn mowers.

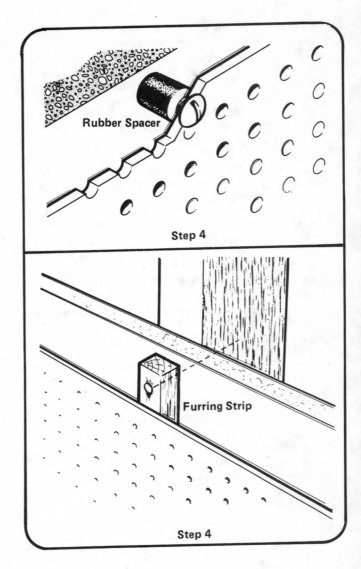

Step 4

Furring Strip

Step 4

Here Is What You Will Need
Materials
• 1/8-inch or 1/4-inch pegboard
• Sandpaper
• Nails, screws, or hardboard adhesive
• Rubber spacers or furring strips
• Expansion or toggle bolts
• Paint
• Moldings
Tools
• Fine-toothed saw
• Hammer
• Screwdriver

1. Most pegboard comes in either 1/8- or 1/4-inch thicknesses. You should require only the 1/8-inch size for home uses, but you may want the 1/4-inch pegboard for especially heavy items like lawn and garden tools.
2. Pegboard comes in 4x8 foot sheets. If you can use a complete sheet, fine; but if not, you will find that pegboard is easy to saw with a fine-toothed blade. A cross-cut is the best hand saw for straight cuts, a coping saw is for making curved cuts, and power saws can provide good results at greater speed. For a smoother cut, pegboard edges can be sanded if necessary. Saw from the finish side with a hand saw and from the back side with a power saw. For the sake of appearance, avoid cutting through any of the holes.
3. Lean the panels against a wall in the room where they are to go, and leave them there for

48 hours to give them time to adjust to existing humidity conditions.
4. You must provide a minimum of 3/8-inch clearance behind each panel to allow for the insertion of most hangers. If you are attaching the pegboard to exposed studs, as is the case in many unfinished garages, you can use nails, screws, or hardboard adhesive to attach the panels directly to the studs. Over a solid wall, though, you must bring the pegboard out some distance to allow the hooks to go in the holes. The rubber spacers sold at hardware stores can serve the purpose. Furring strips nailed to the wall will also do the job. Locate the studs behind the wall and then fasten the strips to the studs with nails, screws, or the adhesive. If you plan to attach the panel to a sheetrock wall with rubber spacers in between, use expansion bolts (Mollys) to hold the pegboard. For 1/4-inch panels that will hold heavy tools, you might consider using toggle bolts.

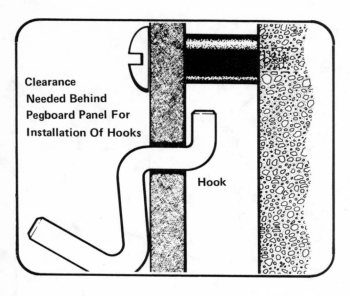

Clearance
Needed Behind
Pegboard Panel For
Installation Of Hooks

Hook

5. When attaching more than one panel, avoid butting the panels tightly together. Moderate contact between the two is all you need.
6. If you want to paint the panel, first attach it to the wall and then apply any paint you would use on wood. Just make sure that the panel is clean and dry before you paint it.
7. If you want to finish off the corners, you can attach inside or outside molding with the same adhesive you use for putting the panel on the wall.

Pegboard need not be confined to walls. You can use it as a room divider or place it on the inside of closet or cabinet doors. Just keep two things in mind: (1) Make sure you attach the panel securely, and, (2) be sure to provide space behind the panel for the hooks.

50. Applying An Artificial Brick Wall

Here Is What You Will Need
Materials
• Synthetic bricks
• Mastic
• Paint
• Sandpaper
• Wall cleaning solvent
• Sealer
Tools
• Measuring tape
• Joint measuring guide
• Putty knife
• Line level

IT USED TO BE that artificial bricks looked extremely artificial, but now there are several manufacturers offering synthetic brick-like materials that are unbelievably authentic in appearance. You can choose from complete lines of brick and stone styles, with most including outside corner pieces. You also have a wide choice of mastic colors, with all resembling actual mortar.

Installation of a real brick wall might compel you to make all sorts of structural changes so that your house could take the additional weight. With the artificial bricks, however, the only preparation you need to make is the surface which you are covering. These bricks can be applied to any surface that is clean, structurally sound, and dry. A wallpapered surface should be stripped of all the wall covering. A porous surface — or any wall not already sealed — must first be painted with an appropriate sealer, and all painted or finished walls should be given a scuff sanding. When cleaning, make sure that you get the surface completely free of all dirt, dust, wax, and grease.

Once you pick out the brick pattern you want, give the dealer the dimensions of the area you wish to cover. He can then help you figure how much mastic — as well as how many flat pieces and corner pieces (if any) — you will need. With the walls prepared and the materials purchased, you are ready to apply your artificial brick wall. Here is all you have to do.

1. If you have decided on a mixed pattern, lay the bricks out on the floor so that you can establish the sequence you want. At the same time, measure the number of bricks per foot, including the spaces for mortar joints. Plot this measurement against the space to be covered to find out about how much you will have to close or open the mortar joints to end up with an even course of bricks. Strive for mortar joints that are about 3/8 of an inch wide. A stick cut to the width of the joint makes a handy guide.
2. Use a wide putty knife to spread on a thin coat of the mastic; all you need is enough to cover the old surface. Avoid starting at an outside

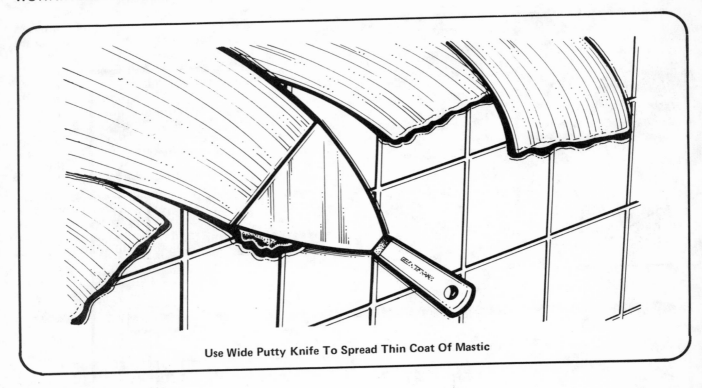

Use Wide Putty Knife To Spread Thin Coat Of Mastic

corner, if possible. Cover an area across the top that is large enough to accommodate two courses (rows). Go down to the floor on the left side, keeping the mastic coat wide enough for only one full brick.

3. Butter the back of each brick with additional mastic.

4. Press each brick firmly into place on the coated surface, and wiggle the brick slightly to set it. Use your stick to measure even mortar joints between bricks.

5. Work all the way across the top with your two rows, and then come back and work down, alternating a full brick with a half brick if that is the pattern you want. This method establishes your horizontal and vertical dimensions. If you discover that you must make some adjustments to make the rows come out even, do your adjusting now while the bricks will still slide.

6. Spread additional mastic, but cover only about four to six square feet at a time. Work across under your two starter courses, adding three or four courses at a time.

7. Step back often and examine the courses, using the previous course as a guide to getting all of them on straight. If you have long walls to cover, a line level (a string stretched taut across the area with a hook-on level) can come in handy. When the bubble lines up, you know the string is level, and the string should line up with each course of bricks.

8. Check all the mortar joints periodically. If they need any smoothing, fix them with your finger.

That is really all there is to it. Some synthetic brick walls require a sealer after the mastic sets, but most are ready immediately.

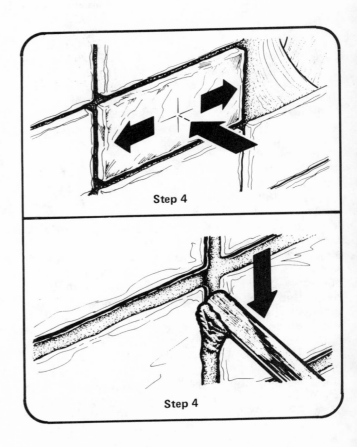

Step 4

Step 4

51. Covering Walls With Fabric

IF PAINTING sounds too messy and wallpapering is more work than you care to tackle, you should consider covering your walls with fabric. Before you decide that such a project is restricted to the professionals, just look at these simple steps.

Here Is What You Will Need
Materials
• Fabric
• Staples
• Shirtboard
• Glue
• Molding strips
• Nails
Tools
• Plumb bob chalk line
• Scissors
• Staple gun
• Hammer

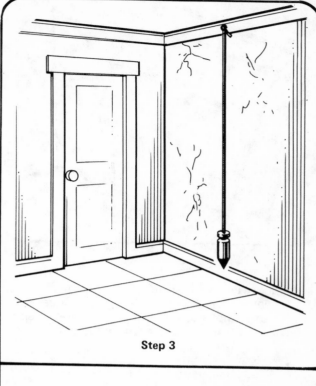

Step 3

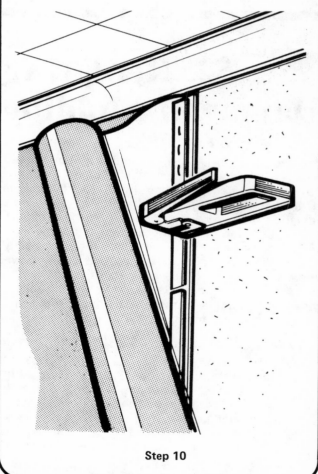

Step 10

1. Select fabric in rolls as wide as possible. Remember when picking a pattern that the panels must match adjacent panels.
2. Since it is unlikely that the last panel will match the first one after you go all around the room, pick out the most obscure corner in which to start.
3. Use a plumb bob chalk line as a guide for getting the first panel straight up and down.
4. Cut each panel to the height of the room plus one inch extra at both top and bottom.
5. Take the first panel, turn an inch of fabric under at the top, and staple the top of the panel to the wall so that the side edge lines up with the chalk line. Unless you plan to cover the top and bottom with molding or ribbon, place the staples as near and as in line with the ceiling as possible. Try to use only as many staples as are required to prevent the fabric from sagging; you can also run a bead of glue across the top to guard against sagging.
6. Staple down both sides of the first panel about 1/4 of an inch in from the edges.
7. Fold the inch under at the bottom, pull the fabric tight, and staple the panel along the baseboard.
8. For the second panel, place the edge face to

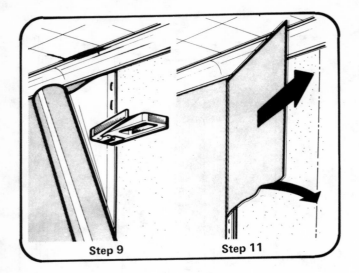

Step 9   Step 11

10. Now staple strips of cardboard (1/2-inch wide) all along the edges you just stapled together. Make sure that the cardboard strips are straight.
11. When you pull the second panel of fabric over into position, you will find you have a hidden seam that is stapled securely in place.
12. Staple down the other edge about 1/4 inch in from the edge.
13. Repeat the same procedure as you continue on around the room.
14. Rough cut the panels for doors and windows, turning the excess under and stapling them as close to the frames as possible. Keep the number of staples to a minimum, using glue wherever possible. With some fabrics, you can glue the entire job.
15. Turn under and glue the last panel in place over the staples you left showing along the edge of the first panel.
16. If you wish to hide the staples at the top and bottom, you can glue a band of the fabric — or even a wide contrasting ribbon — around these seams. You can also attach molding strips to cover the staples.

face with the first panel. In other words, the reverse side of the second panel faces out.

9. Staple the second panel at several spots about 1/2 inch in from where the edges of the two panels meet.

52. Replacing Damaged Molding

MOLDING IS ALMOST a panacea for botched-up wall seams and joints. Of course, it can be decorative as well, but generally its main function is to hide cracks. When the molding itself gets damaged, however, you cannot hide the problem; you must replace at least a section of the molding and perhaps the entire piece. Since the most easily damaged moldings are the baseboards — down where they can be hit by all sorts of things — the following instructions describe how to replace baseboard molding, but you can apply the same technique to other moldings in other places.

1. First, you must remove any shoe molding, the quarter-round piece that fits against both the baseboard and the floor. Since it is nailed to the subfloor, apply gentle prying pressure with a putty knife at one end of the shoe molding to get it started. Then you can use a screwdriver with a wood block for leverage. Once started, the shoe molding should come up fairly easily. Try not to be too rough, though, or you can break it, adding to your

Here Is What You Will Need

Materials

- Wooden wedges
- Replacement moldings
- Finishing nails
- Paint

Tools

- Putty knife
- Screwdriver
- Wood block
- Pry bar
- Hammer
- Pliers
- Miter box
- Backsaw or hacksaw
- Coping saw
- Nailset
- Paintbrush

replacement costs and troubles.

2. Next, pry out the damaged baseboard. Start at one end, inserting a small flat pry bar between the baseboard and the wall. Pry gently, and move further down the line whenever you can, slipping small wooden wedges in the gaps. Work all the way along the baseboard prying and wedging. Then work back between the

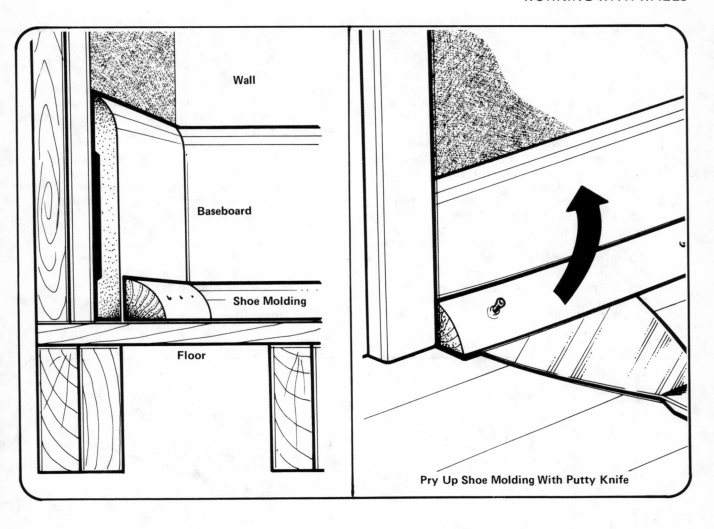

Wall

Baseboard

Shoe Molding

Floor

Pry Up Shoe Molding With Putty Knife

wedges, tapping the wedges in deeper as the baseboard comes out more. The baseboard soon will come off.

3. Check to see if any nails pulled through either the shoe molding or the baseboard, and if so, pull out the nails completely.

If the old baseboard came out intact, you can use it as a pattern for cutting the new one. If part is missing or if it is badly damaged, however, you must cut the new moldings to fit without the aid of a pattern. You will need a miter box to cut the moldings; an inexpensive wooden miter box will be adequate for this work. The slots allow you to cut 45-degree angles, and you should use either a backsaw or a fine blade in a hacksaw. Be sure to place the molding you are about to cut next to the molding against which it will rest in order to make certain that the cut you plan to make is the right one. Then follow these instructions to cut the new molding.

1. Place a scrap of wood in the miter box.
2. Make sure that the lip of the miter box presses against the edge of a table or bench so that

you can hold it steady.
3. Hold the molding tightly against the side of the miter box to prevent it from slipping as you saw.
4. After you make the cut, the molding should fit

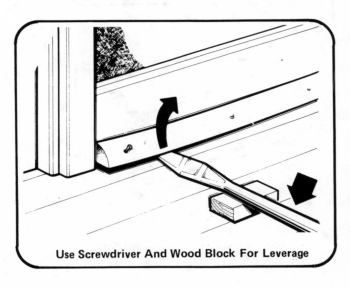

Use Screwdriver And Wood Block For Leverage

perfectly against the other mitered piece to form a right angle.

If you need an inside right angle, though, you could go crazy trying to get the two angled pieces to fit. The solution to this vexing problem is called a coped joint. Here is how you make such a joint.

1. Cut one piece of baseboard to fit precisely in the space.
2. Lay this piece of baseboard flat on the floor with its backside facing up.
3. Place another piece of baseboard molding down against the back of the piece on the floor. The tapered end of the top molding should point to the edge of the bottom piece. If it does not, turn the top piece end for end. Now it is in place.
4. Trace the contour of the top piece onto the bottom piece.
5. Use a coping saw to cut along the pattern.

6. When cut, the two pieces will fit closely together to form a false miter — referred to as a coped joint — that creates a perfect inside corner.

When you finish all the mitering and coped joints, you are ready to install the new baseboard molding and to reinstall the shoe molding.

1. Fit all the pieces together before nailing to make sure that you cut them correctly.
2. Nail the baseboards in place with finishing nails. Then use a nailset to drive the nail heads below the surface of the molding.
3. Reinstall the shoe molding with finishing nails as well. Remember, shoe molding must be nailed to the floor and not to the baseboard. Drive the nail heads below the surface of the shoe molding with a nailset.
4. Paint all new moldings to match the color of your walls.

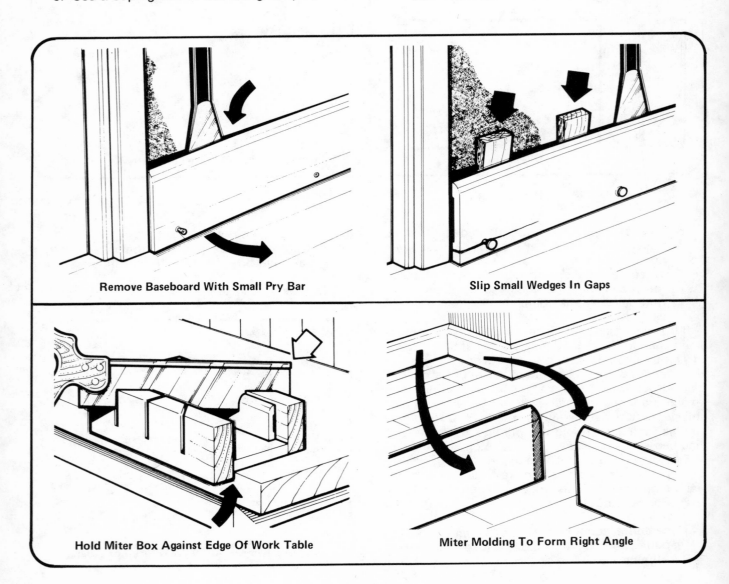

Remove Baseboard With Small Pry Bar

Slip Small Wedges In Gaps

Hold Miter Box Against Edge Of Work Table

Miter Molding To Form Right Angle

53. Replacing A Ceramic Tile

GENERALLY, the hardest part about replacing a cracked ceramic tile is finding a new tile that matches. Some colors are not easy to find. If your tile is very old, you may have to go to a wrecking yard to find a match. Once you have the right tile, however, just follow these directions for removing the cracked one and putting in its replacement.

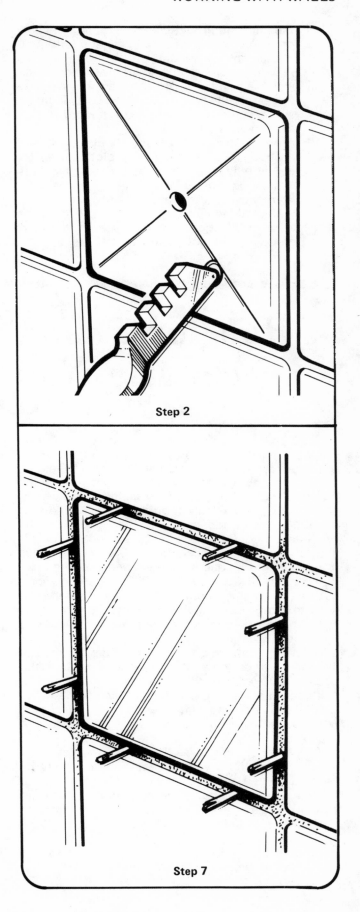

Step 2

Step 7

Here Is What You Will Need

Materials

- Replacement tile
- Tile mastic
- Tape or wooden toothpicks
- Tile grout
- Sponge
- Terry cloth towel

Tools

- Power drill with carbide tip
- Glass cutter
- Cold chisel
- Hammer
- Knife
- Putty knife

1. The best method for removing the old tile is to drill a hole in its middle with a carbide bit in your power drill.
2. Next, score an "X" in the tile with a glass cutter.
3. Take a cold chisel and hammer, and break away the tile without damaging any of the surrounding tiles.
4. Clean the bed on which the old tile rested, removing all the bumps to make the surface as smooth as possible. Then remove any loose grout around the opening.
5. Purchase tile mastic at a hardware store, and spread it over the back of the new tile. Keep the mastic about a half inch away from all four edges.
6. Hold the tile by its edges and ease it into place. Press until the new tile is flush with the surrounding tiles.
7. Position the tile to provide an even space all around it, and then either tape it in place or insert broken toothpicks to keep gravity from pulling the tile down before the mastic sets up.
8. Allow enough time for the mastic to cure, and

then mix tile grout according to the directions on the package. Be sure to mix the grout until it is completely smooth.

9. Fill in the space all the way around the tile with the grout mix. Dip either a sponge or your finger into the mix, and apply it so as to fill the space entirely. You will do no harm if you get the grout on other tiles.

10. After the grout has set for about a quarter of an hour, take a damp terry cloth towel and gently remove any excess on the other tiles. Just be careful not to dig out any of the grout from between the tiles.

11. Wait until the next day, and then rub the damp towel more vigorously to remove all traces of grout and to polish the tile. If the tile you

replaced is in a shower, make sure that you avoid getting any water on it until the grout has set up completely.

You can remedy loose tiles the same way, except that you eliminate steps 1, 2, and 3. Use a knife to scrape out all the grout around the loose tile, and then gently pry out the tile with a putty knife. Follow all of the steps above to replace it.

While you are working on the one tile, check all the others to see if they are loose. Loosened tiles usually are caused by shifting in foundation, and, therefore, several tiles often come loose at the same time. Light tapping on the tiles with a putty knife handle will show you where any loose ones are.

54. Hanging Things On The Wall

Here Is What You Will Need
Materials
• Picture hangers
• Cellophane tape
• Plastic wall anchors
• Expansion (or Molly) bolts
Tools
• Magnetic stud finder
• Hammer
• Drill
• Screwdriver

THE OLD SAYING, "What goes up must come down," need not apply to things you hang on the wall. Most homes today have hollow wall construction, and that means something like sheetrock is nailed to studs within the wall. When you drive a nail into such a wall to hang something, the weight of the hanging will probably pull the nail out of sheetrock before too long — unless you drive the nail into a stud. Generally, studs are located on 16-inch centers, which means that there are 16 inches from the center of one stud to the center of the next. You can usually locate studs with a magnetic finder, but frequently the studs are not located where you want to hang your pictures, mirrors, etc. What you want to know then is how to hang things where you want them when there are no studs available.

To hang lightweight pictures, use a picture hanger. All you need do is place the plate flat against the wall and drive the nail through it. The nail goes in at an angle, and the angled nail and the flat plate will hold most lightweight objects securely. When you drive the nail in, though, be sure to place a tab of cellophane tape over the spot to prevent the surface from crumbling as the nail penetrates it.

For hanging lightweight objects like drapery rods, use plastic wall anchors. Buy the anchors made for the size screws you have, and examine the package to find out what size drill bit to use for the holes. Then, to install these anchors, just follow 1, 2, 3.

1. Drill a hole in the wall to accommodate the plastic anchor.
2. Tap the anchor in all the way.

3. Insert the screw through the item it is to hold, and then turn it into the anchor. The screw expands the anchor to make it grip the sides of the hole.

As you get into heavier hangings, such as shelves and mirrors, the best device is the expansion anchor — commonly called the Molly. Mollys come in different sizes to accommodate differences in wall thickness and in the weight of the things they are to hold. Once you get the right Molly, here is how to install it.

1. Consult the package to see what size drill bit to use, and then drill a hole in the wall.
2. Lightly tap the Molly in place with your hammer.
3. Turn the slotted bolt clockwise.
4. When you cannot turn it any more, back it out. The Molly is then secure against the inside of the wall, and you are ready to hang your shelves, mirror, etc.
5. Put the bolt through the item or the item's

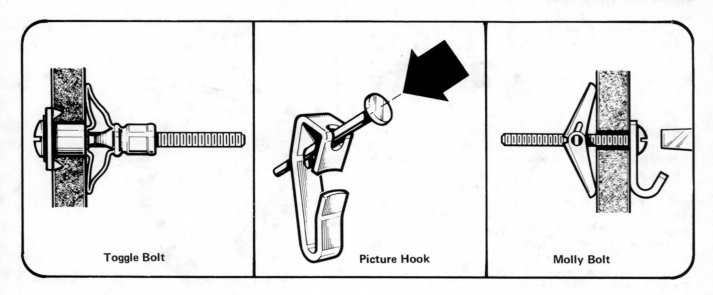

Toggle Bolt **Picture Hook** **Molly Bolt**

hanger, and reinsert the bolt in the Molly. That is all there is to it. One Molly can support up to five hundred pounds.

For really heavy installations — such as cabinets or a bookshelf unit — use toggle bolts. Available in several sizes, toggle bolts also require that you drill holes in the wall. If you buy the packaged kind, you will find the size of the hole specified on the package. Here is how to install them.

1. Drill the hole.
2. Remove the bolt from the flange.
3. Put the bolt through the object to be hung or through its hanger before you insert it into the wall. You cannot remove the bolt after the toggle bolt device is in the wall without the flange falling down between the wall. Reinsert the bolt in the flange.
4. Crimp the flange with your thumb and forefinger and push it into the hole. Of course, you must hold the object you are hanging right next to the wall as you insert the toggle bolt. When the flange goes through, pull it back toward you until you feel it hit the back of the wall.
5. Turn the bolt clockwise until the hanger or the item itself is flat against the wall.

For specialized hanging problems, chances are that you will be able to find an inexpensive anchor of some kind to do the job. Check your local hardware store.

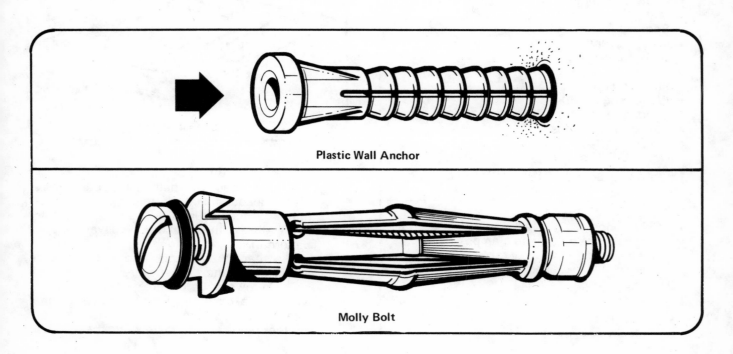

Plastic Wall Anchor

Molly Bolt

55. Framing A Picture

Y OU NEED NOT own a priceless art collection to have plenty of attractive wall hangings. If you pay to have all your treasures framed by a custom framer, however, you will find youself spending considerable sums of money. If, on the other hand, you make you own frames, you can save somewhere near 75 percent of what a professional charges. After you get the hang of it, your frames will look custom made and you will have the satisfaction of turning out a product of your own creativity. You can even create "one-of-a-kind" frames suited exactly to the picture you are hanging.

The basic picture frame is made from decorative moldings. These moldings, available at lumberyards and some home centers, are quite inexpensive and they come in many sizes and shapes. Try to find a store where you can select the moldings yourself. That way, you can be assured of getting straight pieces without pockets of sap, knots, warps, and bows. To start, buy a two-part frame, consisting of a sub-frame and moldings for the decorative outer frame. Here is how it goes.

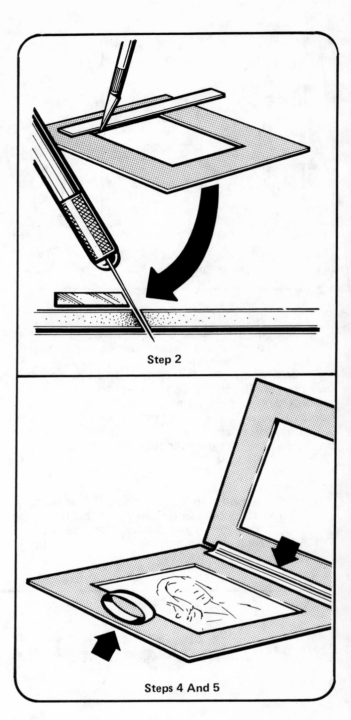

Step 2

Steps 4 And 5

Here Is What You Will Need

Materials

- Decorative moldings
- Mat
- Spray glue
- Masking tape
- White polyvinyl glue
- Fasteners
- Finishing nails
- Wood putty
- Sandpaper
- Nonreflective glass
- Brads
- Heavy brown paper
- Picture hanger or wire and screw eyes

Tools

- Artist's knife
- Straightedge
- Corner clamps or framing clamps
- Miter box and hand saw or table saw
- Nailset
- Hammer
- Scissors

1. You must decide whether the painting or photo needs a mat. In many cases, a mat enhances the picture. After selecting the color and texture of the mat board you want, draw a pattern of the picture on the mat.
2. Use a sharp artist's knife and a straightedge to cut along the line you drew. As you cut, bevel in toward the picture.
3. Next, cut a backing piece to match the mat size. You can use heavy cardboard, but another piece of mat board works best. Mount

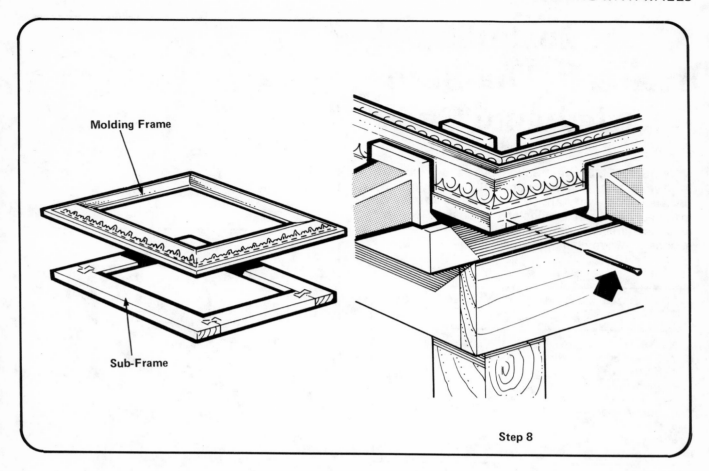

Molding Frame

Sub-Frame

Step 8

the picture on the backing with spray glue.

4. Make a hinge out of masking tape by running it along the edges of both the mat and the backing.

5. Form a loop out of masking tape with the sticky side out to hold the other mat in place.

6. Now you are ready to make the sub-frame. The opening of this part must be slightly larger than the mat and mounting. Cut the four pieces and glue them together (white polyvinyl glue works well) in simple butt joints, clamping the corners with inexpensive corner clamps or framing clamps. While the clamp is holding the corner, attach a fastener to secure the joint.

7. The moldings must be wider than the material used in the sub-frame and must overlap toward the center a quarter of an inch to form a rabbet into which the picture will fit. Miter the molding very carefully. A wooden miter box and a hand saw will do, but if you have a table saw, you will be able to set it for a more accurate miter. When all four pieces are cut, check them against the sub-frame before gluing.

8. Glue and clamp the frame moldings, and while the clamps are on, drive tiny finishing nails into the frame so that they go into the ad-

joining pieces.

9. Use a nailset to drive the heads below the surface.

10. Fill the holes over the nails and sand.

11. Attach the two frames together with glue and nails.

12. Finish the frame in any manner you like.

13. When the finish is dry, insert a piece of glass cut 1/8 of an inch less than the frame in both width and length to compensate for any irregularities. Nonreflective glass is best for paintings and photos. With the glass in place, insert the mounted picture.

14. Use brads to hold the picture and its backing in the frame. Drive in two brads per side, and make sure that both the picture and glass are as snug against the front of the frame as possible.

15. Next, add the dust cover, which is a piece of heavy brown paper glued to the back of the frame to seal in the picture. After the glue sets, take a damp cloth and rub lightly over the dust cover. The cloth must not be wet enough to soak through, however. When it dries the paper will shrink, creating a tight dust jacket.

16. The frame itself is finished. Now you can add either a hanger or wire in screw eyes and hang your new creation.

56. Installing A Between-The-Studs Medicine Chest

MOST HOME construction over the past thirty years has been of the dry wall type. If you have dry wall type walls and if your bathroom lacks a medicine chest, you can install one easily. Recessed medicine chests come sized to fit inside the 16-inch spaces between wall studs.

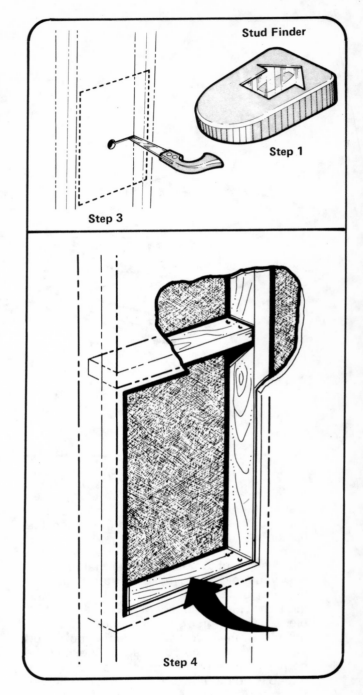

Stud Finder

Step 1

Step 3

Step 4

Here Is What You Will Need
Materials
• 2x4's
• New medicine chest
• Screws
Tools
• Stud finder
• Drill
• Keyhole saw
• Screwdriver

1. You must first find the studs. An inexpensive tool called a stud finder utilizes a magnet to help you find the hidden nails. Once you find a line of nails, you know that there is a stud behind the wall to which these nails are attached.
2. When you locate two consecutive studs in the right area, hold the chest where you want it to go and draw an outline around it.
3. Drill a hole inside the outline and saw from the hole toward either stud, using a keyhole saw. When you reach one of the studs, cut along the outline you drew.
4. Cut a pair of 2x4's into 16-inch lengths, and toenail them in place at the top and bottom of the opening. Toenailing means driving nails at an angle. Position these crossbraces so that they are behind the surface of the wall but right at the edge of the hole.
5. Set the cabinet unit in the hole, and drive in screws on all four sides to hold the new medicine chest securely.

Cabinets wider than the space between two adjacent studs are available, but they require some special installation procedures. You must saw out sections of the studs that interfere with the cabinet, and then nail in crosspieces (headers) to regain the support lost by the missing stud sections. If you discover plumbing or wiring behind the wall at the spot where you want you medicine cabinet to be, you should forgo a recessed model and install a surface-mounted unit instead. Unfortunately, the selection of surface units is not nearly as large as the choice of recessed cabinets. If you cannot find a suitable surface-mounted medicine chest, you should look into the kits that let you install a sleeve around a recessed model so that you can mount it on the wall's surface.

57. Mildew

EVEN THE NICEST homes can have mildew, an ugly looking mess that can also produce an unpleasant odor. Mildew is a fungus that floats in the air until it finds the right conditions to start growing on the wall. What are those right conditions? Mildew spores must have moisture and dirt to feed on; soap scum is one of mildew's choice dishes. The bathroom walls, of course, are among the most common places for mildew to settle, but you can get rid of the fungus easily if you follow these simple steps.

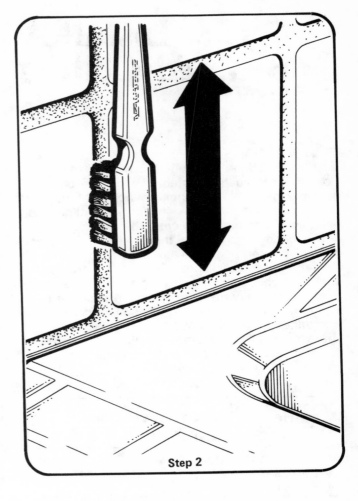

Step 2

Here Is What You Will Need

Materials

- Household bleach
- Plastic squeeze bottle
- Household ammonia
- Dehumidifier or exhaust fan
- Trisodium phosphate
- Powdered detergent

Tools

- Toothbrush
- Stiff brush or broom
- Garden hose

1. Cover all the mildew spots you can see with household bleach. Since most of the fungus will be along the grout lines between tiles or in corners, a good way to apply the bleach is with a plastic squeeze bottle (such as a shampoo or dish detergent bottle). Be sure to observe all of the caution notices on the bleach bottle regarding dangers to your skin and respiratory system.
2. Most of the mildew spots will disappear in a few minutes, but stubborn spots may need additional bleach and perhaps a light scrubbing. An old toothbrush is ideal for scrubbing between tiles and in the corners.
3. When all the mildew is gone, rinse all the bleach away with water.
4. When you are sure that none of the bleach remains on the walls, wash the walls with household ammonia. **REMEMBER: YOU MUST NEVER MIX BLEACH AND AMMONIA.** The combination releases potentially fatal chlorine gas. The ammonia will kill the spores of the fungus, preventing the mildew from making a speedy return.

Of course, new mildew can get started unless you eliminate the conditions that allow it to thrive. Find out what is causing the excess moisture. If the mildew occurs in a bath, kitchen, or laundry room, you know where the moisture comes from, and your problem then is to discover a way to exhaust the excess moisture. A dehumidifier or an exhaust fan may be the answer, or regular airing of the room may do the job. If the moisture comes from a leak under the house or bad drainage, you must correct the problem to eliminate your mildew problem for good. Naturally, it is always a good idea to keep walls free of dirt, grease, and soap scum.

Mildew also forms outside. Many people think that they can kill the fungus when they paint their homes with a mildew-retardant paint. Usually, however, they see the mildew growing back through the paint in a matter of weeks. No paint can kill mildew; you must kill mildew before painting. Here is how to get rid of fungus from exterior walls. Mix 2/3 cup TSP (trisodium phosphate — available at most paint stores), 1/3 cup powdered detergent, and one quart liquid household bleach. Add enough warm water to make one gallon of solution, and scrub the affected areas with a stiff brush or broom; then hose them off. Be sure to trim back trees and bushes that prevent air and sunlight from reaching mildew-prone areas.

58. Install A Beamed Ceiling

MANY ROOMS can achieve real character with the addition of a rough hewn beamed ceiling. Not long ago such a project would have been impossible for the average homeowner, but today it is an easy do-it-yourself task. In fact, you will not even need an assistant to help carry the beams.

The change is due to the advent of synthetic beams made of a rigid polyurethane foam. Although available in wood finishes, some beams are obtainable unfinished and ready to take any oil-based paint or stain. You buy the fake beams in sections or in kits, and you attach them to any sound, dry surface with adhesive. All you have to do is select a design, figure the number of beams you will need, and follow these steps to install a beamed ceiling.

Here Is What You Will Need

Materials

- Polyurethane foam beams
- Deglosser
- Panel adhesive

Tools

- Measuring tape
- Hand saw

---

1. Make sure that the surface is sound, dry, and clean. If the surface is glossy, apply a deglosser.
2. Measure the length the beams are to span, and cut them to fit. You can cut the beams with a hand saw.
3. Mark the position of all beams with light pencil marks on the ceiling.
4. Hold each beam in place to make sure that they fit.
5. If you plan to install corner beams, attach them first. Corner beams are half the size of the regular U-shaped ceiling beams. To install them, run a 1/8-inch bead of adhesive in a wiggly line along the back of the beam. Some manufacturers suggest running an additional bead on the ceiling or wall. If you have the beams with adhesive already on them, you just peel the coating paper off and stick the beams to the ceiling.
6. After you apply the adhesive, press the beam against the ceiling in line with the pencil marks. Push firmly to flatten the adhesive.
7. Remove the beam to allow the adhesive to cure.
8. When the adhesive starts to get tacky, replace the beam and press it firmly in place.
9. Apply some sort of temporary support until you are sure that the adhesive has set up completely.
10. Next, put up the center pieces. If you are installing an odd number of beams, put the middle beam up and then work to each side. Before you know it, you will have a beautiful beamed ceiling.

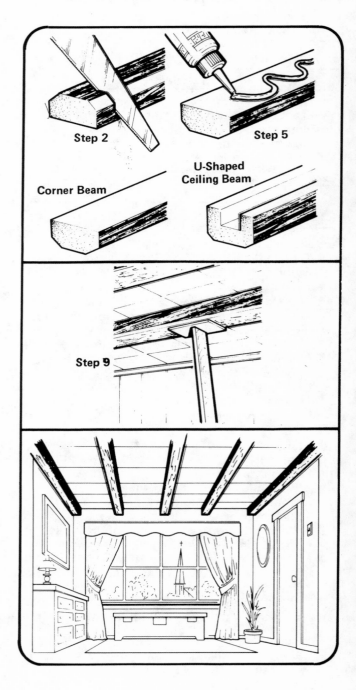

Step 2

Step 5

Corner Beam

U-Shaped Ceiling Beam

Step 9

59. Installing A Tile Ceiling

THE EASY WAY to have a new ceiling — as long as the old surface is sound and you do not wish to lower it — is to install ceiling tiles. Some ceiling tiles can absorb a good deal of the noise in the room, but you should realize that not all tiles are acoustical tiles. If your reason for wanting a tile ceiling is noise reduction, then you must do some very careful comparison shopping.

You apply ceiling tiles in one of two ways, either with staples or with adhesive. A sound ceiling of wallboard or plaster takes adhesive well, but if a plaster ceiling is unsound, you must install furring strips and then staple the tiles to the strips. Staples can also be used on wallboard. Different tile manufacturers have different systems for joining tiles together, but the installation principles are all about the same.

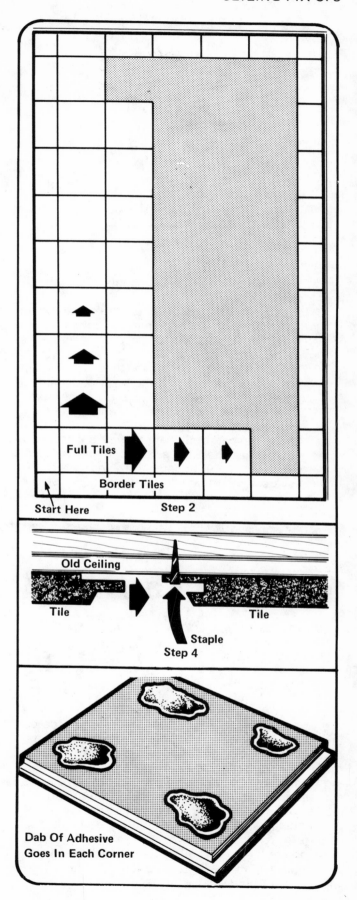

Full Tiles

Border Tiles

Start Here

Step 2

Old Ceiling

Tile

Tile

Staple

Step 4

Dab Of Adhesive Goes In Each Corner

Here Is What You Will Need

Materials

- Ceiling tiles
- Staples or adhesive
- Furring strips
- Nails

Tools

- Measuring tape
- Chalk line
- Staple gun
- Fiberboard knife or a fine-toothed saw
- Hammer

---

1. You must find out how large your border tiles are to be. You do not want to end up with less than half a tile at the borders, and you want the borders at each end to be the same width. Here is what you do. Measure each wall, disregarding the number of feet involved but paying close atttention to the number of inches. For example, suppose that one wall measures ten feet three inches. All that counts is the number three. Add twelve to that and then divide by two. The result — 7½ — is the border tile width for each end. Now if the other wall measures ten feet, eight inches, the borders along the other sides would be ten inches

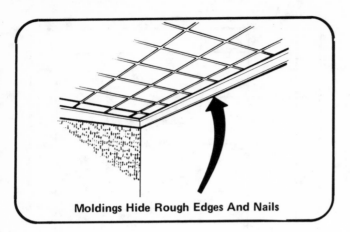

Moldings Hide Rough Edges And Nails

flange will be covered by the interlock of the next tiles.

5. Now staple a complete course of cut border tiles along one wall, nailing the back sides in place.
6. Run the border tiles along the other wall.
7. Work in rows with the full tiles, stapling them as you go.
8. Border tiles at the other end will have no staple tabs. Nails plus the interlocks will hold them in place.

If you are applying the tile ceiling with adhesive, then follow these steps.

1. Apply four dabs of adhesive to the back of a tile about an inch and a half in from each corner.
2. Place the tile near either the chalk line or the next tile, and slide it into place.
3. Press the tile with your hand to make sure it adheres firmly against the ceiling. If a tile seems uneven, pull it back down and adjust the amount of adhesive to compensate for any irregularities.

Be sure to cut holes in the tiles for ceiling light fixtures. Remember that since the fixture's plate will cover the opening, the hole you cut need not be a work of art. When you get all the tiles up, place molding in the corners and you will hide all the rough edges as well as the nails. You should have a great looking ceiling!

(eight inches plus twelve equals 20 divided by two equals ten).

2. Pick a corner to start in, measure out the width of the border tiles, and snap a chalk line each way. It is also a good idea to snap a chalk line at the center as a guide.
3. If you are going to staple the tiles in place, cut the corner tile first with the staple tabs aimed toward the center. Use a sharp fiberboard knife or a fine-toothed saw for cutting, and cut with the tile turned face up.
4. Staple the corner tile, after placing it carefully against the chalk lines. You can nail the back sides in place because any nails will be covered by molding later on. The staple

60. How To Install A Suspended Ceiling

IF YOU EVER thought about converting a garage or basement into a family room, chances are you were discouraged by what you considered the impossibility of covering up all the wires, ducts, and pipes in the ceiling. And in an already finished room you might have thought that the existing ceiling was in such bad repair that it would have to be completely refinished before the room could be made useful once again. You can surmount all of these obstacles, though, by installing a suspended ceiling.

Suspended systems allow you easy access to pipes and ducts when you need to reach them, and special lamp units that you place in the ceiling in

Here Is What You Will Need
Materials

• Wall angles	• Wire
• Nails	• Main tees
• Ceiling panels	• Cross tees
• String	• Light fixture ceiling panels
• Screw eyes	

Tools

• Measuring tape	• Hammer
• Chalk line	• Tin snips
• Level	• Utility knife

place of certain panels make lighting the room a snap. There are several different systems on the market, all claiming to be the easiest to install. Since all work on about the same principles and all go up fairly easily, however, make your choice of suspended ceiling systems based on some other factor than ease of installation. Here is how to install a typical suspended ceiling system.

1. Determine the height you want the ceiling to be, and snap a chalk line around the perimeter of the room. Use a level to make sure that the line does not slant.
2. Nail the metal pieces called wall angles all the way around the room at the chalk line.
3. Measure the room to determine the size of the border tiles. Most suspended ceiling panels are 2x4 feet. Decide which way you wish the longer dimension to run, and divide the room length by four and the width by two. What is left over is your border area. Since your borders should be the same size at both ends, divide the remainder by two. Measure out from the wall the proper distance for the border panel, and stretch a string from one wall angle to the other at that point. If the ceiling joists above are exposed, run the string across perpendicular to them.
4. Drive screw eyes or nails into the sides of the joists. If you are installing a suspended ceiling over an existing ceiling, use screw eyes which are long enough to go through the ceiling and into the joists. Attach wires to the screw eyes or nails, and bend the wires at the level of the string.
5. When you finish attaching all of the wires along that line, install one of the metal pieces called a main tee (available in 12-foot lengths). Place one end of the main tee on the wall angle, and attach the wires through the holes in the tee.
6. Proceed with the other main tees at four-foot intervals all across the room. Cut odd lengths with tin snips, and check the tees regularly with a level.
7. When all of the tees are in place, start installing the cross tees. Cross tees are four-foot sections that fit perpendicular to the main tees and lock in place with a twist. Work your way across the room from wall to wall, installing all the cross tee sections.
8. Cut and snap each end of the cross tee pieces into the main tee.
9. Attach the remaining rows of cross tees every two feet all across the room.
10. When the entire grid system is hooked together, just tilt the panels to fit above the grids and then lower them into place.
11. You can cut the end panels easily with a sharp utility knife.
12. Attach light fixtures to the joists above or — if you have the kind equipped with special brackets — attach them to the grid system. A special translucent panel lets the light through to the room.

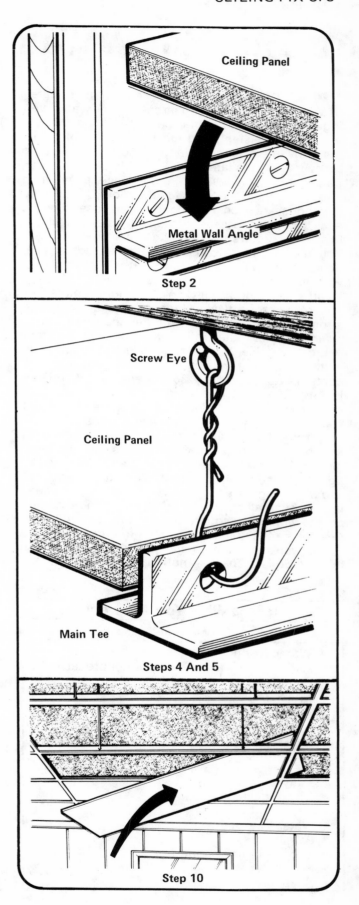

Ceiling Panel

Metal Wall Angle

Step 2

Screw Eye

Ceiling Panel

Main Tee

Steps 4 And 5

Step 10

61. Papering A Wall

WALL COVERINGS can make a dramatic difference in a room's appearance. Vinyl wall coverings are the most popular because they are washable, fade resistant, and most are strippable. That last advantage looms large when you have to recover the walls later on. Strippable coverings can be peeled off the wall all in one piece, eliminating messy steaming, soaking, and scraping. Prepasted coverings are also very popular because they are easy to use and less messy than unpasted coverings. Prepastes require the use of a water box, however. You must put the strip in the water box to activate the paste. If you select a covering that is not prepasted, you must be sure to use the prescribed type of paste. If you are applying a vinyl covering, for example, use one of the special vinyl adhesives that are much stronger and mildew resistant than the wheat paste.

Figuring how many rolls to buy is strictly a mathematical exercise, but you have to know the rules. No matter how wide the roll is, any wall covering roll contains approximately 36 square feet. A roll 24 inches wide is 18 feet long, while a roll that is 27 inches wide is only 16 feet long. Because of trim and waste, though, you can never use all 36 square feet on a roll. The actual yield is usually only about 30 square feet. To figure how many rolls you will need, measure the perimeter of the room and multiply that figure by the room's height. That gives you the square footage. Deduct one roll for every two openings — such as doors and windows — and then apply the yield of 30 square feet against the total. The final figure is the number of rolls to order.

Now you are ready to start to work. But the first thing to do is prepare — not paper — the surface.

Here Is What You Will Need
Materials
• Wall covering
• Adhesive (if wall covering is not prepasted)
• Sandpaper
• Spackling
• Sizing
Tools
• Measuring tape
• Steamer
• Putty knife
• Chalked plumb line
• Scissors
• Water tray
• Paintbrush
• Sponge or smoothing brush
• Roller
• Razor blade

1. A paper wall covering can be applied over old paper, provided that the old covering is sound. If it is not sound, remove any spots of loose paper and feather the edges. If there are more than two layers of old paper, or if you are applying a vinyl wall covering, you should remove all of the old covering. Removing old paper is no easy job, however. You can rent a steamer from the wallpaper store, but you still have to scrape off most of the covering with a wide putty knife.

2. An unpapered wall that is textured should be sanded to remove all the bumps. You need not

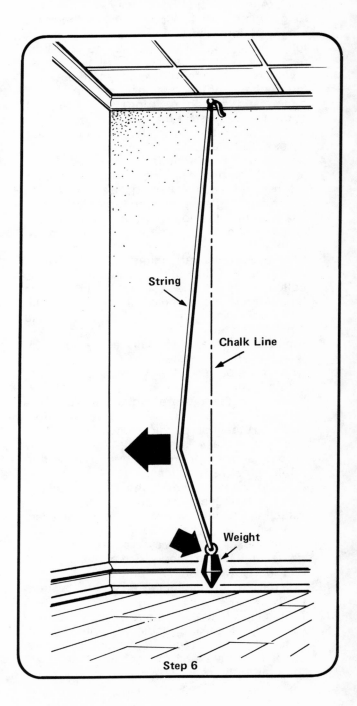

String

Chalk Line

Weight

Step 6

sand it as slick as glass, but you must get most of the bumps off. Remove the gloss from any enameled surfaces.

3. Fill all cracks and holes.
4. Apply sizing (a sort of glue) over the wall. Absolutely necessary on new wallboard, unpainted plaster, and other such surfaces that would absorb paste, sizing also works well on most other surfaces. Talk to your wall paper dealer; he can tell you which sizing is compatible with the adhesive you are using.
5. Now you are ready for papering. Select the most inconspicuous corner in the room, and

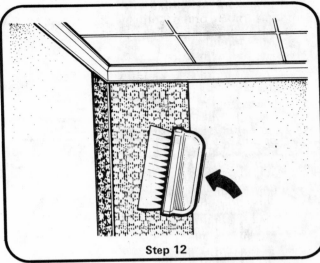

Step 12

measure out along the wall adjacent to that corner a distance one inch less than the width of your roll.

6. Drop a chalked plumb line from that point, and snap it to show the true vertical. A plumb line is nothing more than a string with a weight on one end. Tack the chalk-coated string at the ceiling so that the weight almost touches the floor. When the weight stops moving, the string is vertical. Hold the bottom end tight and snap the string to place a vertical chalk line on the wall.
7. Now you are ready to put up your first strip of paper. Measure the height of the wall, and cut your strip about four inches longer.
8. If you have the prepaste type of wall covering, put the rolled-up strip in the water tray and leave it there for the prescribed amount of time. If you must apply the paste yourself, put the strip face down on a large table and start brushing on the paste at the top. Cover the top half, and then fold the top over — paste against paste — making sure not to crimp or crease the paper. Do the bottom half and fold it over the same way. This technique allows you to carry and work with the strip without getting the paste all over you.
9. When you get to the corner, unfold the top half of the paper strip, position the edge next to the chalk line, and be sure it lines up. This step is very important. If the first strip does not line up, the whole room will be out of line. Leave about half of the extra four inches of length sticking out at the ceiling. Start smoothing over toward the corner, using your hand, and work over the entire top half. When you get to the corner, you will find that an extra inch of wall covering remains; take the extra amount around the corner and stick it to the other wall.
10. When the top half is smooth, unfold the bottom

Smoothing Brush

Seam Roller

Step 8

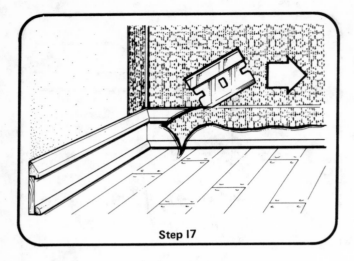

Step 17

tually pound it against the corner to push the paper back in the corner until it sticks.

13. Use the same pounding technique along the baseboard and at the ceiling. Do not trim the top and bottom yet.

14. Now unroll some new paper, and make sure it lines up according to the pattern before you cut the second panel.

15. After you prepare the second panel for hanging, place it right next to the first, and then slide it over to butt against the edge.

16. Roll the seams after you smooth each panel.

17. Wait until after you put up and smooth the next panel before trimming the previous one. Use a sharp razor blade, and change blades when you start to notice the blade getting dull.

18. Continue on all the way around the room. Do not skip any areas around doors or windows.

19. When you come to doors and windows, hold the strip over the door and use a hard object to crease an outline of the frame in the wall covering. Then trim the panel to fit, and paste it in place. You can trim it more precisely with a razor blade later.

half and apply it the same way.

11. Use a sponge or smoothing brush to force out excess paste and air bubbles. Always work toward the edges.

12. Hold the smoothing brush vertically, and ac-

62. Repairing Wallpaper

AFTER A WHILE, you may notice some wallpaper problems. If not remedied, a loose seam, a slight tear, or a bubble will surely become a bigger and more unsightly aspect of your walls. When you think back to what you went through in putting the paper up originally, you will certainly prefer to repair than to repaper.

1. You can simply repaste seams that come unstuck. Save a small container of the paste for that purpose, and squirt a bit under the loose flaps or spread it on with a small artist's brush. Then use a seam roller to press the paper back down.

2. If you have overlaps in a vinyl covering that refuse to stay down, buy some of the special paste made for vinyl-to-vinyl adhesion. An application of this special paste will do the job.

3. Just when you think you did the world's smoothest papering job, you see some bubbles! Do not despair. Merely slit them twice to form an "X" across the center of the blister. Then peel back the tips of the slit and squirt paste into the blister. The tips may overlap a

Here Is What You Will Need
Materials
• Wallpaper paste
• Vinyl-to-vinyl paste
• Razor blades
• Pin
• Rye bread or kneaded eraser
• Sponge
• Mild detergent
• Colored ink pens
Tools
• Small artist's brush
• Seam roller

little, but such overlapping is seldom noticeable. If you notice the blister shortly after you finish papering — but after the paste has dried — the thick blob under the blister may still be wet paste. Try sticking a pin in the blister and then forcing the paste out. If that trick does not do the job, slit and repaste.

4. Patching a torn section of wallpaper is easy to do — provided you saved the scraps from the original papering job. Select a scrap section that matches the pattern, and tear the patch in an irregular shape so that the edge can be feathered back under the patch. Such a patch

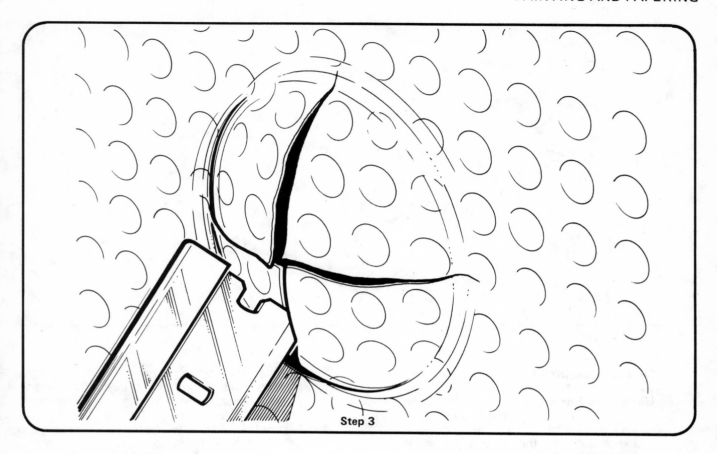

Step 3

blends in much better than if it were cut evenly.

5. When nonwashable paper gets dirty, use a blob of rye bread or a kneaded eraser (available at an art store) to rub away the dirt. Incidentally, nonwashable wallpaper can be made washable with an application of a transparent coating now on the market. Be sure to test the coating on a scrap before

covering the entire wall with it, however. You can sponge washable wall coverings with a mild detergent and even scrub some vinyls, but to find out just how much elbow grease your paper can take, work on a scrap first.

6. If some of the wallpaper's design has rubbed off and you do not have the scraps to patch over it, you might try using colored inks to redraw the design.

63. Papering A Ceiling

MOST PEOPLE like the contrast of a painted ceiling and a papered wall, especially when they find out that papering a ceiling is rather difficult. Nevertheless, if you plan to repaper a room — including both walls and ceiling — you should know how to do the job right. Always do the ceiling first, and follow these steps.

Here Is What You Will Need

Materials	
• Wall covering	• Sandpaper
• Sizing	• Spackling
• Adhesive (if wall covering is not prepasted)	

Tools	
• Scaffold	• Scissors
• Chalkline	• Water tray
• Measuring tape	• Paintbrush
• Steamer	• Roller
• Putty knife	• Razor blade
• Sponge or smoothing brush	

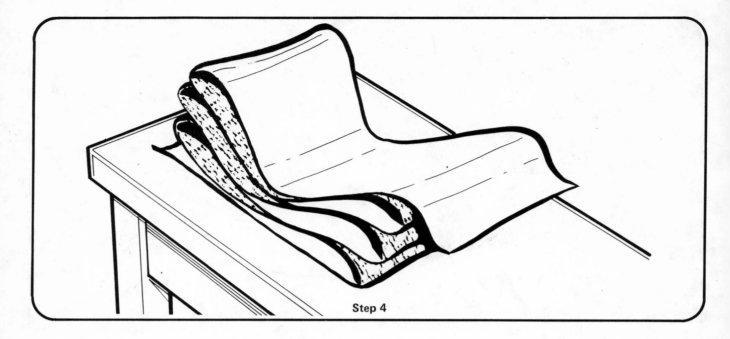

Step 4

1. Do the same preparation work you would for papering walls.
2. Hang the strips crossways rather than lengthwise. One of the major difficulties in papering a ceiling is handling those long strips.
3. Measure out from the edge of the ceiling an inch less than the width of the roll, and make your chalk line.
4. After putting paste on the strip, accordion fold it, paste against paste.
5. You will need a scaffold to make it all the way across the room without having to get down off a ladder. Make the height of the scaffold so that your head is about six inches below the ceiling.

Start at the right-hand corner if you are right handed, and unfold about three feet of the pasted paper. Smooth it down with your hand. Meanwhile, use your left hand to support the rest of the folds. A spare roll of paper in your left hand can be a great help in keeping the folds from sagging. Be sure to place the strip right on your chalk line.

6. After you work all the way across, unfolding and smoothing about three feet at a time, go back to the beginning and work out the bubbles. Now is the time to smooth carefully.
7. Put up the other strips, following the same techniques as you would for papering walls.

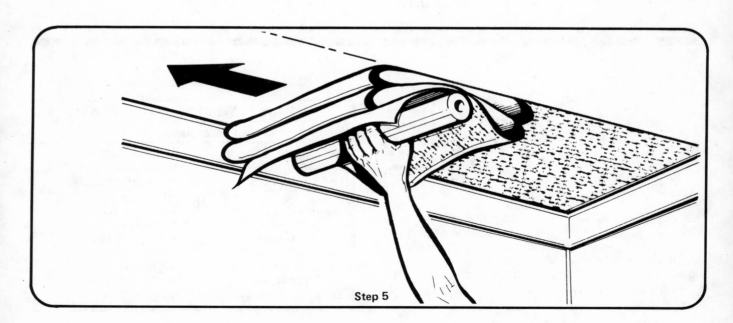

Step 5

64. Interior Painting

DO YOU HAVE interior walls that need repainting? Few do-it-yourself projects can make such a dramatic improvement in the appearance of your home and few can save you so much money over having the job done professionally. Painting can be fun, and it is easy to do well if you follow the rules. Even if you have never painted before, you can produce professional results by just following some simple directions.

Always buy top quality paint. In most cases, latex paint is your best bet. It goes on easily, dries fast, and cleans up with soap and water. After the paint dries fully, you can wash the surfaces without fear of damaging the appearance of your walls and ceilings.

The first key to a good paint job is preparation. Here are the basic steps for interior wall and ceiling prepartion.

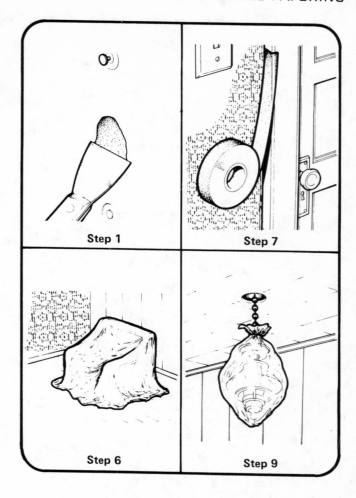

Step 1   Step 7

Step 6   Step 9

Here Is What You Will Need

Materials

- Spackling paste
- Wall cleaner
- Liquid deglosser
- Drop cloths
- Masking tape or shirtboard
- Plastic bags
- Latex interior paint
- Latex enamel
- Primer

Tools

- Hammer
- Putty knife
- Paint scraper
- Screwdriver
- Measuring tape
- Mixing stick
- Roller with extension handle
- Roller tray
- Paintbrushes

1. Inspect walls and ceilings for any protuding nails. If you find any, drive them back in and cover them with spackling paste.
2. Patch any cracks or holes.
3. Scrape away any loose or flaking paint.
4. Clean the wall and ceiling surfaces. If they are merely dusty, brushing may be all that you need to do. If there are grease spots or other dirt, however, wash your walls and ceilings.
5. Degloss any shiny surface. You can buy liquid deglossing preparations at a paint store.
6. Move all furniture, pictures, drapes, and rugs out of the room if possible. Protect everthing that must stay in the room with drop cloths or newspapers.
7. Mask all trim which is adjacent to wall areas that you will paint.
8. Remove wall outlet plates and switch plates.
9. Loosen light fixtures and let them hang down. Then wrap the fixtures in plastic bags.

With the preparation completed, you are ready to start painting. Do the ceilings first, walls next, and woodwork last. Use a roller with an extension handle for painting ceilings, and follow this procedure.

1. Mix the paint thoroughly.
2. Use a brush to paint a border along the edge of the ceiling. This technique is called "cutting in."
3. Fill up the roller tray with paint, load the roller, and roll it across the tray grid to remove ex-

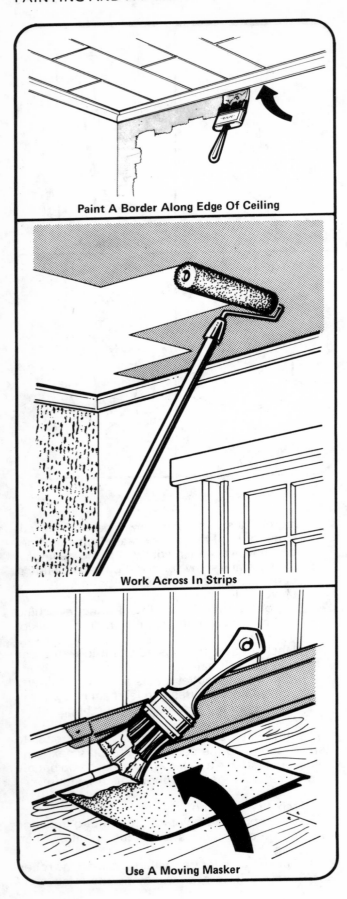

Paint A Border Along Edge Of Ceiling

Work Across In Strips

Use A Moving Masker

cess paint.

4. Start painting with the roller right next to the cut-in strip. Use slow steady strokes, working back and forth over the width of the ceiling. Fast strokes spin the roller and can sling paint. Use cross strokes to smooth the paint on the ceiling.
5. Keep working in strips across, always working against the wet edge of previously painted strips. If you allow a strip of paint to dry, you may leave streaks when you paint over it. Therefore, be sure to paint the entire ceiling without stopping.

For wall painting, follow the same procedure just described for painting ceilings.

1. Cut in along corners and around doors and windows.
2. Start in the left-hand corner if you are right handed. Begin at the top and work up and down all the way, moving across as you finish each strip. Again, use cross strokes to smooth; always work against the wet edge; and avoid having to stop in the middle of a wall.
3. Roll horizontally to paint the narrow strips over doors and windows.
4. If you did not mask the woodwork with tape, use a shirtboard as a moving masker. Should you happen to get some wall paint on the trim, use a rag to wipe it off as you go.

When you finish all the wall, you are ready to go to work on the woodwork. You should use an enamel on the trim, and it should have some gloss to it. A glossy enamel is easier to clean than a flat paint.

1. Clean all trim surfaces and remove the gloss by sanding or by applying a surface preparation chemical available at the paint store. These chemicals degloss and also leave a tacky surface which makes the new paint adhere better. Be sure to follow the directions on the label.
2. Mix the enamel paint thoroughly.
3. Although you can use rollers or foam pads to paint large flat areas, appropriately sized brushes are better for painting most woodwork.
4. Start with the baseboards and use a moving masker as you paint.
5. Do the windows next, but be sure to mask the panes of glass and to open the sash about three or four inches before you start painting. Then, after you paint but before the paint starts to set, move the sash up or down to prevent window from sticking.
6. Do the doors and door frames last. Remove all hardware before painting the doors, and make sure that the enamel is dry before reinstalling the hardware.

65. Exterior Painting

THE SAME TRICKS of the trade for interior painting apply to exterior painting as well. Preparation is again a big part of a successful paint job. Here are the steps to follow to prepare exterior walls for a fresh coat of paint.

Here Is What You Will Need
Materials
• Caulk
• Sandpaper
• Primer
• Latex or oil-based exterior paint
Tools
• Caulking gun
• Paint scraper or wire brush
• Hammer
• Garden hose
• Ladder or scaffolding
• Mixing stick
• Paintbrushes

Step 1

1. Caulk around all doors and windows and any other joints that might let in moisture or air.
2. Repair or replace any damaged wood or other exterior siding material.
3. Remove all loose paint with either a scraper or a wire brush. Feather any chipped edges by sanding away the sharp edges of the remaining paint.
4. Reset any loose nails.
5. Prime all bare spots with a primer suggested for use with the paint you have selected. Latex exterior paint offers the same ease of application and cleaning as latex interior paint, and — when used properly — it provides long lasting coverage. Nevertheless, some people still prefer oil-based paint for exterior use.
6. Be sure to remove any mildew on exterior surfaces. Add a mildicide to the paint if mildew has been a problem, but do not expect the mildicide to kill the existing fungus. You must do that before you paint.
7. Make sure that all surfaces you intend to paint are clean. Hose off any loose dirt.
8. Wait until the surfaces are dry before starting to paint.
9. Cover walks, drives, patios, and shrubs with tarps. Plastic suit bags from the dry cleaners are very handy for wrapping shrubbery.

You will get the best results if you paint the outside of your house when the temperature is mild, the humidity is low to moderate, and when no rain is forecast. Naturally, you must take the proper safety precautions. If you are going to rely on a ladder, make sure that it is sturdy and that it is tall enough for

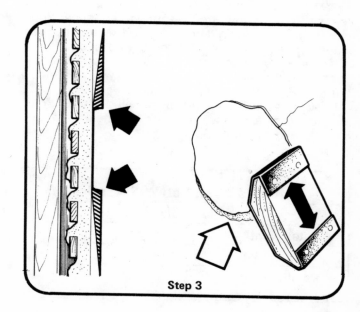

Step 3

you to reach all areas without stretching. Although buying scaffolding for a job you do only once every few years makes no sense, renting scaffolding does. Most rental outfits can provide the scaffolding you need at very reasonable rates.

With all the preparation completed, you are ready to start painting your house. Follow these simple steps for professional results.

1. Mix the paint well.
2. Try not to paint in the hot sun.
3. Start at the top, completing all broad main areas first. Work in a band across the width, painting a swath of about three to four feet wide, and continue painting such bands all the way down.
4. When you finish the main part of the house, go back and paint the trim. Pad the ends of a straight ladder that must rest against the newly painted areas in order not to mar the new paint job.
5. Wait to apply a second coat until the first one is fully dry.

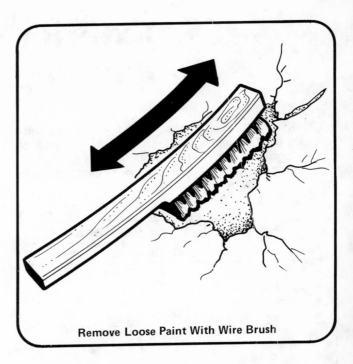

Remove Loose Paint With Wire Brush

66. Painting Doors, Windows, And Shutters

WHEN IT COMES to putting a coat of paint on doors or windows, you will get much better results if you follow the prescribed sequence. You may have been lucky and had good results before without even knowing that there was such a sequence, but by following these guidelines you can be certain that your doors and windows will come out looking professionally painted.

First, consider painting a paneled door. You should arrange to have the time to finish the door completely without stopping.

Here Is What You Will Need
Materials
● Latex paint
Tools
● Paintbrushes

Panel Door

1. Start with the inset panels at the top, painting all the panels and the molding around them.
2. Next, paint across the top rail.
3. Work on down to cover other horizontal rails.
4. Finish the door by painting the side rails.

5. If both sides of the door need painting, follow the same sequence before painting the edges.
6. Now, paint the top edge, followed by the hinge and latch edges.

Here is the step-by-step procedure for painting double-hung windows.

1. Raise the bottom sash more than half way up, and then lower the upper sash until the bottom rail of the upper sash is several inches below the lower sash.
2. Paint the lower rail of the upper sash and on up the sides (stiles) as far as you can go.
3. Next, paint the outside and inside channels as far as you can go above the lower sash.
4. Paint across the head jamb.
5. Now lower both windows, and paint the outside and then inside channels on both sides.
6. Raise both windows and paint the remainder of the two channels.
7. Lower the bottom sash and finish the stiles and top rail of the upper sash.
8. Raise the lower sash a few inches and paint it.
9. Be sure to move both the upper and lower sash before the paint can dry, sealing the sash and causing them to stick.

Shutters seldom require much of a sequence, but they usually turn out much better if you remove them from the wall before painting.

1. Examine the shutters to see how they are attached. Decorative shutters are often nailed in place (even to brick walls).

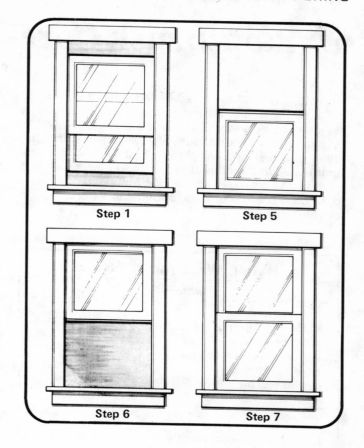

Step 1   Step 5

Step 6   Step 7

2. Do whatever you must to remove the shutters, and then lay them on a flat surface.
3. Use a narrow brush to paint the louvers first, the frame second, and the edges last.

Lay Shutters On Flat Surface

107

67. Paintbrush Care

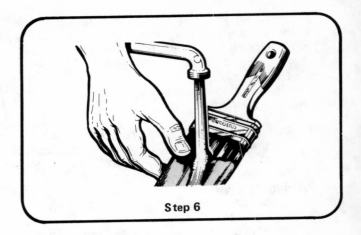

Step 6

ALMOST EVERY so-called painting expert recommends buying only top quality brushes. You would be wise to follow the experts' advice. If you fail to take proper care of your brushes, though, even the best ones might not last beyond the first paint job. On the other hand, a good paintbrush can give you years of service when you take proper care of it. Here are some rules to follow to extend the life of your brushes.

Here Is What You Will Need

Materials

- Soap or detergent
- Paint thinner or turpentine
- Wood alcohol
- Lacquer thinner
- Aluminum foil
- Linseed oil
- Brush cleaner

Tools

- Wooden mixing paddles
- Comb
- Wire brush or putty knife

---

1. Never use your brush to stir paint. To do so could cause it to become floppy. Instead, use those wooden mixing paddles available free at the paint store.
2. Never dip your brush into the paint bucket more than half way up the bristles. You should try to prevent paint from getting into the heel.
3. Never paint with the side of your brush. That causes curling.
4. To remove excess paint, tap the brush against the inside of the can instead of drawing the brush across the edge of the can. The latter method can cause the bristles to finger, which means that they separate into clumps.
5. Never leave the brush in the bucket. Its own weight will bend the bristles against the bottom of the can and cause them to curl.
6. If you stop painting for a short period of time while applying a latex paint, wrap the brush in a damp paper towel or insert it in a plastic sandwich bag. Latex paint dries quickly, and partially dried paint in a brush can stiffen the bristles.
7. Pick the right brush for the job. For example, use only nylon brushes for latex paint. No

brush is capable of doing all your painting, and forcing a brush to do things it is not shaped or sized to do will damage the brush.

The best way to get the most mileage out of a brush is to clean it immediately after each use. Here are the basics of brush cleaning.

1. The solution in which you clean your brush can make a big difference. For latex paints, use soap or detergent and warm water; avoid putting nylon brushes in solvents. For oil-based paints, use paint thinner or turpentine. For shellac, use wood alcohol. For lacquer, use lacquer thinner. For varnish, use paint thinner or turpentine.
2. Let the brush soak for a few minutes to saturate the bristles completely. Make sure to use enough cleaner to cover all of the bristles. Suspend the brush in such a way that the bristles do not rest on the bottom of the container.
3. Work the brush against the side of the container for several minutes to get the paint out.
4. Squeeze the bristles with your hands. Start at the heel of the brush and work to the tip.
5. Work the brush against a section of newspaper to remove excess solvent and to check whether all the paint is gone. If there is still some paint present, repeat the cleaning process.
6. With latex paint, you can just rinse the brush out by holding it under a faucet.
7. When the brush is clean, shake out the excess solvent or water and comb out the bristles.
8. Wash solvent-cleaned brushes in warm soapy water, and comb them again to separate the inner bristles and to allow the brushes to dry straight.

Even a clean brush must be stored correctly or it will go bad before you need to use it again. Here are some storage hints.

1. Always let brushes dry by suspending them

Suspend Brush In Cleaning Solvent **Comb Out Cleaned Bristles**

with the bristles down.

2. Wrap natural bristle brushes in aluminum foil after they have dried. Wrap carefully to hold the brush in its proper shape during storage, and pour in a little linseed oil before crimping the foil around the handle.

If you neglected your brushes and now they are hard with caked paint, here are some steps you can take to restore them to usefulness.

1. Go to the paint store and buy a commercial brush cleaner. Some are liquid, while others are dry and must be mixed with water.
2. Let the brush soak in the cleaner. If there is dried paint up under the metal ferrule, make sure that the brush gets into the cleaner that

deep.

3. When the cleaner has softened the paint sufficiently, use a wire brush or putty knife to scrape the residue away. Work from the ferrule downward.
4. Rinse the brush in the cleaner. If you still can see caked paint, soak the brush some more and repeat the cleaning steps.
5. Now follow all the steps as if you had just finished painting with the brush.

You will not be able to reclaim all your old brushes caked with paint, but it is worth a try because brush cleaner costs much less than new brushes. If you treat your paintbrushes properly from the start, of course, you need never worry about getting in such a fix again.

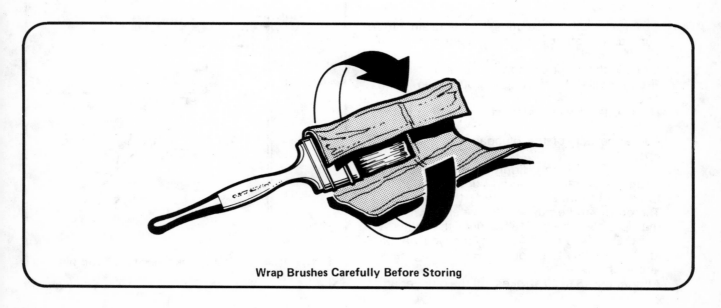

Wrap Brushes Carefully Before Storing

68. The Clogged Drain

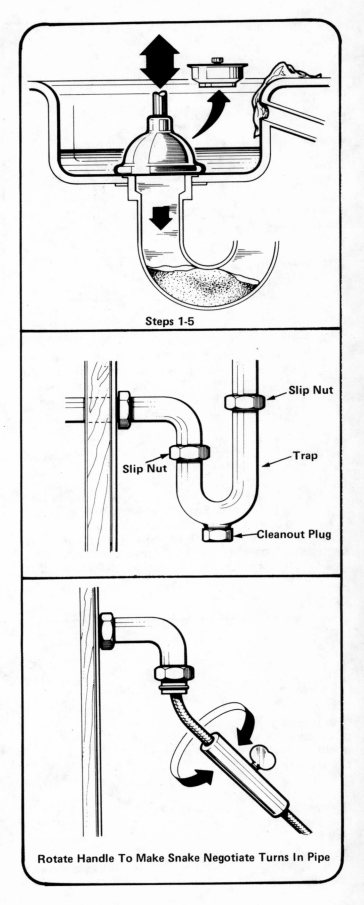

Steps 1-5

Slip Nut

Slip Nut

Trap

Cleanout Plug

Rotate Handle To Make Snake Negotiate Turns In Pipe

I T IS NOT surprising that home drain lines get clogged up. People put all kinds of things down the sink: grease, followed by coffee grounds, leftover salad, table scraps, and even cigarette butts. Once these items wash down the drain and disappear, who worries about them? Then one day, the kitchen sink goes on strike and refuses to take any more.

You should be able to clear the clogged drain with a plumber's friend or plunger. Since many clogs are close at hand, the plumber's friend can usually build up enough force and direct it against the clog to solve the problem. There are aerosol drain openers on the market that do the same thing, but they are no more effective than the plunger and are considerably more expensive. Just make sure that the rubber cup is big enough to cover the opening in the sink, and then follow these directions.

Here Is What You Will Need

Materials

- Aerosol drain opener
- Chemical drain cleaner
- Pipe joint compound or petroleum jelly

Tools

- Plumber's friend (plunger)
- Plumber's snake (auger)
- Adjustable wrench

---

1. Cover any other openings to the drain pipe such as the other side of a double sink or an overflow drain.
2. Remove the stopper and/or strainer.
3. Brush aside the garbage around the drain opening.
4. Have at least an inch of water standing in the sink.
5. Place the cup of the plunger over the drain opening.
6. Position the plunger firmly in place over the drain, and start an up-and-down motion to force the the water back and forth in the pipe. The down stroke pushes the water down, and the up stroke creates a vacuum that pulls it back. Once you build up a rhythm, you will be able to feel the force of the water going back and forth.
7. After about 15 to 20 strokes, lift the plunger up.

8. If the water does not swirl on out of the sink and down the drain, try the plunger procedure at least once again.

The next thing most people try on a clogged drain is a chemical drain cleaner. These chemicals are caustic and they can be dangerous. If they fail to do the job, they remain in your pipes, and you must be very careful not to splash this water on you or on anything that would be damaged.

The next best step to take after using the plunger is to drive a plumber's snake or auger into the drain pipe. The tool is so flexible that it can make its way around all the curves inside a drain pipe until it reaches the clog. Here is how to use the plumber's snake.

1. Remove the stopper and/or strainer in the sink.
2. Feed the snake into the drain.
3. When it hits a turn, slide the handle up to within a few inches of the opening, tighten it, and start turning the snake until it negotiates the turn.
4. Loosen the handle and slide it back out of the way.
5. Keep feeding the snake in until it hits either another turn or the clog. Set the handle once more.
6. When you finally do hit the clog, work the snake back and forth while at the same time turning the handle.
7. When you feel the clog break loose, pull the snake back and forth a few more times, and then remove it from the drain pipe.

8. Flush the line with hot water.

If you cannot get the snake down the sink drain, you can remove the trap under the sink and insert the snake there. The trap is that U-shaped pipe under every sink or basin. It is a good idea in general to know how to remove the trap because rings and contact lenses often go down the drain and get caught in the trap. Here is how to remove the trap.

1. Place a bucket under the trap to catch all the water in the sink and in the trap.
2. If you see a plug in the bottom of the trap, turn it counterclockwise with an adjustable wrench to remove it. If there is no plug, you must remove the slip nuts holding the trap to the sink and drain pipe. You will need either large pliers or a large adjustable wrench to turn the nuts counterclockwise. Make sure that you do not lose the washers under the nuts.
3. Check to see if the clog is in the trap itself. If so, clean it out with a piece of wire or with the plumber's snake.
4. If the clog is not in the trap, run the snake in at the cleanout plug or into the pipe leading into the wall, following the same procedures as above.
5. When replacing the trap or plug, smear some pipe joint compound (available at the hardware store) or some petroleum jelly on the threads.
6. Run the water for a few minutes to make sure that you have the trap all back together properly so that it will not leak.

69. Unclogging A Toilet

Here Is What You Will Need
Materials
• Wire coat hanger
Tools
• Plumber's friend (plunger)
• Closet snake (auger)

FOR SOME REASON, children have a tendency to put things in the toilet — like toys, teddy bears, etc. — that clog up the john. Adults can be guilty as well, placing items on the tank lid that then accidentally get knocked into the bowl. The good old plumber's friend, or plunger, will usually clear the clog. You should be aware, though, that there is a plunger made especially for toilets. It has a special tapered lip that fits down snugly into the bowl. If you have frequent toilet clog troubles in your home, invest in a toilet plunger and then follow these steps.

1. Make sure that there is enough water in the bowl to cover the plunger, and then place the

plunger over the outlet in the bottom. Keep in mind that you must allow room for the extra water the plunger will bring back into the bowl.
2. Push down on the plunger's handle, and start a steady up and down motion.
3. When you can feel that the force created by the plunger has the water rocking back and forth, lift the plunger out and check to see if

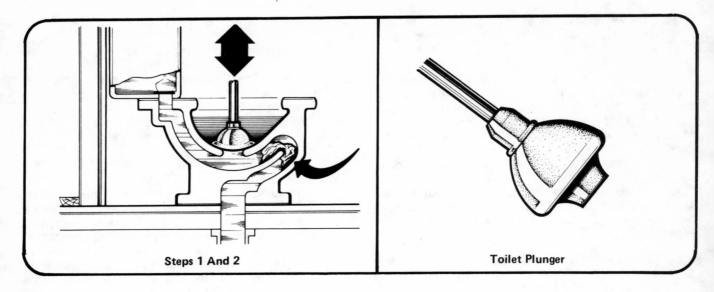

Steps 1 And 2

Toilet Plunger

any matter has been dislodged. If you unclog the drain, some of the water will probably rush out. If you dislodge a big wad of paper, use a wire coat hanger to break it up.

4. Pour some water from another source into the bowl; do not trip the handle to flush the toilet. Flushing the toilet while the clog is still present will produce an overflow, while pouring

in some water from another source will tell you whether your work with the plunger did the job.

Stubborn clogs often require the use of a closet snake, a shorter version of the plumber's snake. Sometimes referred to as a closet auger, the closet snake has a crank at one end with a hollow metal

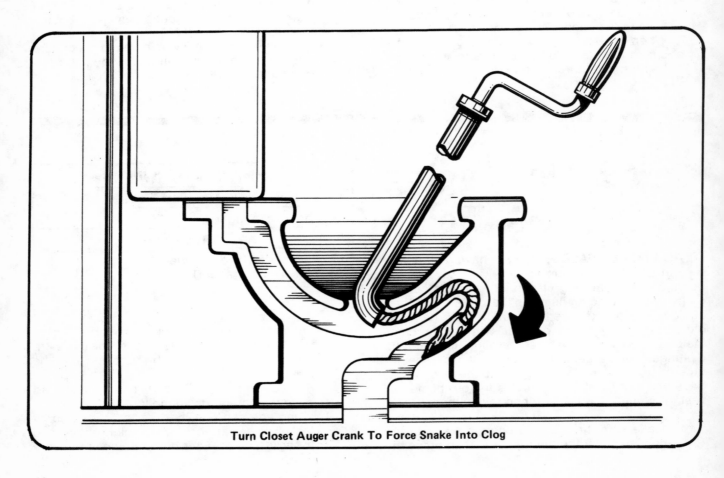

Turn Closet Auger Crank To Force Snake Into Clog

tube housing the snake itself. You do not need a long snake for toilets, since the blockage cannot be very far away. Just be careful not to bang the auger against the bowl; it could break the porcelain. Here is what to do with the closet auger.

1. Insert the snake into the outflow opening.
2. Push it in until it hits the clog.
3. Turn the crank, forcing the snake to move forward into the clog.
4. Reverse the direction of the crank every few turns to prevent compacting whatever is causing the clog.

5. Once the snake works its way through the clog, keep advancing and reversing the tool to be sure you remove everything that once blocked the drain.
6. Pour water in the bowl from another source to make sure that the toilet drain is clear.

Another useful tool for clearing toilet clogs is one you can make yourself. Just straighten a wire coat hanger, but leave the hook at the end. You can generally fish out paper clogs, teddy bears, and whatever else is blocking the drain with the coat hanger hook.

70. Toilet Tank Repairs

A FAULTY TOILET tank can send thousands of gallons of water down the drain and take a great deal of money out of your pocket to pay for the wasted water. In addition, the noise of the ever-flowing toilet can get on your nerves. Although the insides of a toilet tank may look very complicated, you can figure out how it works with no difficulty whatsoever.

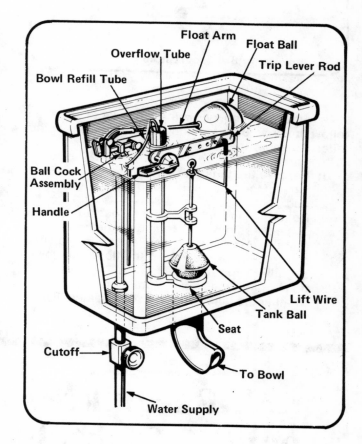

Here Is What You Will Need
Materials
• Replacement guide wires or trip lever
• Replacement tank ball
• Wet-dry emery paper or steel wool
• Replacement washers for valve of ball cock assembly
Tools
• Knife

1. You push the handle to flush.
2. The handle raises the trip lever inside the tank.
3. Since the trip lever is attached to the lift wires, they go up too.
4. The lift wires raise the tank ball from where it rests in an outflow hole, allowing water in the tank to run out into the bowl and clean it.
5. Meanwhile, the float ball — which had been floating on the top of the water in the tank —

drops as the water in the tank rushes out.
6. The float arm moves down with the float ball, opening the valve which lets new water flow into the tank.
7. The tank ball falls back in place in the overflow hole, causing the new water to fill the tank.
8. As the water rises in the tank, it picks up the float ball and moves the float arm back up until the valve closes and no more water can enter.

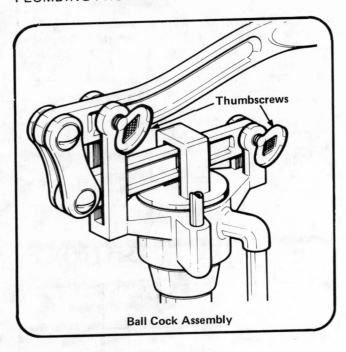

Thumbscrews

Ball Cock Assembly

cannot tell by looking, turn off the water supply under the tank. A toilet that continues to run is one in which water is seeping out around the outflow opening. Make sure that the guide is in place so that the wires are directly above the opening. Rotate the guide until the tank ball falls straight down into the outflow hole. If you see any bent wires or a trip lever that is not exactly where it shoud be, bend the parts back in shape or install new ones. Occasionally the tank ball wears out, but it is easy to replace too. If all the parts seem to be in good shape, inspect the valve seat for corrosion on its lip. Such corrosion may be preventing the tank ball from sealing the opening. You can remove the residue with wet-dry emery paper, steel wool, or even a knife.

4. If the toilet continues to run, then something is probably wrong with the valve in the ball cock assembly. This valve has one or more washers (often including a split leather washer) that can be replaced. To get at the washers, remove the two thumbscrews and lift the valve out. Replace any and all faulty washers.

Here are some other basic repairs for toilet tanks.

1. If the toilet makes a screaming noise as it fills, but works properly otherwise, replace the washers in the ball cock assembly valve.
2. If the flush is inadequate, make certain that the level of water in the tank is sufficient; it shoud be about a half inch below the top of the overflow tube. If the water level is too low, bend the float arm up slightly. An inadequate flush might also result from the tank ball not going up far enough. Raise the guide to give the tank ball more room.

Now that you know how the tank works, you can follow the procedure for fixing a continually running toilet.

1. Remove the tank lid very carefully, and place it out of the way where it cannot fall or be stepped upon.
2. Reach in and lift up on the float arm. If the water stops running, you know the problem is that the arm does not rise far enough to shut off the valve. Merely bend the float arm down slightly to correct the situation.
3. If the float arm is not the problem, look to see whether the tank ball is properly seated. If you

71. Recaulking Around A Bathtub Or Shower

Here Is What You Will Need
Materials
• Bathtub caulking
• Cleaning solvent
• Rags
Tools
• Putty knife
• Knife

WHEN YOUR CAULKING breaks loose, the crack that forms around the tub may not look terrible, but you should fix it immediately. As long as there is a gap between the tub and wall, you are letting water seep in. The seepage can rot the walls, cause mildew with its musty odors to form inside, damage the ceiling below, and even loosen the tiles above the tub. Here is how to fix the crack.

1. Purchase a tube of the caulk made especially for bathtubs; it differs from the regular caulk. Some manufacturers of tub caulk offer their

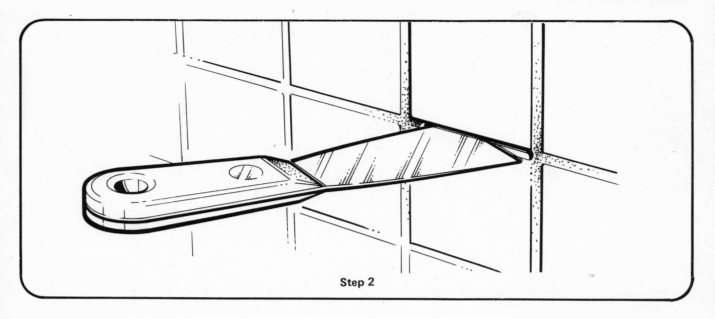
Step 2

product in colors, allowing you to match the color of the tub. If you cannot find the right color, white caulk will look fine no matter what color the tub is.

2. Remove all of the old caulk. Use a putty knife, and be careful not to chip the surface of the tub or the edges of the bottom row of tiles.
3. Use a solvent to clean away any soap residue.
4. Rinse away the solvent with water.
5. Make sure that the surface is completely dry by wrapping a cloth around the putty knife blade and running it through the seam.
6. Cut the nozzle of the tub caulk tube at an angle and at a point where the size bead that comes out will be slightly wider than the cavity around the tub.
7. Squeeze the caulk in one continuous bead all around the tub.
8. Wrap a rag around your index finger, dip your finger into a glass of water, and then press the caulk into the cavity. Keep dipping as you go

whenever the rag loses its moisture. Smooth the caulk as you push it in.

Done correctly, a caulk job should last for a long time. Quality caulk has elasticity, allowing it to stretch and compress as the weight in the tub changes.

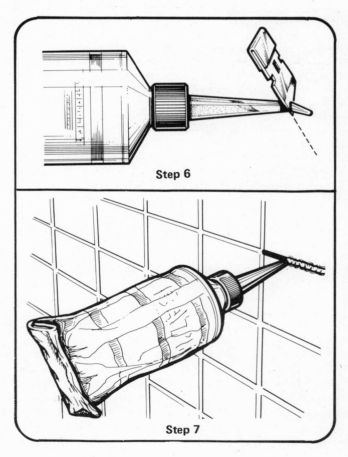
Step 6

Step 7

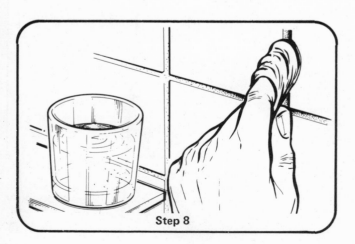
Step 8

72. Plumbing Pipe Leaks

WHEN A PIPE bursts, it can do tremendous damage to your home. But there are measures you can take to prevent major destruction. If you act quickly and follow these steps, you can turn a potential disaster into an easy do-it-yourself repair job.

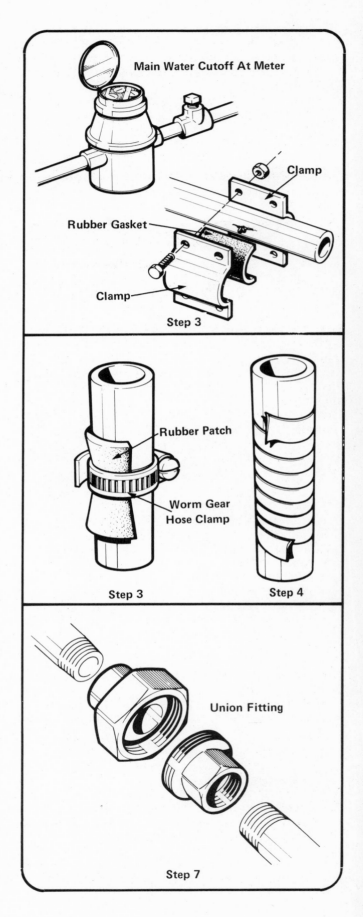

Main Water Cutoff At Meter

Clamp

Rubber Gasket

Clamp

Step 3

Rubber Patch

Worm Gear Hose Clamp

Step 3   Step 4

Union Fitting

Step 7

Here Is What You Will Need

Materials

- Pipe patching kit (clamps, rubber pad, and bolts) or inner tube scrap and worm gear hose clamp
- Waterproof tape
- Epoxy metal
- Pipe joint compound
- Solder
- New pipe
- Union fitting
- Solvent weld compound

Tools

- Pipe wrench
- Propane torch
- Hacksaw

1. Cut off the water. If there is a cutoff for just that section of pipe, shut it off. If not, go to the main water cutoff for your home and turn it off.
2. Locate and examine the leaky section.
3. If the leak is in the middle of a length of galvanized pipe, there are several ways to clamp a patch over the hole. You can buy a kit at the hardware store that includes a pair of clamps, a rubber pad, and bolts. Or you can apply the same sort of patch with a scrap of inner tube and a worm gear hose clamp.
4. For a temporary repair of a small leak, you can wrap waterproof tape around any type of pipe. The tape should cover several inches to either side of the hole.
5. You can apply epoxy metal to any metal pipe. Be sure to allow the pipe to dry completely, and then follow the directions for curing time.
6. Leaks around pipe joints are more common than burst pipes. Galvanized pipe joints are threaded, and sometimes they just need to be tightened. If tightening fails to stop the leak, loosen the fitting, apply pipe joint compound, and retighten. A compression fitting that leaks

probably just needs a slight tightening; but joints in copper tubing that leak must be removed, all the old solder cleaned away, the tubing dried completely, and then the joint resoldered.

7. A bad section of pipe should be replaced rather than patched. Cut the bad part out, and replace it with two shorter pipe sections joined by a fitting — called a union — that goes in the middle.

8. If the leak is in plastic pipe, try to use solvent weld compound to seal the leak. If the compound does not do the job, replace the bad section of pipe.

73. Repairing A Dripping Faucet

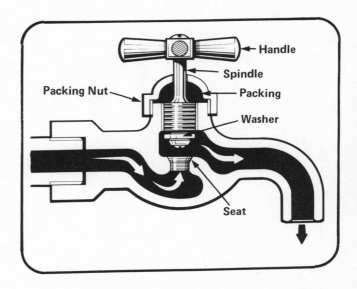

AMONG THE MORE harmless of household problems is the dripping faucet. Most people reason that a drip just amounts to a few drops of wasted water, so why worry? Yet, if you stop to add up how much water is wasted in a year, the cost can mount up to around $50 right down the drain. If you call for a plumber to fix it, of course, he will charge you $15 to $25, but you can repair a dripping faucet in a few minutes, and the parts cost no more than a dollar. You will find it an easy repair if you follow these steps.

Here Is What You Will Need
Materials
• Masking tape
• Replacement washer
• Replacement seat
• Petroleum jelly
• Replacement packing
• Repair kit for single-handle faucet
Tools
• Adjustable wrench
• Screwdriver
• Reseating tool or valve seat grinder

1. Shut off the water at the cutoff below the sink or at the main cutoff where the water supply pipe enters your home.

2. Remove the packing nut with an adjustable wrench. You may first have to flip up a button, remove the screw under it, and slip the handle off to expose the packing nut. In some cases, you will find a set screw holding the handle; remove it and the handle to get at the packing nut. If the packing nut is highly visible or made of chrome, protect it from the wrench by wrapping it with masking tape.

3. With the packing nut off, turn the spindle out.

4. At the bottom of the spindle you will see the washer held in place by a brass screw.

5. Remove the brass screw, and replace the washer with a new one of the same size. Reinstall the brass screw.

6. Inspect the seat down in the faucet. If it is scarred or corroded, either clean and reface it with an inexpensive reseating tool or replace the seat itself. The reseating tool or valve seat grinder has cutting teeth. Insert the tool in the faucet and install the packing nut over it; then turn the handle to screw the tool down against the seat, causing the cutting teeth to grind the seat smooth. Make sure that the seat is smooth and shiny after using the tool.

7. Coat the threads of the spindle with petroleum jelly.

8. Reassemble the faucet, and turn the water back on.

If your faucet leaks around the handle only when the water is turned on, you need to replace the packing. Here is how to do that simple repair procedure.

1. Remove the spindle as in steps 1, 2, and 3 above.

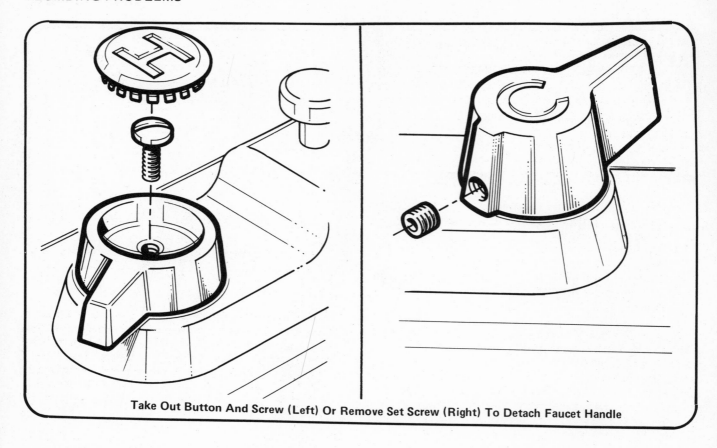

Take Out Button And Screw (Left) Or Remove Set Screw (Right) To Detach Faucet Handle

2. If you have not already removed the handle to get to the packing nut, remove the handle now.
3. Slide the packing nut up off the spindle.
4. The blob under the packing nut is the packing. It may be a solid piece, or it may be a string of black graphite material that is self forming. Replace the old packing with new packing of the same type.
5. Coat the threads of the spindle with petroleum jelly.

6. Reassemble the faucet and turn the water back on.

Another type of faucet that is very popular in newer homes is the single-handle version. One lever controls both the hot and cold water. Every maker of such faucets markets a repair kit containing all the parts that you might have to replace. The kit also offers detailed instructions on how to work with the faucet. All you have to do is find a company that carries your brand of faucet, buy the repair kit, and then follow the instructions.

74. Taking Care Of A Hot Water Heater

POSSIBLY THE sturdiest appliance you will ever own is your hot water heater. Most new units carry a guarantee on all parts, with an even longer guarantee (often up to 10 years) on the tank. Whether you have a gas, electric, or oil-heated unit,

usually the only maintenance you need to do is dra periodically to prevent sediment from building up the tank. In many areas you may need to d monthly, depending on the hardness of the and on the type of chemicals added. Here is h drain your hot water heater.

1. Make sure that the drain valve turns e does not, it may have frozen from used for a long period of time. If it is tach a garden hose to the faucet s you do get the drain open and close it readily, you will be abl water either into a drain or out
2. Perform this maintenance st

Here Is What You Will Need

Materials

• None

Tools

• Garden hose
• Bucket or small container

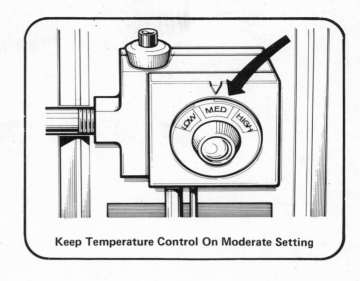

Keep Temperature Control On Moderate Setting

morning before anyone has used the hot water to insure that the sediment has settled to the bottom of the tank.

3. Open the drain and let a few pints of water flow into a bucket or small container.
4. Keep draining until the water runs clear. When it does run clear, your draining chore is done.

Once you do this task several months in a row, you will know how often it needs to be done. Sometimes, twice a year is all the draining required. By keeping the sediment out, you will have a more efficient and less noisy hot water system, and you will prevent future problems from developing in the tank and in the hot water pipes.

For a more efficient and longer lasting hot water heater, keep the heat control at a moderate setting. The temperature control knob on most heaters has "warm," "normal," and "hot" settings. The "normal" setting, usually about 140 degrees, is about all the heat you need. If you set the water heater control too high, it can create steam and cause knocking noises in the pipes.

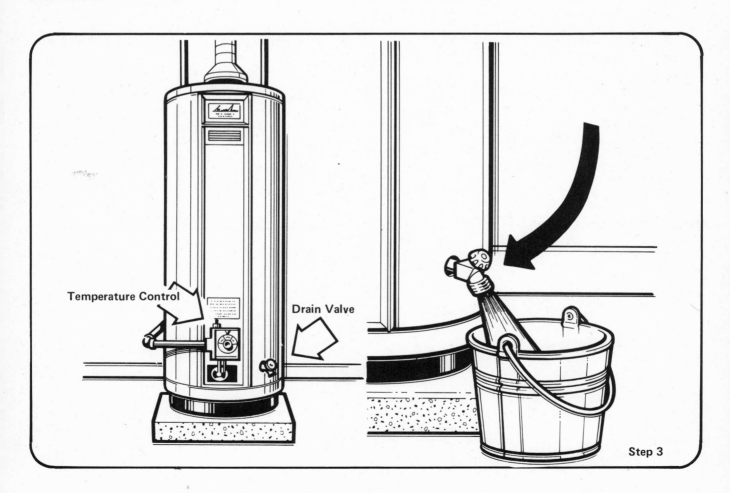

Temperature Control

Drain Valve

Step 3

75. Troubleshooting A Fluorescent Light Fixture

FLUORESCENT LIGHT fixtures are quite popular these days because they burn much cooler and consume less electrical current. There are three basic types of fluorescents: the pre-heat, the rapid start, and the instant start. Pre-heat units use a starter mechanism, while the other two types do not. Every fluorescent unit, though, contains a component called a ballast, a sort of transformer that converts house current into a current of its own that produces light. The type of ballast is also your guide to purchasing all replacement components — tubes, starters, or the ballast itself. You must have the exact replacement parts or you will never enjoy properly working fluorescent light fixtures.

If you get no light at all from your fluorescent fixture, follow these basic steps.

Here Is What You Will Need
Materials
• Replacement starter
• Replacement tube
• Sandpaper
• Replacement ballast
Tools
• Pliers

1. Make sure that the house current is on and that the circuit is live by checking the fuse or circuit breaker box.
2. Next, make sure that the fluorescent tube is inserted properly in the lamp holder.
3. If you have another fluorescent fixture that is working, try the nonfunctioning tube in the good fixture to see whether the tube is burned out.
4. If the tube is still good, replace the starter — provided you have a pre-heat fluorescent fixture. The starter is an inexpensive and easy component to replace. Just be sure to buy the right replacement for your fixture.
5. If a new starter fails to make the light work, replace the tube. Again, be sure to get the proper size.

If the light blinks off and on, here is the procedure to follow.

1. Make sure that the temperature in the room is more than 65 degrees Fahrenheit.
2. Check to be sure that the tube is seated firmly in the lamp holder.
3. Inspect the pins on the ends of the tube to see that they are free of dirt or corrosion. If they are not, sand them lightly. If the pins are bent, use a pair of pliers to straighten them gently.
4. Cut the current to the fixture at the fuse or circuit breaker box, and inspect the wiring for loose connections.
5. If none of the above steps stops the light from blinking off and on, replace the starter and then the tube.

If the tube is dark in the middle but the ends light up, or if the ends are discolored to more than just a brownish tinge, these steps should restore the lamp to proper working order.

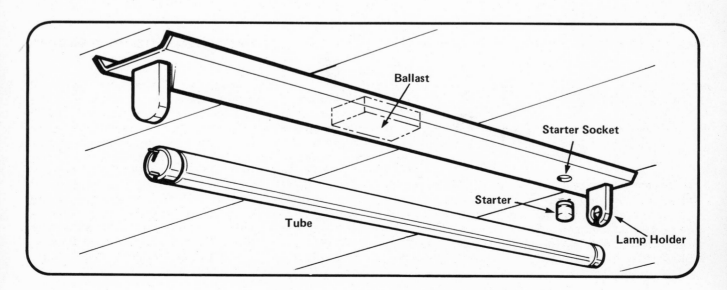

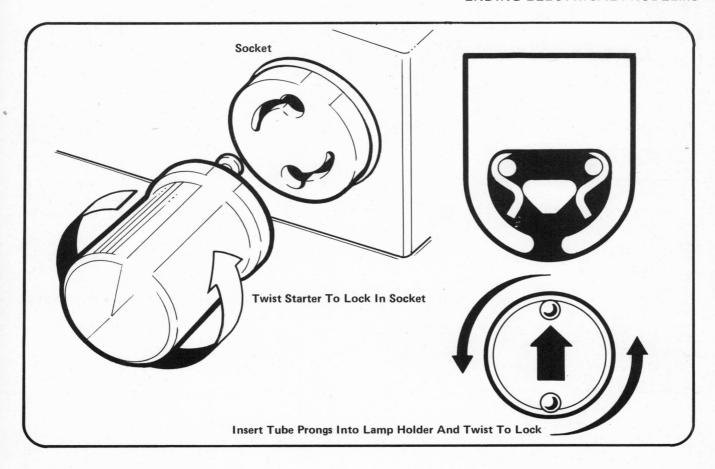

Socket

Twist Starter To Lock In Socket

Insert Tube Prongs Into Lamp Holder And Twist To Lock

1. Be sure that the room temperature is high enough. It should be 65 degrees or higher.
2. Replace the starter.
3. Remove the tube and reverse it in the holder end for end.
4. Cut off the circuit that supplies current to the fixture, and check the wiring inside the unit.

If there is a pronounced flicker in the light, try these basic steps to get it working right.

1. If it is a new tube, the flicker will go away soon. New tubes often flicker at first.
2. Shut the fixture off and then turn it back on.
3. Replace the starter.
4. Cut off the current and check the wiring inside the fixture.

If you experience any problems right after you replace parts, check the legend on the ballast to verify that the parts are the right ones for the fixture.

76. Conquering The Home Blackout

ALTHOUGH IT IS annoying when the electricity goes out, most people just flip the circuit breaker or put in a new fuse and forget about it. That may be all that is necessary. On the other hand, you should know that a tripped circuit breaker switch or a blown fuse is a warning that something is wrong within your electrical system. Fuses blow and circuit breakers trip when there is too much heat in the wires of a particular circuit; the fuse or circuit breaker then acts as a safety device to keep a fire from starting. The excessive heat can be caused by an overload or by a short circuit.

An overload generally means that you have too many devices operating on that one circuit, but it can also mean that you have a temporary overload that occurs when a large appliance motor (like a refrigerator) comes on. It takes about three times as much current to get a motor started as it does to keep it going. A short circuit occurs when a bare

Here Is What You Will Need

Materials

- Replacement fuses: regular, reset, or time-delay
- Dry piece of wooden board

Tools

- None

wire touches either another wire or something metal. The short can be in an appliance, a lamp, or in the house wiring itself.

If you have fuses, you will keep blowing new ones every time you put them in, if you fail to find the cause. Here is how to track down the reason for a fuse blowing or a circuit breaker switch tripping.

1. The first thing to do is check everything on that particular circuit. Test each outlet by plugging in a lamp, and be sure to check all the overhead lights too. Make a list of everything on the blown circuit.
2. Now turn off or disconnect every appliance or light on that circuit.
3. Go to the service entry box (fuse box), and locate the blown fuse or tripped circuit breaker switch.
4. Replace the fuse or push the switch back to the "on" position. If the fuse blows or the switch trips immediately, you know that there must be a short in the wiring since no lights or appliances are hooked to the circuit. Check light fixtures, outlets, and wall switches for shorts. Look for either a loose connection or a frayed or bare wire. If you cannot locate any such problem after checking all the wiring you can find, the problem is probably within the walls. Unless you have some electrical expertise, this is the time to call in the professional electrician.
5. If the fuse did not blow or the switch did not trip, go back in and start plugging in or turn-

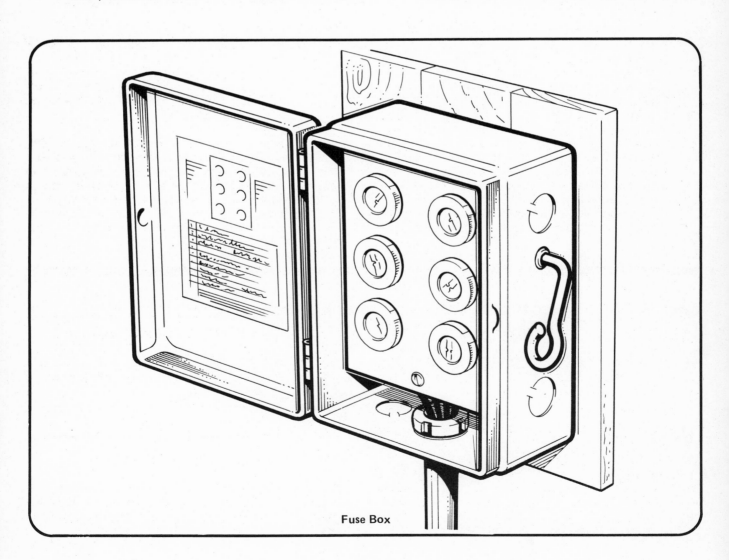

Fuse Box

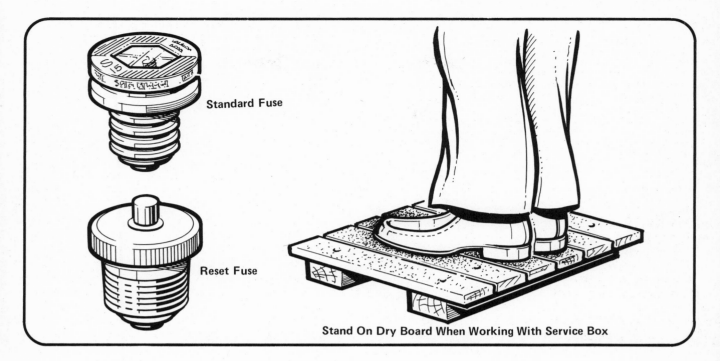

Standard Fuse

Reset Fuse

Stand On Dry Board When Working With Service Box

ing on each appliance or light one at a time. When you get to the one that has a short, the circuit will blow again. Unplug that light or appliance and get it fixed. Now you can plug everything back in and restore the power once more.

6. If nothing you plugged in or turned on indicates a problem, go back and plug in all of the things that were on at the time of the blackout. If you have a blackout again, you know that the circuit is overloaded. All you need do is move some of the devices to another circuit.

7. If the fuse blows often and you notice that it occurs when a motor (such as an air condi-

tioner or a refrigerator) comes on, you know you have a temporary overload. Replace the regular fuse with a time-delay fuse. A time-delay fuse can withstand a short-term overload without blowing, but it still gives you the protection you need.

Never replace a fuse with one that is rated to carry more amps than the one you took out. In addition, never put a penny behind a fuse or try to bypass it in any other way; you would be asking for an electrical fire. One more thing: respect the service entry box. Stand on a dry board, have dry hands, and use only one hand to trip switches or change fuses.

77. Replacing A Wall Switch

Here Is What You Will Need
Materials
• Replacement single-pole or three-way switch
Tools
• Screwdriver

WHEN YOU WALK into a dark room, flip the switch, and nothing happens, your first impulse is to change the bulb. Usually that is the problem, but one of these days you just might discover that the switch has gone bad. Never fear, replacing a broken wall switch is an inexpensive and easy do-it-yourself repair job.

If the switch is the only one that controls the fix-

ture, it is called a single-pole switch. If there are two switches that control the same light, then it is called a three-way switch. Here is how to replace a single-pole switch.

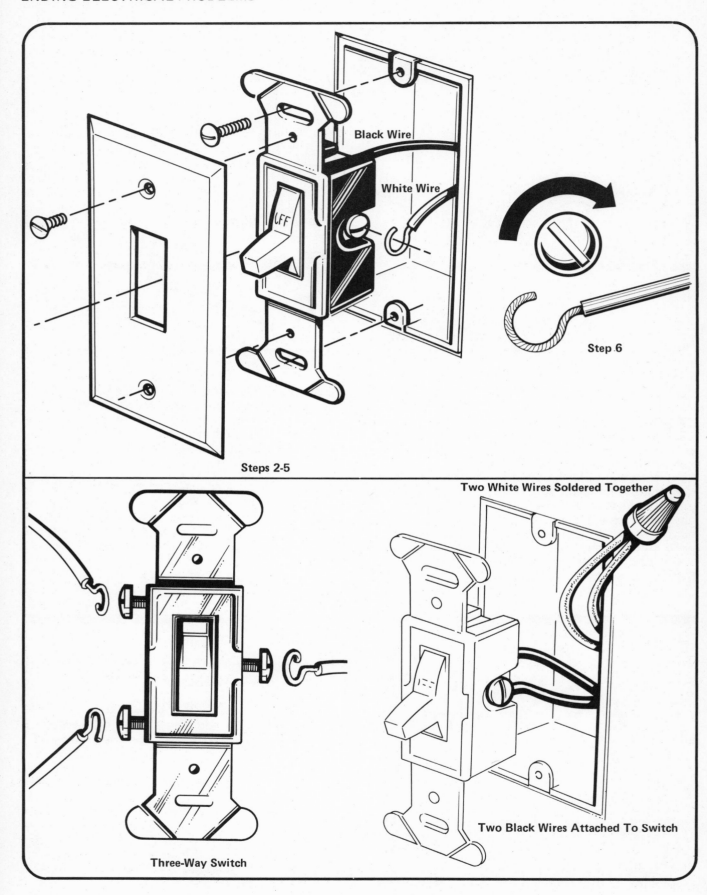

Black Wire

White Wire

Step 6

Steps 2-5

Two White Wires Soldered Together

Three-Way Switch

Two Black Wires Attached To Switch

1. Cut off the power to the switch; unscrew the appropriate fuse or trip the appropriate circuit breaker switch.
2. Remove the cover plate by turning the screws on its face counterclockwise.
3. Remove the two screws holding the switch to the junction box.
4. Grasp the switch and pull it out from the box. It should come out several inches.
5. Remove the two wires to the switch by turning the screws counterclockwise.
6. The new switch has two screws. Put the wires under the screws with the curls going in the same direction — clockwise — you turn the

screws to tighten them. Tighten the screws.
7. Push the wires back into the junction box, and press the switch back against the box. Reinstall the screws that hold the switch in place.
8. Replace the cover plate with its face screws.
9. Restore the power.

If you have a three-way switch, very little more is involved. The difference is that a three-way switch has an extra wire, usually a red one. All of the same safety precautions apply to changing such a switch. All you do differently is make a note of where each wire is attached to the old switch, and then attach the wires the same way to the new three-way switch.

78. Replacing A Lamp Socket

DO YOU HAVE a lamp that flickers, one that refuses to come on until you jump up and down on a certain board in the floor, or one that just will not work no matter what you do? The problem could be a defective bulb, plug, wiring, or socket. If you find that the socket is the culprit, you can repair it easily and safely. Socket repairs are made without any electrical current flowing to the lamp. It makes no difference whether your lamp has a pull chain, a push button switch, or no switch at all; all conventional sockets are installed in the same manner. Even three-way sockets hook up the same way.

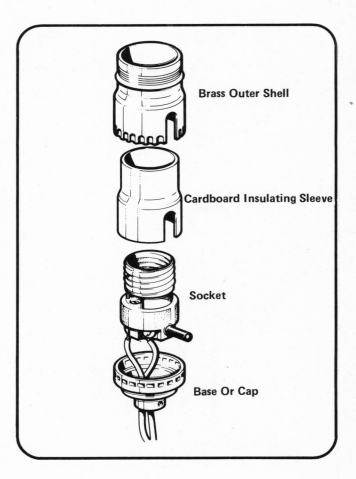

Brass Outer Shell

Cardboard Insulating Sleeve

Socket

Base Or Cap

Here Is What You Will Need	
Materials	
• Replacement socket	
Tools	
• Screwdriver	• Insulation stripper or knife
• Wire cutters	

1. Unplug the lamp.
2. Remove the bulb.
3. Remove the old socket from its base or cap. Usually all you have to do is press on the brass outer shell with your thumb and forefinger, but stubborn sockets may require that you pry them out with a screwdriver.
4. Slide off the cardboard insulating sleeve.

5. Loosen the screws that hold the two wires to the socket.
6. Check the wires. The tiny strands must be twisted to form a single unit with no stray strands. If the ends are in disarray, snip them off and strip the insulation back to expose about 3/4 of an inch of bare strands. Twist the strands into one neat wire.

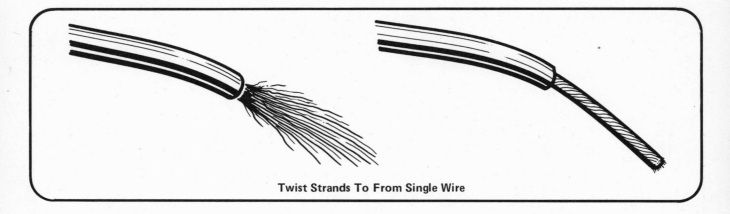

Twist Strands To From Single Wire

7. Curl the wire ends in a clockwise direction to fit around the screws of the new socket.
8. Tighten the screws.
9. Replace the insulating sleeve and outer shell back over the socket.
10. Snap the entire unit back into the lamp base, and check to make sure that it is in good and tight.
11. Install the bulb, plug in the lamp, and take a moment to marvel at your repair skills.

Many ceiling and wall fixtures possess the same type of sockets as found on standard table lamps. The installation is just about the same, but since you cannot unplug a wall or ceiling fixture, you must unscrew the fuse or trip the circuit breaker to make certain that no current goes to the fixture while you are working on it.

79. Fixing A Doorbell

Here Is What You Will Need
Materials
• Replacement button
• Cleaning solvent
• Replacement bell unit
• Replacement transformer
• Replacement wiring
Tools
• Screwdriver
• Knife
• 12-volt test light
• Electrical testing light

IT IS AMAZING how many people shy away from even trying to fix a faulty doorbell, considering what a simple hookup is involved. There are only four components to check, and the first one you look at — the push button — is usually the problem. Fortunately, the button is also the easiest component to fix. The other components are the bell or chime unit, the transformer, and the wiring.

You should be aware of how much electric current you will be facing. A doorbell runs on very low voltage. A single button unit may operate on only 12 volts, while a unit with separate buttons at the front and back may involve from 16 to 24 volts. Most doorbell repair experts will tell you that these voltages are too low for you to bother cutting the power to the circuit, but even though none of these voltages can harm you, 24 volts is enough to make you feel the shock. Therefore, try to avoid touching the wires while troubleshooting, and then cut the power while doing the repairs.

1. First, check the button. Buttons wear out and go bad before any of the other components in most cases. To check the push button, remove its face plate.
2. Disconnect the wires to the button unit.
3. Touch the two wires together. If the bell rings, you know that everything else is in good shape. The trouble is in the button itself.
4. Scrape the ends of the wires and sand the contact points on the button to get rid of any corrosion.
5. Hook up the wires again and try the button. If it

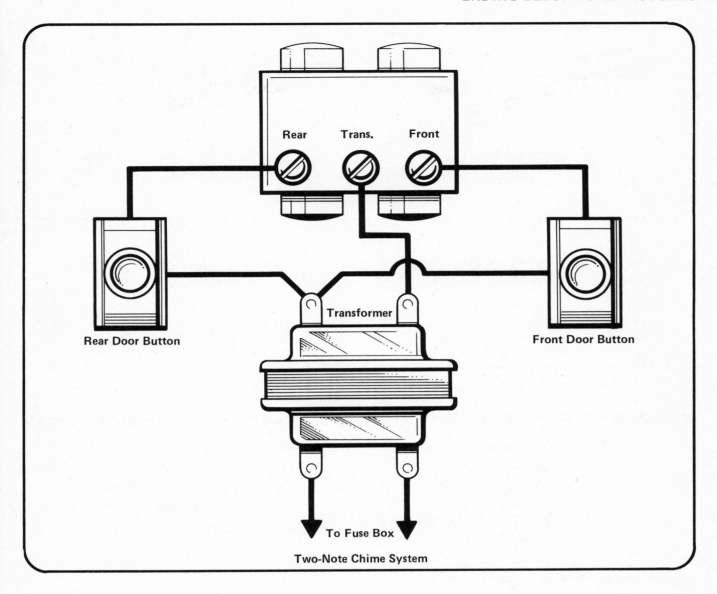

Rear **Trans.** **Front**

Transformer

Rear Door Button

Front Door Button

To Fuse Box

Two-Note Chime System

still fails to work, go buy a new button.

6. On the other hand, if the bell failed to ring when you touched the wires together, you know that the problem lies elsewhere. The next part to check is the buzzer or chime unit.

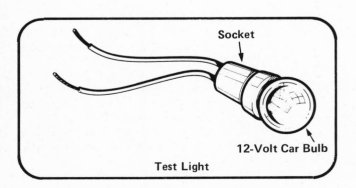

Socket

12-Volt Car Bulb

Test Light

Check the connections going into the unit to make sure that the wires are clean and that the terminals are tight. Inspect the bell clapper to make certain that it is close enough to the bell to hit it. If you have a set of chimes, clean the striker rods carefully with a solvent. After cleaning and checking the connections, disconnect the bell unit from its circuit and hook up a 12-volt test light (you can make one with a 12-volt auto bulb in a socket with two wires coming from it) to check the bell unit itself. If the light glows when you push the doorbell, you need a new bell. With a unit that has a back door button, remove only the wire marked "transformer" and one other — either the one marked "front" or "rear" — and hook them to the light. If the doorbell button lights the bulb, you can be doubly certain that the trouble is in the bell unit.

7. If the unit checks out, meaning the light fails to go on when you push the door buttons, you must next test the transformer. Keep in mind that there are 110 volts on one side of the transformer; therefore, be sure to unscrew the fuse or trip the circuit breaker before you touch the transformer.

8. With the power turned off, hook the test light to the low voltage side of the transformer. Restore the power. If the light comes on, you know that the transformer is all right. If not, you will need a standard electrical testing light to check the other side of the transformer for current flow from the power source.

9. If the transformer checks out, then the trouble must be in the wiring. When you locate the bad section, inspect it to see if it can be repaired. If not, replace the faulty wire. To run new wire inside the walls, splice the new to the old wire. As you pull the old wire out from the other end, it will pull the new wire through the walls and into position.

80. Heating And Air Conditioning Units

THERE ARE SOME problems in a central heat and air conditioning unit that should not be tackled by the novice do-it-yourselfer. On the other hand, there are a number of things that you should do and which you can do with a minimum of tools, training, and experience.

The biggest enemy of your central heating and cooling system is dirt. Many homeowners know that there is a filter in the unit that needs to be cleaned or changed periodically, but most rely on the preseason inspection by a serviceman for filter maintenance. Once or twice a year, though, is not enough. If fact, many units need a filter change once a month. If your heating/cooling unit has a permanent type filter, clean it according to the instructions on the unit itself. Many models must be sprayed after you clean them with a filter coating chemical available at hardware stores. Fortunately, most units have disposable filters that are very inexpensive and easy to change.

1. The filter is usually located in the furnace unit between the blower and the return air vent. Look right next to the blower, and when you find it, remove the filter access panel on the front of the unit.

2. Remove the old filter. It is either held in place by some sort of device that you can see, or it is in a slot. The size of the filter should be printed on its sides or ends. If you have a poor memory, write the size on a piece of tape and attach it to the filter access panel.

3. Install the new filter. Make sure that the arrow on the filter is aimed in the same direction that the air flows.

4. Be sure to replace the access panel.

Here Is What You Will Need
Materials
• New filters
• Filter coating chemical
• Household bleach
• Duct tape
• Lightweight oil
• Belt dressing
Tools
• Screwdriver
• Toothbrush
• Brush
• Canister vacuum cleaner
• Suede brush
• Hand mirror

What most homeowners fail to realize is that there are other places besides the filter where dirt can disrupt your heating/cooling unit. The blower or fan that moves air from the unit out through the ducts can get dirty, too. This is particularly true with a squirrel-cage type fan. When the openings get clogged, the fan cannot move enough air, and the system runs inefficiently. Here are some blower cleaning instructions.

1. Turn off all electric power to the unit by tripping the circuit breaker switch. Make sure the current is off before you start working on the blower.

2. Remove the filter access panel. The fan is usually held in a track by sheet metal screws. Remove the screws.

3. The fan unit will slide out.

4. If the electric cord to the fan unit is not long enough for you to slide the unit all the way out, disconnect the wires after noting exactly how they are hooked up.

5. To clean the blower, you must brush off each fan blade. An old toothbrush may be the biggest brush you can get into the spaces between blades.

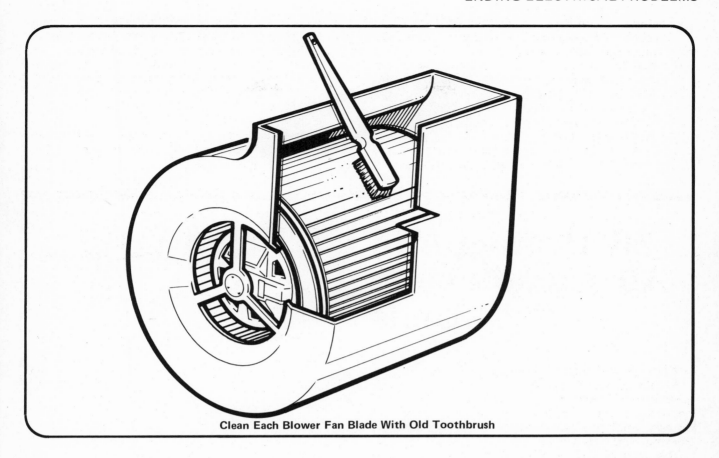

Clean Each Blower Fan Blade With Old Toothbrush

6. Also brush the entire area around the blower; here you can use a larger brush.
7. Go over the fan unit with a hose type vacuum cleaner to remove all the dirt you loosened.
8. Replace the fan assembly; make sure that you secure it with the screws or bolts you removed earlier.

With an air conditioning unit, you have additional cleanup chores outside as well as those inside. The inside cleanup concerns the evaporator, which is rather difficult to reach. The evaporator is located just forward of the furnace in a small metal box called a plenum. The blower sends air through the furnace and then through the evaporator just before the air goes into the duct system. If you change filters monthly, the evaporator should never get very dirty, but you should clean it every year in any case. Here is how to reach and then clean the evaporator.

1. Cut the electric power to the unit by tripping the circuit breaker switch. Make sure that the current is off before you start working.
2. Remove the foil wrapped insulation at the front of the plenum. It is probably taped in place. Remove it carefully because you will have to replace it later.
3. Once the insulation is off, you will see the access plate which is held on by several screws.

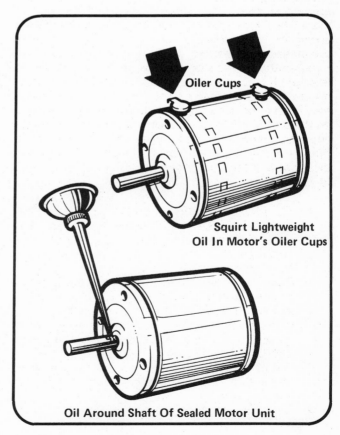

Oiler Cups

Squirt Lightweight Oil In Motor's Oiler Cups

Oil Around Shaft Of Sealed Motor Unit

Blower Unit Slides Out For Cleaning And Lubrication

Blower

Filter

Return Air Vent

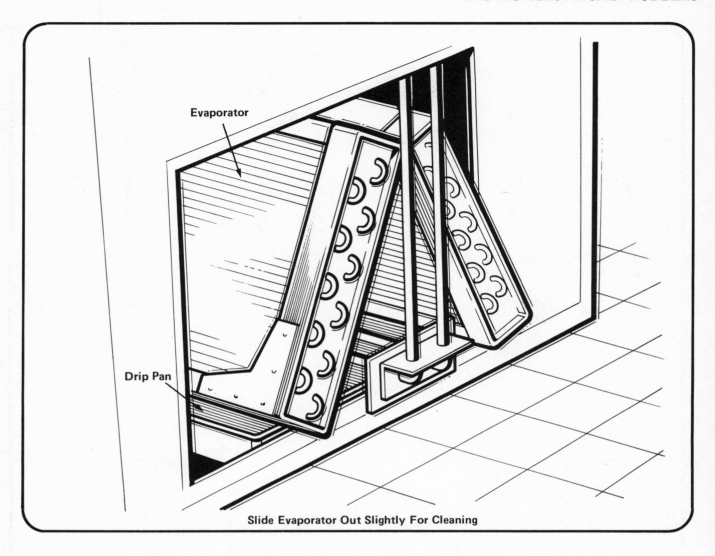

Slide Evaporator Out Slightly For Cleaning

Remove the screws and the plate will come off.

4. In some cases, you will now be able to reach all the way back to clean the entire area. If not, slide the evaporator out a little. You can slide it even though the evaporator has rigid pipes connnected to it, but be sure not to bend the pipes.

5. Use a suede brush to clean the entire underside of the evaporator unit. A large hand mirror can be very helpful in letting you see what you are doing.

6. Clean the tray located below the evaporator unit. This tray carries away condensation from the evaporator, and if it gets dirty it can clog up. Next, pour some household bleach into the hole in the tray to get rid of any fungus that may be forming.

7. Put the evaporator unit back in place, reinstall the plate, and tape the insulation back over it. Check for any air leaks and cover with duct tape.

The outside cleaning must be done at the condensing unit. The unit has a fan that moves air across the condenser coils. You must clean the coils on the intake side. Check while the unit is running to ascertain which direction the air moves across the coils. After you know this, then you can start cleaning.

1. Cut all the electric power to the unit by tripping the circuit breaker switch. Make sure that the current is off before you start working.

2. Cut down any grass, weeds, or vines that have grown up around the condensing unit. They could be obstructing the flow of air.

3. Use a brush to clean away all the dirt that has collected on the fins. Brushing works better than spraying with a garden hose because water can turn part of the dirt into mud and compact it between the fins.

In addition to cleaning, you should be sure to lubricate parts of your heating/cooling unit. Cut off the power if you have to reach inside to oil. Here are the spots to lubricate.

1. The blower motor has oiler cups. Lift the cups and squirt in from five to ten drops of lightweight oil at the beginning of each season.
2. If the blower motor is belt driven, spray belt dressing on the belt once a year and any time you hear the belt squealing.
3. Apply lightweight oil to the fan motor in the condensing unit at the start of each season. If the fan blade is aimed upward, look for a rubber or plastic cover over the oiler cup. Lift the cover to oil, and put in no more than five to ten

drops. If the fan faces out, look for oiler cups on the motor housing. To reach them, you must remove the access plate. If there are no oiler cups, you may have a sealed unit. Sealed units do not need oiling, but it is a good idea after about four years to squirt oil around the spot where the shaft enters the motor. A felt pad there tends to dry out.

These simple care and maintenance steps will make your unit work more efficiently and thus reduce your utility bills. They should also cut down on those very expensive repair bills you were paying every year.

81. Checking And Changing Your Thermostat

IF YOU HAVE a thermostat in your home that controls the heating and/or cooling of your house, you may be perfectly happy with it. If the thermostat is no longer calibrated properly, however, you can never be sure that you are heating or cooling your house to the temperature setting you desire. Here is how to check your thermostat's calibration.

Here Is What You Will Need

Materials

- Tape
- Tube-type thermometer
- Padding
- Replacement thermostat

Tools

- Plastic squeeze bottle
- Screwdriver
- Knife
- Level

---

1. Tape a glass tube thermometer to the wall a few inches from the thermostat. Place a small tab of padding under the thermometer to prevent it from actually touching the wall.
2. Wait about ten to fifteen minutes for the thermometer to stabilize.

3. Compare the reading on the glass thermometer with the needle showing the temperature on the thermostat.

If there is a variance of more than one degree, you need to do something about the thermostat. Remove the face plate — usually held in place by a snap-in friction catch — and inspect the mechanism inside for dust particles. If there is dust inside, blow it away either with your breath or with an empty plastic squeeze bottle. Do not use a vacuum cleaner.

If there is no dust problem, you must decide whether to replace the thermostat or just learn what each setting means in terms of real temperature. If you wish to put in a new unit, here are the basic steps.

1. With the face plate off of the old unit, look for the mounting screws. Remove the screws to release the unit from the wall.
2. Remove the wires coming from the wall by turning the screws on the back of the thermostat unit counterclockwise. Take care not to let the loose wires fall down between the walls.
3. Clean the exposed wires by scraping them with a knife until the wire ends shine.
4. Attach the wires to the new thermostat. Be sure that the new unit operates on the same voltage.
5. Push the excess wire back into the wall.
6. Tape up the opening to prevent cold air inside the walls from affecting the thermostat.
7. Install the mounting screws to secure the new unit to the wall. If the thermostat has a mercury tube, set the unit against a level during installation. A mercury tube thermostat is more accurate when it is level.
8. Snap the face plate in place.
9. Make sure that the new thermostat turns the heating/cooling unit on and off when you change the temperature setting.

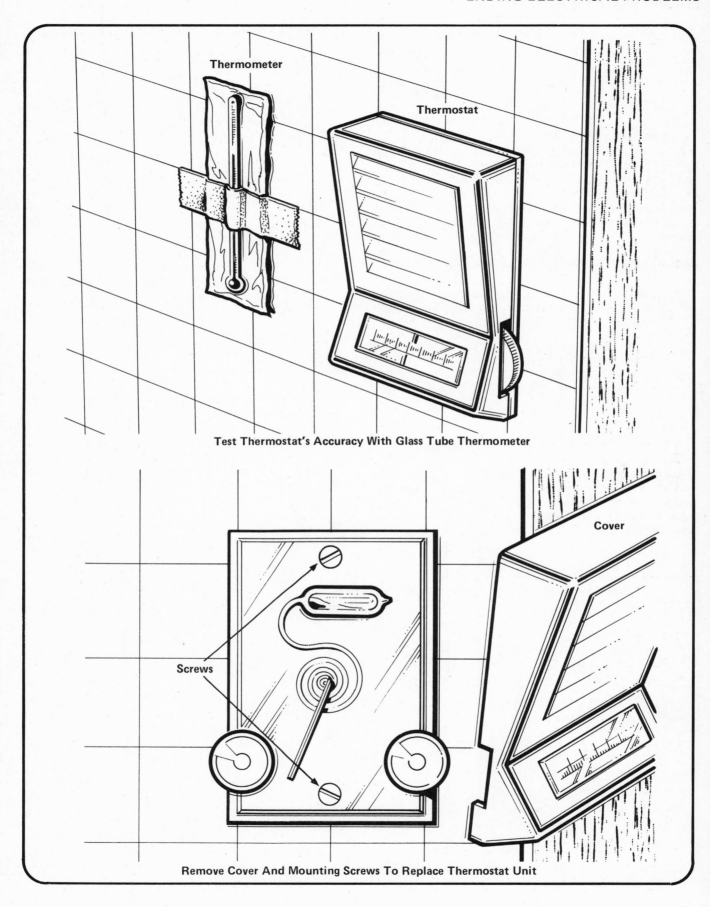

Thermometer

Thermostat

Test Thermostat's Accuracy With Glass Tube Thermometer

Cover

Screws

Remove Cover And Mounting Screws To Replace Thermostat Unit

82. Replacing A Wall Outlet

Here Is What You Will Need

Materials

- Replacement grounded or ungrounded receptacle

Tools

- Screwdriver

VERY OFTEN, PEOPLE plug in an appliance and when nothing happens they mistakenly blame the appliance for malfunctioning when the real culprit is the wall outlet. If you have a faulty outlet, the first thing you need to determine before trying to replace it is whether you need to buy a grounded or ungrounded receptacle. It is easy to tell the difference. The grounded outlet has a third hole for a three-pronged plug. Once you purchase the proper replacement, just follow these steps to install it.

1. Cut off the power to that circuit by either unscrewing the fuse or tripping the circuit breaker.

2. Remove the single screw in the middle of the face plate that holds the plate to the wall.
3. With the face plate off, remove the two screws that hold the outlet to the junction box.
4. Pull the outlet from the box. The outlet's wires will allow it to come out several inches.
5. Before loosening the screws to remove the wires, take note of how each wire is con-

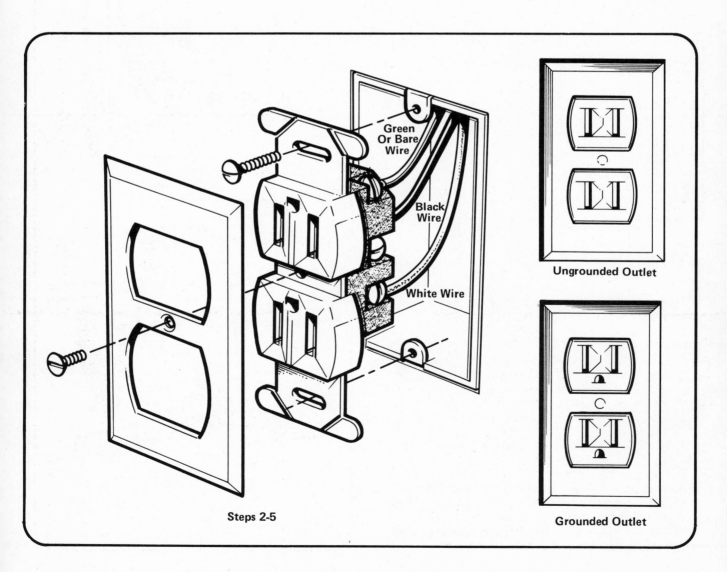

Green Or Bare Wire

Black Wire

White Wire

Ungrounded Outlet

Grounded Outlet

Steps 2-5

nected. You must attach the new outlet the same way. Hook any black wires to the side with the brass screws, and white wires to the side with the silver screws. Attach the green or uninsulated wire to the green screw of a grounded outlet.

6. Push the unit back in place in the junction box and secure it with the two screws.
7. Reattach the face plate with its screw.
8. Restore the power.

83. Troubleshooting Appliances

IF YOUR RADIO is silent, your waffle iron cold, or some labor saver refusing to labor, you may be able to fix it without knowing anything about how it works. There are certain things that you can and should always do before calling the repairman. Here is a list of things to check before you call for help.

Here Is What You Will Need
Materials
• Replacement outlet
• Replacement fuse
• Replacement cord
• Owner's manuals
Tools
• Screwdriver
• Knife or insulation stripper

1. First of all, make sure that any electrical device is still plugged in. A child or pet could accidentally have unplugged it, or an appliance that vibrates — like a washer — could have worked the plug loose.
2. If there is a reset button on the appliance, check to see if it is tripped.
3. Test the outlet with another appliance that you know works. The outlet could be faulty, the circuit breaker could be tripped, or the fuse could be blown.
4. Next, check the cord and the plug for any visible flaws.
5. Wiggle the cord while the appliance is turned on. If the unit works intermittently, you need to replace the cord.
6. If you still have the owner's manual, read it for some specific troubleshooting steps. Since reading the manual is also a good way to learn a great deal about your appliance, you would be wise to save these booklets.

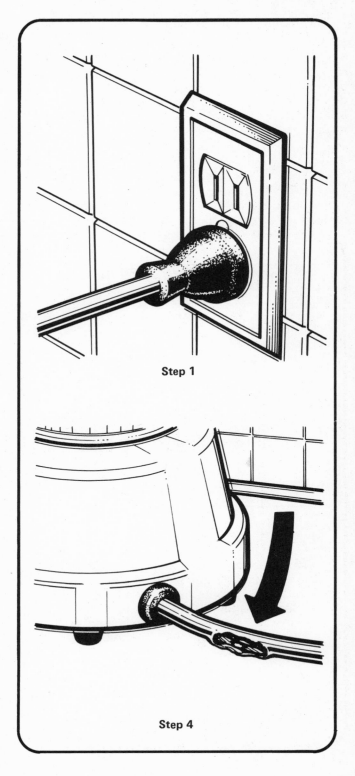

Step 1

Step 4

84. What To Oil And When

EVERY HOME has dozens of things that need lubrication. Many people just wait until they hear squeaking and groaning before even thinking about lubrication, but by lubricating on a regular basis you will never hear such squeaks or groans or be forced to replace prematurely worn parts. Why not set up one time each year to go through your house to oil or grease everything that might need it?

You can assemble a small lube kit for just a few dollars. An empty soft drink carton can tote about all the items you will need, including machine oil, penetrating oil, powdered graphite, an all-purpose spray lube (such as LPS or WD-40), an aerosol can of silicone spray, and a wax candle. If you have special oiling instructions for a particular appliance or motor, place the proper lube in your carton as well.

Assemble Lube Kit In Soft Drink Carton

Here Is What You Will Need

Materials

- Empty soft drink carton
- Machine oil
- Penetrating oil
- Powdered graphite
- All-purpose spray lube
- Silicone spray
- Wax candle or bar soap
- Steel wool
- Belt dressing
- Vegetable oil or glycerin

Tools

- Hammer
- Screwdriver

---

1. Start with door hinges. Remove the hinge pins and rub them with steel wool to remove any rust. Buff until the pin is shiny, and then coat with powdered graphite or silicone spray.
2. Send a shot of graphite powder into each keyhole, and run the key in and out a few times to distribute the lubrication.
3. Small motors often come with a tag or booklet telling you what kind of oil to use. You can generally apply machine oil or a spray lube, however, if you cannot find the recommended type. It is always a good idea, though, to save the owner's manual that comes with any new appliance. This manual will tell you exactly what lubricant to use, when to lubricate, and where the lubricant should go.
4. Any belt-driven appliance needs a shot of belt dressing from time to time. Each time you spray be sure to check the belt's tension.
5. Wooden drawers often need help even when they do not give you trouble. Rub the edges and tracks with wax or bar soap, or apply a silicone spray.
6. Windows can become balky unless you lubricate the tracks. Rub wax into the track of a wooden window, and move the window up and down. A silicone spray will do the job for either a wooden or a metal window.
7. Spray the tracks of sliding doors with silicone spray.
8. Kitchen appliances that need lubrication can be a problem because you do not want the lubricant to come in contact with your food. Some people use vegetable oil in such cases, while others use a drop or two of glycerine. Neither poses any health hazard, and neither will alter the taste of food.

85. Keeping Your Tools Sharp

ALTHOUGH IT MAY seem hard to believe, a sharp tool is actually much safer than a dull one. A dull tool forces you to use more muscle, which means that you have less control over it. A sharp tool is not only safer, of course, but it also allows you to do better work. Sharpening is not a difficult task, and the tools required are not expensive.

The basic implements needed for sharpening are files, stones, and grinding wheels. A grinding wheel is basically a shaping tool. It does not give you a razor sharp edge. After you shape the edge, you add the sharpness with a stone. The whetstone is the basic sharpening stone. You hold it stationary as you sharpen by drawing the tool over the stone's surface. Slip stones, on the other hand, are moved along the edge of the tool's blade. Files can be used for both shaping and sharpening when a bevel is all that is needed for cutting. If you do not know the specific degree of bevel that is best suited for a particular cutting edge, just try to recapture the shape of the original cutting edge put there by the manufacturer. Unless the edge is severely nicked and worn, you should be able to spot sections that have retained their original shape.

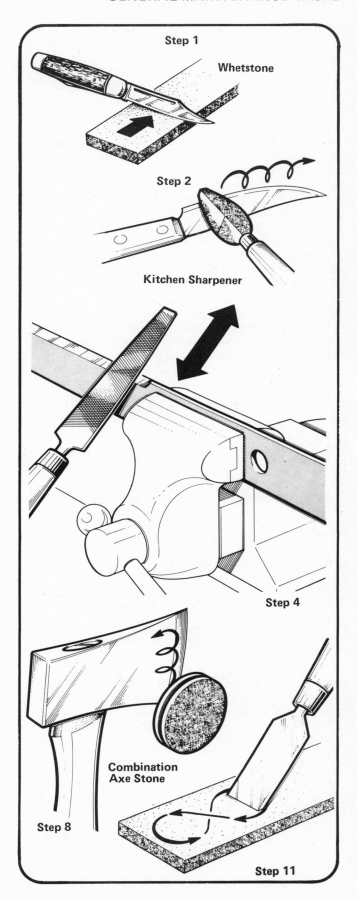

Step 1 — Whetstone

Step 2 — Kitchen Sharpener

Step 4

Combination Axe Stone

Step 8

Step 11

Here Is What You Will Need
Materials
• None
Tools
• Grinding wheel
• Whetstone
• Slip stones
• Files
• Kitchen sharpener
• Sharpening steel
• Vise
• Combination axe stone
• Drill jig
• Saw set

1. The most basic cutting tool, the pocket knife, is one of those blades that can overheat if you grind it. Instead, use your whetstone to hone it regularly. Set the blade at about a 30-degree angle to the stone with the cutting edge turned away from you, and move the cutting edge into

the stone. Draw the blade in a diagonal direction beginning at the heel and ending at the point. At the end of each stroke, flip the blade and hone the other side the same way but with the blade moving toward you.

2. For sharpening kitchen knives, purchase the special teardrop shaped stone with a handle called a kitchen sharpener. Hold the kitchen sharpener at about a 30-degree angle against the cutting edge, and stroke the stone against the knife edge in small circular motions going from the heel to the tip of the blade. Now reverse the blade and repeat the same motions on the other side.

3. To sharpen carving knives, use a long bar called a sharpening steel. Place the heel of the blade on the tip of the bar at about a 30-degree angle, and then swing the blade down to the hilt of the bar, using a light curving stroke in order to hone the entire length of the blade. Alternate sides of the bar with each stroke to sharpen both sides of the knife.

4. To restore the cutting edge on the blade of your rotary lawn mower, remove the blade and put it in a vise. Then use a file to remove any nicks and to reestablish the original bevel.

5. Stroke scissors on a whetstone with the bevel flat against the stone. Always move the blades away from you into the stone.

6. Clippers and shears are not supposed to be extremely sharp. They are just beveled, which

you maintain by filing. Stroke forward, starting at the heel and going all the way to the tip.

7. Ice picks, awls, and other sharply pointed tools can best be sharpened by rotating the point against the side of the whetstone.

8. Sharpen an axe or hatchet with a special round stone called a combination axe stone. The combination axe stone has a coarse side and a fine side. Move the stone across the blade in a circular fashion, starting with the coarse side and finishing with the fine side.

9. To sharpen drill bits properly, use a jig that adjusts to the bit size and also positions the bit for exact grinding. There is also an electric tool for sharpening drill bits that works much like an automatic pencil sharpener.

10. Saw blade sharpening also requires special tools. Each tooth must be sharpened with a file. There is a tool designed to set the file at the precise angle you need, and there is another tool (called a saw set) to bend the teeth to the correct angle after filing.

11. Chisels must be held at the proper angle and sharpened on a whetstone. There are jigs designed to hold the chisel at this angle and roll with the chisel as you move it back and forth in a sort of figure eight pattern over the stone.

12. Gouges — or any tool with a curved cutting surface — must be sharpened with slip stones that have curved or tapered surfaces.

86. Installing A Plastic Laminate Counter Top

Here Is What You Will Need
Materials
• Plastic laminate
• Finish remover
• Sandpaper
• Laminate adhesive
• Brown paper
Tools
• Fine-toothed hand saw or power saw
• Utility knife with laminate blade
• Roller or mallet and wood block
• Fine-toothed file

CERTAINLY ONE OF the most trouble-free and attractive materials for kitchen counters is plastic laminate. Although putting in a new counter top used to be a project restricted to specialists, modern materials and adhesives are so easy to work with that the job is well within the capabilities of an inexperienced — but handy — homeowner. After you select the plastic laminate in the thickness and the pattern and the color you want, here is what to do to install it.

1. If the surface to which you want to attach the laminate was previously finished, remove all the paint or varnish right down to the bare wood. The surface must be sanded smooth,

and it must be clean. Never try to cover over badly dented surfaces; the dents will show through the counter top before long.

2. Cut the laminate to fit the counter top. To cut the material, hold a fine-toothed hand saw at a low angle, and always cut with the good side of the laminate facing up. If you plan to use a

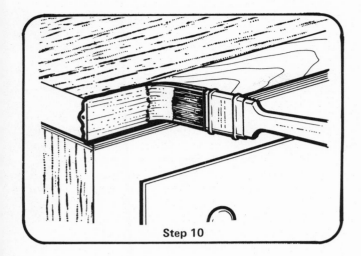

Step 10

power saw, be sure to insert a fine-toothed blade and to position the laminate so that the teeth cut into the good side for less chipping. You can also score and then break plastic laminate with a utility knife equipped with a special laminate blade. No matter how you cut, though, always leave a tiny margin that you can trim later, and be sure to support the sheet as you cut it.

3. Scuff the surfaces lightly with sandpaper, and then apply a contact cement made for laminates to both the surface of the counter and to the back of the laminate.

4. Let both surfaces dry the prescribed amount of time or until they become tacky. Examine the area of counter top to make sure that it still has a glossy look to it. If it does not, some of the adhesive has soaked in and you should put another coat over that area.

5. Now comes the tricky part. As soon as the two cemented surfaces touch, they will be stuck together permanently. Since you only get one chance, you must make sure that the laminate goes on the counter at the exact spot that it should go. The key to doing the job right is to place large sheets of brown paper on the counter to prevent the laminate's adhesive from coming in contact with the counter's adhesive until you get everything lined up. The paper will not stick.

6. After you line up the two surfaces, lift up one edge of the laminate and pull the first sheet of paper out, making sure not to move any more of the laminate than you must.

7. Press that end of the laminate down into the adhesive. Then continue to pull out the sheets of paper until the entire sheet of laminate is in place.

8. Use a roller or a mallet and wood block over the entire area to eliminate any air pockets and to attach the plastic laminate securely.

9. Use a fine-toothed file to remove the excess plastic laminate around the edges.

10. Apply adhesive to the edges of the counter top.

11. Cut strips of laminate to fit the edges, and coat the backs of the strips with the adhesive.

12. When the mastic gets tacky, put the edge strip in place carefully. Make the first contact at the center of the strip for better control.

13. Roll the edge strip to press it firmly in place.

Step 1

Step 2

Step 2

Step 3

Step 6

Step 8

87. Insulation

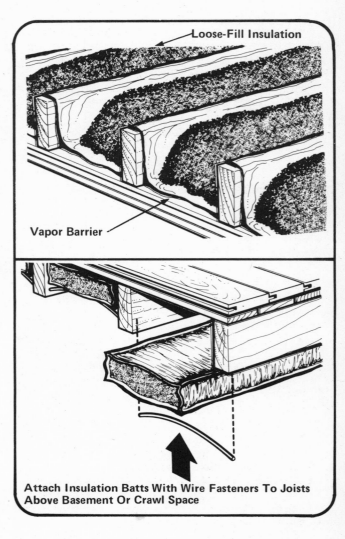

Loose-Fill Insulation

Vapor Barrier

Attach Insulation Batts With Wire Fasteners To Joists Above Basement Or Crawl Space

A S THE ENERGY crisis brings with it soaring utility rates, the homeowner needs to do whatever he can to reduce his heating and cooling costs. The best thing he can do is to make sure that his home is insulated properly; insulation will actually pay for itself in long-term energy savings. There are other good reasons for having proper insulation, though. Good insulation makes your home more comfortable, deadens outside noise, and acts as a fire retardant.

If you are building a home, you face no problem in placing insulation everywhere it needs to go: within all outside walls, throughout the attic, and under your new floors. In an existing house, however, you cannot reach all those places easily, but you can insulate the one place where you lose the most efficiency during both winter and summer — the attic. In most cases, you can insulate your attic yourself with little difficulty.

There are two basic types of insulating material, blanket and loose-fill. Blanket insulation comes in rolls or in batts, and you can buy it in widths that fit exactly between the attic joists. Loose-fill comes in bags, and you pour it in place.

Here is how to go about installing blanket insulation in an unfinished attic.

Here Is What You Will Need
Materials
• Blanket and/or loose-fill insulating material   • Wide boards   • Polyethylene sheeting   • Staples   • Insulation support wires
Tools
• Staple gun   • Knife

1. Lay wide boards across the joists to serve as walkways. The surface between the joists is the ceiling of the room below, and unless you stay on the walkways, you could damage that ceiling severely.
2. If there is no insulation whatsoever in the attic at present, you should install a vapor barrier. You can buy blanket insulation that has a vapor barrier on it, or you can put down a two mil polyethylene sheeting. Place the vapor barrier right next to the ceiling with the insulation on top. If you are merely adding to the thickness of the existing insulation, you can install blankets that do not have a vapor barrier.
3. Blankets need not be attached. Just lay them between the joists. If the blanket insulation comes in rolls, cut what you need to fit a specific length. Be sure not to cover the eave vents.
4. Fill odd spaces that will not accommodate a complete blanket either by cutting a section of blanket to fit or by stuffing scraps into the opening.
5. Work around obstructions like ducts, wiring, or pipes. If you cannot work the blankets around a particular obstruction, try placing a single bag of loose-fill insulation in the problem area.
6. Be careful not to let the material fall through or cover the eave vents.

If the attic floor is finished or if you plan to finish it later, use blanket insulation and staple it between the rafters. Once again, keep the vapor barrier toward the inside of the house.

To insulate under the floors of an existing home, go down to your basement or crawl space and staple batts of insulation to the joists. Instead of stapling, though, you can use the special wires made for this purpose. The wires have points to go into wood, and they are bowed in order to hold the insulation between the joists.

Putting insulation between the walls of an existing home is not a do-it-yourself job for the average homeowner. The insulation should be blown in. Firms that do this sort of work make openings in the walls between each pair of studs and then blow the material in. If you are building an addition onto the house or finishing a garage or basement, however, you can install wall insulation by stapling the blanket type in place when only the framing is up. Be sure to save all the scraps for use around windows, doors, and electrical outlets and switches.

88. Be Your Own Chimney Sweep

THE HOME fireplace chimney usually requires little in the way of repairs, but you should clean it every so often. Although not one of your more pleasant jobs, cleaning the chimney will make your fireplace operate more efficiently next winter. Here is how to make cleaning the chimney a do-it-yourself project.

Here Is What You Will Need
Materials

- Plastic sheet or plywood scrap
- Masking tape
- Burlap bag filled with straw, excelsior, or wadded paper
- Bricks
- Rope

Tools

- Hand mirror
- Flashlight
- Vacuum cleaner

1. Open the damper.
2. Seal off the fireplace opening from the room by attaching a heavy plastic sheet or a scrap piece of plywood with masking tape. Make sure that there are no cracks or leaks.
3. Fill a burlap bag with straw, excelsior, or wadded paper, and then put in a brick or two for added weight.
4. Fasten the bag securely to a rope.
5. Climb up on the roof on a day you are certain that the roof is completely dry. Be sure to wear sneakers for good traction; some people even tie a rope around themselves and the chimney.
6. Lower the bag down one corner of the chimney until it hits bottom.
7. Raise the bag up and down several times.
8. Now move the bag around the perimeter of the opening (move it about a foot each time) and repeat step 7. Then get down off the roof.
9. If your fireplace has an outside door, open it and remove the soot that you loosened.
10. Wait for an hour or so while the dust settles before removing the plastic sheet or plywood covering from the fireplace opening.
11. With the opening uncovered, take a large hand mirror and a flashlight and hold them so that you can inspect the chimney. Look for any obstructions.
12. Put on gloves, reach over the damper to the smoke shelf, and gently clean away the debris.
13. Vacuum out the fireplace, and if you have an attachment that will reach the smoke shelf, vacuum it as well.

89. Termites And What To Do About Them

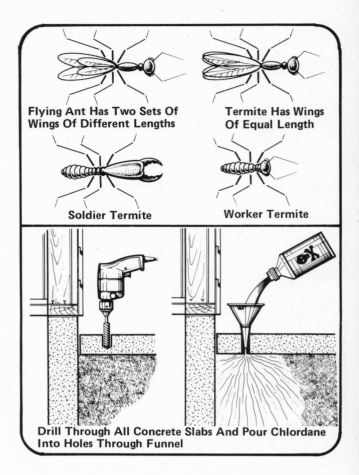

Flying Ant Has Two Sets Of Wings Of Different Lengths

Termite Has Wings Of Equal Length

Soldier Termite

Worker Termite

Drill Through All Concrete Slabs And Pour Chlordane Into Holes Through Funnel

IT IS ESTIMATED that termites do about a half billion dollars in property damage every year. When you add that to the amount of money that dishonest exterminators cheat homeowners out of, the unseen, unheard, little bugs turn out to be very costly indeed. Since termites operate completely out of sight and since they never bite or buzz, many people find it hard to see the urgency in getting rid of the pests. If they are working at your house, however, termites can do great structural damage. You must stop them. Although extermination is not always a do-it-yourself project, you should know something about termites to save yourself from being bilked. Of course, not all termite control companies are dishonest. There are some very reputable firms in the business. But it never hurts to be knowledgeable, even if you have a first-rate professional exterminator do the work for you. Here is what to look for if you think there might be termites in your house.

Here Is What You Will Need

Materials

- Chlordane — liquid or cartridge
- Concrete patch mix
- Garden hose

Tools

- Ice pick
- Shovel
- Power drill with masonry bit
- Soil injector tool or watering can

---

1. Spring through early summer is the termite mating season. At this time, reproducing termites swarm in search of a place to set up another colony. If you see the swarm or if you see a great many discarded wings, you know that termites are in the area.
2. Next, look for grayish mud tubes going from the ground up to wooden parts of the house. These tunnels — usually found on foundations, basement walls, or piers under the house — are half round and can be from about 1/8 inch to 1/2 inch wide. Check both inside and outside your house for the mud tubes.
3. Inspect any cracks in the foundation or walls, including joints where a slab (such as a porch, patio, or garage) abuts the house wall.
4. Look under all scrap lumber around the house. Remove all this debris.
5. Use an ice pick and probe wooden areas that are close to the ground. Include the underside of porches, lower steps in a basement stairway, supporting posts, thresholds, window boxes, sill plates, trellises, and fences that touch the house. If the point of the pick goes into the wood easily to a depth of about a half inch, investigate more closely.

The way to control termites is to build a barrier around your home. The termites are living in a subterranean colony and come up to your house each day to feed. The barrier you build is made of a poison, usually chlordane. The barrier must be complete because if there are any gaps, the termites will find a way to get around it and to the wood of your home.

Chlordane is applied to the soil, not to the wood. The barrier traps some of the termite colony, and they die. The rest of the colony, unable to cross the barrier to get to your house, must find another place to feed. If you use liquid chlordane to create the barrier, here are the steps to take.

1. First, start outside. Dig a slanting trench about

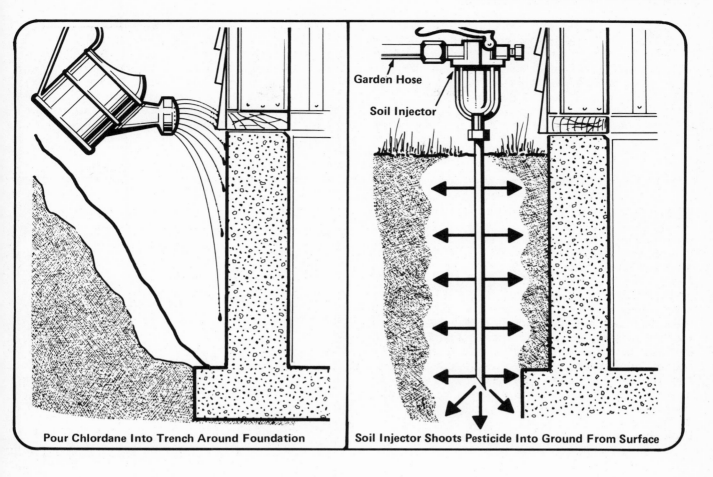

Pour Chlordane Into Trench Around Foundation

Garden Hose

Soil Injector

Soil Injector Shoots Pesticide Into Ground From Surface

six inches wide and two feet deep all the way around the foundation. Do not go below the level of the footing, however.

2. Mix the chlordane with water according to the directions on the package.

3. Pour the chlordane solution into the trench at the rate specified.

4. After you fill the trench, mix additional chlordane with the fill dirt.

5. In addition to making a chlordane trench completely around the perimeter of your house, trench and treat around all porch support pillars.

6. Now you have to treat the ground under all slabs — such as patios, walks, and garage floors — that are adjacent to the foundation. Use a power drill and masonry bit to drill holes six inches out from the foundation and spaced twelve inches apart.

7. Pour the chlordane into these holes through a funnel at the rate suggested.

8. After the treatment, patch up the holes with concrete.

9. Now you are ready to go inside. If your home is on a slab — or if you have a concrete floored basement — drill and treat as you did the patio, walk, and garage floor. Be sure to avoid drilling through plumbing in a slab, however. If

your home has a crawl space, you must trench and treat inside along the foundation wall and around each pier. You must be very careful as you work, and you must observe all the caution notices regarding the use of the pesticide.

There is another extermination method which is

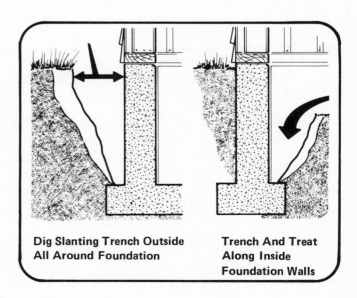

Dig Slanting Trench Outside All Around Foundation

Trench And Treat Along Inside Foundation Walls

much easier than working with liquid chlordane. You can inject chlordane into the soil with a soil injector, thereby doing away with digging. Since the soil injector tool uses cartridges, mixes the pesticide with water from your garden hose, and uses the water to force the chemical into the soil, you avoid doing all the messy work yourself. You make the injections inside and out and through holes in slabs just as with the liquid method. The injector method costs a little

more, but it makes your work easier.

If after looking over the problem you decide to call on a pro, here are some things you should know. According to the Better Business Bureau, no reliable termite control firm prices the job by the quantity of chemical that will be required. In addition, even among the most reliable companies, rates can vary widely; it is always wise, therefore, to get more than one estimate on the job.

90. Lighting And Maintaining Pilot Lights

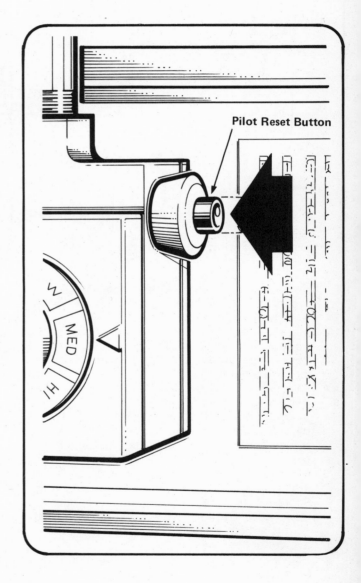

Pilot Reset Button

MOST APPLIANCES heated by natural gas have pilot lights to provide instant heat when you need it. No matter whether the pilot is on a hot water heater, a furnace, a range, or a clothes dryer, they are all quite similar. While the best guide for any appliance is the owner's manual, here are some general tips for lighting and maintaining pilot lights.

Here Is What You Will Need
Materials
• Matches
• Replacement thermocouple
Tools
• Wrench

1. If the pilot is out, check to be sure that the gas cutoff valve and the gas cock (the "on-off" knob at the gas valve) are both at the full "on" position.
2. Unless otherwise specified, turn the gas cock to its "off" position and wait five minutes.
3. Turn the gas cock to the "pilot" position.
4. Hold a lighted match to the pilot and push the reset button down. Keep the button depressed for 30 seconds, and make sure that the pilot stays lighted during the entire interval.
5. Release the reset button; the pilot should keep burning.

If you cannot get the pilot lighted, there is probably something obstructing the flow of gas. Check

the tiny orifice for clogging, and clean it if necessary.

If the pilot catches but goes off when you release the reset button, try holding the button down again for an additional 10 to 15 seconds. If it still fails to stay on, you either have a thermocouple that is

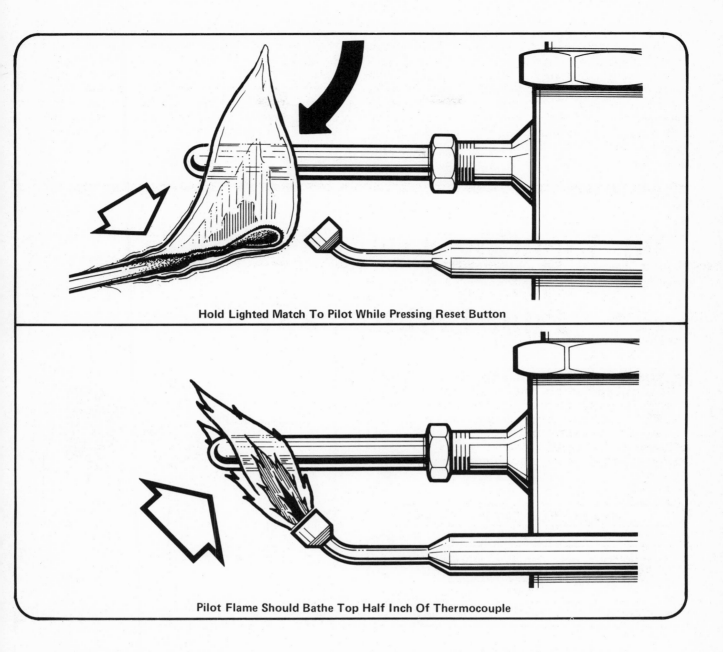

Hold Lighted Match To Pilot While Pressing Reset Button

Pilot Flame Should Bathe Top Half Inch Of Thermocouple

defective or one that is not positioned properly in the flame of the pilot. The flame from the pilot should bathe the top half inch of the thermocouple rod (the sensor tube). If it does not, loosen the bracket nuts and reposition the rod. In case you are wondering what the thermocouple does, it acts as a safety cutoff for the gas valve. When the pilot is lighted, the heat generates a slight electric current in the thermocouple which then allows gas to come from the gas valve. When the pilot goes out, the thermocouple stops sending the current, and the gas supply stops. If the thermocouple is faulty, replace it .

1. Purchase a new thermocouple of the same type, making sure that the lead-in tube is the same length as the old one.
2. Remove the bracket nut (or nuts) that hold the thermocouple unit next to the pilot.
3. Unscrew the connection nut that holds the other end of the thermocouple to the gas valve.
4. Position the tip of the new unit so that about its top half inch will be bathed by the pilot flame. Secure it with the bracket nut or nuts.
5. Be careful not to kink the thermocouple's lead-in tube when maneuvering the other end into position at the gas valve.
6. Turn the connection nut finger tight, and then just a quarter turn more with a wrench.
7. Relight the pilot.

The pilot flame should be steady, blue in color, and strong enough to reach out beyond the tip of the thermocouple.

91. Wobbly Table Legs

WHILE MOST chair rungs are glued in position, table legs are generally held on with bolts. Often as not, all the wobbly table leg needs is a little first aid in the form of your tightening the nut. In that case, your repair is as simple as step 1. If you have to proceed to steps 2 or 3 or beyond, however, it is worth the effort. A wobble today can develop into a collapse tomorrow. Here are the steps for successfully stabilizing your table.

Here Is What You Will Need
Materials
• Wood putty or wooden toothpicks and glue • Glue blocks • L-Shaped mending plates
Tools
• Adjustable wrench • Screwdriver • Drill

1. Check the nuts under the table to see whether the loose leg is caused by a loose bolt. If so, tighten the nut with an adjustable wrench.
2. As long as you are under the table, tighten all four bolts.
3. If the leg still wobbles, flip the table over and remove the bolt.
4. Examine the bracket; sometimes it can slip out of its slots. Reset the bracket and reinstall the bolt.
5. If the bracket is not at fault, examine the hole to see if it has become enlarged. If that is the case, either fill the hole with wood putty and start a new hole, or dip wooden toothpicks into wood glue and wedge them into the hole. Break the toothpicks off at the hole's surface, and reinstall the bolt when the glue starts to set up.

If the leg is glued in place, follow the same gluing ideas found in the chapter on loose chair parts. In addition, you can strengthen glued legs by adding glue blocks. Just make sure to redrill the holes if you are going to use screws as well as glue for holding the blocks. Other methods for strengthening glued legs include: countersinking screws in the apron adjacent to the legs; adding a bracket; or using L-shaped metal mending plates to hold the legs or the apron to the top.

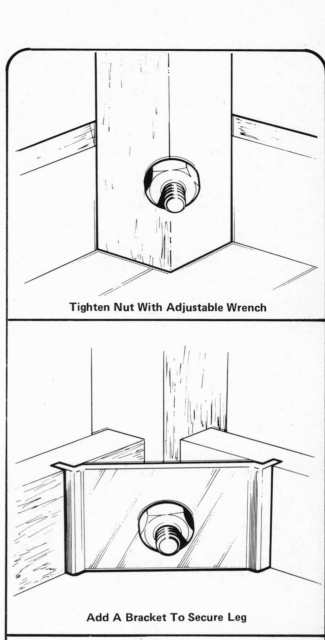

Tighten Nut With Adjustable Wrench

Add A Bracket To Secure Leg

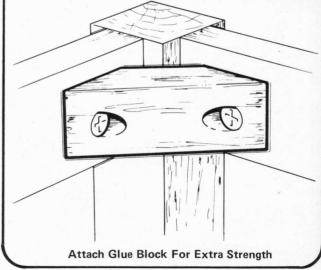

Attach Glue Block For Extra Strength

92. Loose Chair Rungs

DID YOU EVER sit down in a chair and start rocking back and forth — and then suddenly realize you are not in a rocking chair? The problem is probably no more than a loose rung, but one loose rung usually leads to every joint in the chair coming loose. Before you do more damage to the chair, take a few minutes to fix it.

Here Is What You Will Need
Materials
• Vinegar
• White polyvinyl glue
• Rope
• Wooden stick
Tools
• Pry lever
• Pocket knife
• Web or belt clamp

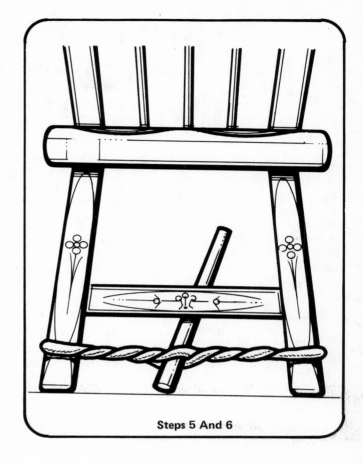

Steps 5 And 6

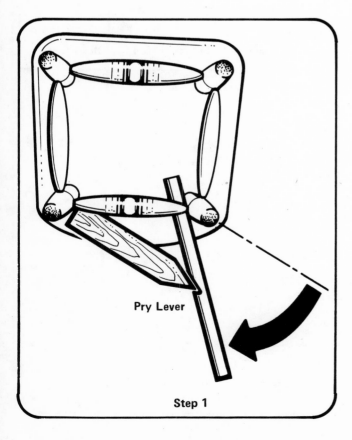

Pry Lever

Step 1

1. Remove each loose rung from the dowel hole. You can often use a homemade pry lever, but in severe cases you may have to disassemble the chair completely.
2. Remove all glue from both the rung and the dowel hole. Hot vinegar will dissolve some glues, but other types require that you scrape them away with a pocket knife.
3. Now you are ready to reglue. A white polyvinyl (like Elmer's) glue is fine. Just be sure that the wood is free of dust before you apply the glue.
4. With the glue applied to both the dowel and the hole, insert the dowel and make sure it goes fully into the hole.
5. Now you need clamping pressure. A web or belt clamp is the proper thing to use, but lacking such a device, loop a rope around the legs and use a stick to create a tourniquet. Tighten the tourniquet around the legs to provide good clamping pressure.
6. Push the stick up until it rests against either the bottom of the seat or another rung; that way, it cannot unwind.
7. Leave the tourniquet in place for 24 hours to give the glue a chance to set up. Now remove the rope, and — if everything went right — you should find no more rocking the next time you sit down.

93. Repairing Broken Furniture Parts

RIGHT NOW, in attics and cellars across the country, there are perfectly good tables and chairs that have been stored away because they have a few broken parts. Probably the most common fracture is a broken rung or broken leg, but if it is a clean split along the grain and the parts fit back together, you can put your sick furniture back on its feet again in no time.

Here Is What You Will Need

Materials

- Resin glue or casein glue
- Plastic wood
- Dowel
- Thread
- Mending plates

Tools

- C-clamp
- Drill
- Belt or web clamp or rope
- Bar clamps
- Dowel centers

---

1. Use a resin glue for a split; apply it to both pieces.
2. Attach a C-clamp to exert clamping pressure on the pieces, but be sure to protect the wood with pads.
3. Wait the full drying time prescribed by the glue maker before removing the clamp.
4. If slivers of wood are missing, fill in the break with plastic wood after the gluing is done. Your alternative to using plastic wood is to use a casein glue for the whole job. Casein glue fills in voids better than the resin glue.

If the break is straight across, there is little chance you can merely fit it back together. Your best bet is to follow these steps.

1. Drill a hole in both pieces to accommodate a dowel.
2. Cut the dowel to fit, and then check the fit before applying the glue.

Apply Glue To Chair Seat And Attach Clamp

Metal Mending Plates Can Strengthen Glued Seat

Use Dowel Centers To Align Parts Precisely

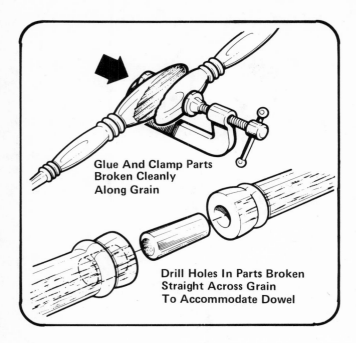

Glue And Clamp Parts Broken Cleanly Along Grain

Drill Holes In Parts Broken Straight Across Grain To Accommodate Dowel

1. If it is only a partial split, consider splitting the piece all the way to make it easier to clean the surfaces, apply the glue, and line up the parts for clamping. In any case, clean off all dirt, dust, wax, and any other foreign matter.
2. Put the pieces back together and clamp without any glue to be sure the parts line up.
3. Apply resin glue to both sides of the split. If it is still a partial split, use a length of strong thread to help get the glue all the way back into the end of the split.
4. Install bar clamps for pressure.
5. Wipe away any glue that gets squeezed out by the clamping pressure.
6. Leave the clamps in place until the glue has cured completely. Read the glue label to find out exactly how long that is.

For a more secure joining, install dowels along the split. Remember, though, that the dowel holes must line up precisely or else the two pieces will be out of alignment. You should have a set of dowel centers, which are little buttons that fit into the dowel holes. When the pieces are lined up, the dowel centers in one piece make a starter hole in the other to indicate exactly where to drill. Another way to strenghten such a split is to attach mending plates underneath.

Of course, sometimes a part breaks off completely, or it gets lost and must be replaced. Unless you are very proficient in wood working, this is probably a job for a pro. Sometimes, though, you can scrounge parts from a similar piece that is too far gone for repairs. If you decide to make parts, try to obtain the same kind of wood, and — if possible — use wood from furniture that is as old as your broken piece.

3. Apply glue to all surfaces involved, and then clamp the pieces together. You can use a belt or web clamp (or a rope) to form a tourniquet.

Large flat surfaces such as a chair seat, table top, or dresser top sometimes develop splits. There are several steps that you can take to repair such a split, the easiest of which is to glue the two pieces back together. With a chair, however, where the split is subjected to strain each time someone sits on it, gluing may not work. It is worth a try, though, Follow this procedure.

94. How To Install Furniture Casters

CASTERS DO a number of good things for furniture. In addition to making pieces easier to move about, these gadgets can stabilize wobbly furniture by compensating for a low place in the floor or for a leg that is shorter than the others. There are three basic types of casters: the stem type, the plate type, and spring adapter type. These designations refer to the methods for installing the casters. Within each type there are several different designs and sizes. The particular style you select depends on the weight it must support, the type of flooring under it, and how often you plan to move the furniture. Generally, you should install the largest caster that will look well on a particular piece of furniture.

Here Is What You Will Need
Materials
• Stem-, plate-, or spring adapter-type casters • Large-head nail
Tools

• Saw	• Screwdriver
• Measuring tape	• Vise grip pliers
• Drill	• Wood block
• Hammer	

Here is how to install a stem type caster:

1. If the present height of the furniture is what you want it to be, you must saw off some of the legs to compensate for the height of the casters. Measure the caster from the bottom of

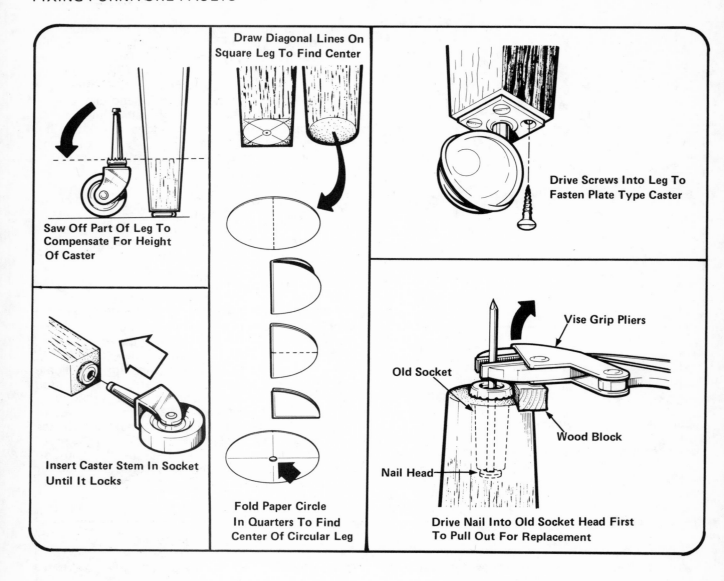

Saw Off Part Of Leg To Compensate For Height Of Caster

Draw Diagonal Lines On Square Leg To Find Center

Drive Screws Into Leg To Fasten Plate Type Caster

Insert Caster Stem In Socket Until It Locks

Fold Paper Circle In Quarters To Find Center Of Circular Leg

Vise Grip Pliers

Old Socket

Wood Block

Nail Head

Drive Nail Into Old Socket Head First To Pull Out For Replacement

the wheel to the top of the socket base, and remove that much from the legs.

2. Find the center of the bottom of each leg: On a square leg, draw two diagonal lines from corner to corner; the point at which the lines cross is the center of the leg. On a round leg, cut out a paper circle to match the circumference of the leg. Fold the paper twice to form a quarter circle. The point thus formed is the center of the circle and, therefore, the center of the leg.

3. Drill a hole of the correct size to accommodate the socket. Insert the socket in the hole.

4. Insert the stem of the caster into the socket until it snaps into a locked position. If the stem fails to lock, tap the caster with a hammer until it does so.

Plate type casters are held by screws driven into the leg through a flat metal plate. Here is how to attach such casters to your furniture.

1. Place the plate against the leg bottom to make sure that there is enough space for the screws to go into solid wood.

2. Mark the screw holes on the bottom of the leg.

3. Drill pilot holes in the wood to make for easier installation and to avoid splitting the leg.

4. Drive the screws into the leg, fastening the plate type caster to the furniture.

The spring type caster, used for tubular metal legs, is held in place against the inside of the leg by a spring device. You must order spring type casters to match the size of the tube.

If you are replacing a caster, pry out the old one with a screwdriver. Then, if the old socket will not accommodate the new stem, drive a nail into the socket head first. Use a nail with a head that is large enough to force open the head of the socket. Once the head goes through, clamp vise grip pliers to the nail and — using a block of wood to give you leverage — pry out the old socket.

95. First Aid For Furniture

YOU OFTEN SEE a piece of furniture that looks so bad you think that only complete refinishing will help it. Although that may be the case, you should do everything you can to avoid the considerable time, money, and mess involved in a complete refinishing job. Before you go the whole route, try some furniture first aid.

Here Is What You Will Need
Materials
• Rags
• Paint thinner
• Fine steel wool (0000)
• Lemon oil
• Furniture polish
• Wood stain or liquid shoe polish
• Crayons or iodine diluted with denatured alcohol
• Blotter
• Ice cubes
Tools
• Toothpicks or artist's brush
• Electric iron

1. Clean furniture that is suffering from a severe wax build-up by rubbing it with a cloth dampened with paint thinner. Paint thinner is a great wax remover.
2. Get rid of cracking and checking in the finish by going over your furniture with four ought (0000) steel wool and lemon oil. Be careful not to rub so hard as to allow the steel wool to cut into the finish, and always rub with the grain.
3. You can often cover scratches. If they are surface scratches (just in the finish and not into the wood), furniture polish usually hides them. If they are down into the stain, you must replace the color. The best way is to apply some stain with a toothpick or a tiny artist's brush. You can also try liquid shoe polish, a crayon, or iodine diluted with denatured alcohol to match the color of the stain.
4. Candle wax on a table can look awful and seem impossible to remove, but a little furniture first aid should do the job. The two best approaches are: (1) Put a blotter over the drippings, and then press the blotter with a hot iron; just make sure that you move the blotter

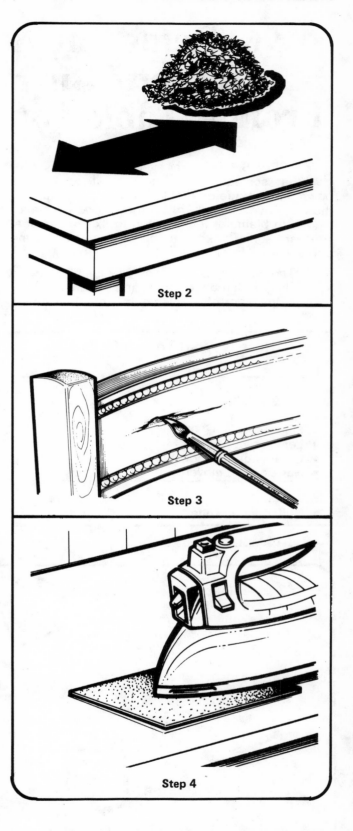

Step 2

Step 3

Step 4

frequently so that a clean and absorbent spot is over the wax drippings at all times. (2) Hold an ice cube against the wax to make it more brittle; then just pry the drippings off.

96. Removing A Cigarette Burn From A Table Top

IT SEEMS THAT after every party you discover that someone inadvertently put a cigarette down on the edge of a table and then forgot it until the table acquired an ugly burned mark. No matter who is to blame, it is up to you to fix the damage. Here are some tricks that you can use to hide the burns in your furniture.

1. The first step is to scrap away the black char. Use a dull rounded knife, and be sure to get all of the black off — even going into the wood.

Here Is What You Will Need
Materials
• Stain
• Stick shellac
• Alcohol flame
• Fine steel wool (0000)
• Lemon oil
• Clear fingernail polish
• Nail polish remover
Tools
• Dull rounded knife   • Clean knife

2. If you go down into the wood on a piece that was stained, you must replace the stain. Your paint dealer should be able to help you match the color. Remember, though, that different stains react differently to different woods. One stain might give five distinctive shades when placed on five different woods.

3. With the stain back in, you are ready to fill in the gouge. Try to make it level with the rest of the table. One way is to fill the low spot with stick shellac. Stick shellac, however, is a little tricky to work with and requires some practice. You put it on by heating a knife over an alcohol flame, touching the hot knife to the stick shellac, and flowing the shellac into the indentation. You should use an alcohol flame because it does not leave sooty deposits on the knife that would mix with the shellac on your table. Flow in enough shellac to make the burned spot higher than the rest of the table. Then use a very fine abrasive (0000 steel wool) and lemon oil to cut it down even with the surface.

If you want to avoid the hassle of using stick shellac, here is another technique. Though not quite as professional in its results, it will do the job. Mix clear fingernail polish and nail polish remover about half and half, and swipe the mixture across the gouge with the polish brush. This will leave a thin coat that dries very fast. As soon as it dries, put on another coat, and keep adding coats until you build up the gouge to a point where it is level with the rest of the table. While the spot may still look a little different from the rest of the table, it will not be as unattractively different as the ugly burn was.

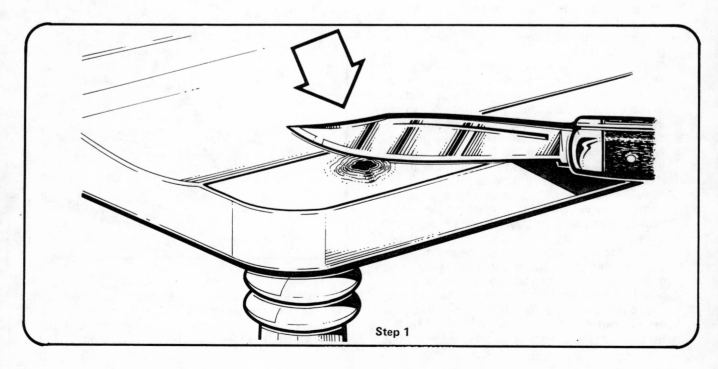

Step 1

97. Removing White Spots From Furniture

THERE ARE ALL sorts of ways to create white rings and spots on your furniture. Setting an iced drink glass down without a coaster under it is one good way. The condensation on the glass drips down, and if left on the furniture long enough, a white ring will form. A hot dish left on a table without a trivet will leave a hazy spot, and spilled hot coffee, alcoholic drinks, and perfume can also cause white or hazy spots. If you thought that there was no alternative but to refinish the whole table top, you have some good news in store. With an abrasive, rubbing oil, and a little elbow grease, you can remove white spots from furniture without refinishing.

Choose a mild abrasive; four ought (0000) steel wool will do. It is extremely fine, and unless you really bear down or use it dry, it will not cut into the finish. You can also use such things as cigar ashes, table salt, tooth powder, or silver polish; each is a mild abrasive. Pure lemon oil is a great rubbing oil, but you can also use petroleum jelly, salad oil, mayonnaise, or even paste wax.

1. Put enough of the rubbing oil on to cover the white spot. If you are using a powdery abrasive, sprinkle it into the oil.

Here Is What You Will Need

Materials

- Fine steel wool (0000) or other mild abrasive
- Lemon oil, petroleum jelly, or other rubbing oil
- Soft cloths
- Furniture polish
- Furniture wax
- Household ammonia

Tools

- None

2. Using a soft cloth or the 0000 steel wool, rub in a circular fashion all around the spot. Keep it up, occasionally moving the goop away with your rag to see how well the spot is coming off.
3. When the spot is gone, take a clean cloth and remove the oily residue.
4. Polish the entire table top with your regular polish. If you normally use wax on the table, you will probably have to rewax the entire surface.

If you can work on alcohol stains right away, you can lift them with a small amount of household ammonia on a soft rag. Squeeze the rag as dry as possible, and then brush it over the stained spot lightly.

Step 2

98. Stripping Furniture

WHEN THERE IS nothing that can be done to revive the finish on an old piece of furniture and when no amount of first aid can make it look nice again, you are faced with having to remove the old finish. There are several ways to strip furniture. Sanding and/or scraping is a sure way to get the old finish off, but it is also a slow and sure way to get a backache. The easier way is to apply a paint and varnish remover that you can buy at the hardware or paint store.

Here are some things to consider in selecting the stripper. If the piece can be turned over — permitting you to work on a horizontal surface at all times — you can get by with a liquid finish remover. The liquid costs a little less than other types. If you have to work on quite a bit of vertical surface, however, get a paste finish remover. And if the piece has veneer on it, avoid any remover that requires you to use water from a garden hose to remove the loosened paint.

Although you must be sure to follow the directions on the label, here are some general pointers on stripping.

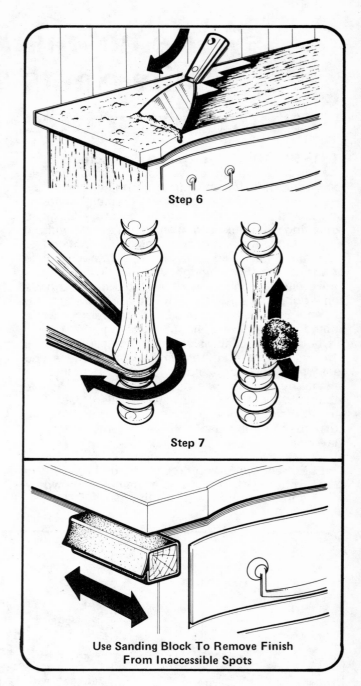

Step 6

Step 7

Use Sanding Block To Remove Finish From Inaccessible Spots

Here Is What You Will Need

Materials

- Liquid or paste finish remover
- Aluminum pans
- Coarse steel wool or burlap rag
- Heavy string or twisted burlap
- Cleaning solvent
- Sandpaper

Tools

- Garden hose
- Rubber gloves
- Inexpensive paintbrushes
- Putty knife or scraper

---

1. Find a spot to work in that can handle the mess. If you have the kind of stripper that requires flushing with water, do the work outside on a day the weather permits. Check the label for caution notices. It may tell you that you need good ventilation, and it may tell you to wear rubber gloves.
2. If you work inside, place plenty of newspaper underneath the furniture.

3. Select older brushes for applying the stripper; even dime store brushes will do.
4. If you are working with a piece of furniture that has legs, set the leg bottoms in flat containers such as those aluminum pans that come with frozen pies. The pans catch any runoff, and you can dip your brush into the pan and use the excess stripper again. Even if you are using a paste stripper, there will always be a little runoff.
5. Brush over an area once only and brush in just one direction. Going back over what you covered will break the thin film that forms,

allowing solvents to evaporate sooner and thus lessen their softening qualities.

6. The label will inform you as to when the remover will start softening the finish underneath it. At about that time, use a putty knife or scraper to check whether the layers of finish are softened all the way down to the bare wood. Incidentally, the best scraper is a flexible putty knife with the sharp corners filed off. Sharper scrapers will probably damage the wood.

7. When the finish is softened down to the wood, scrape the mess away. For rounded areas where the putty knife is of little value, use coarse steel wool to cut through the sludge; just be careful not to scratch the wood. You can substitute for the steel wool by using a burlap rag to mop the residue away. In narrow places, try a piece of heavy string or a twisted strip of burlap.

8. If the directions tell you to clean the stripped furniture with a solvent, do not skip this step just because the piece looks clean. The solvent is recommended to remove all traces of an invisible wax put in the remover to retard evaporation.

In some cases, you must go over parts of the furniture for a second time with the finish remover. You may also find that there are small spots which you can remove more easily by sanding than by stripping.

99. Staining Wooden Furniture

YOU CAN FIND many good reasons for staining furniture. Sometimes you want a darker shade of wood, while in other cases you think that the natural wood lacks an interesting grain pattern. If you do not know whether to stain or not because you do not know exactly how the bare wood will look after you put on the finish, you can get a good idea with what is called the "wet test." Dampen a cloth with turpentine and rub it over the surface. While it is still wet, the wood resembles what it will look like after you apply the finish. The wetness brings out the grain and shows the contrasts. If you do not like what you see, then you should stain the furniture.

There are a number of types of stains on the market. The neophyte in furniture staining should stick with a pigmented wiping stain. It is the easiest to use and yields the best results. It is also preferable because wiping stain allows you to correct most of your mistakes. Here are the simple steps to follow for getting good results with wiping stains.

1. Be sure you have a smooth surface for the stain. If the furniture has any blemishes, the stain will bring them out and make them more pronounced.
2. If the piece has just been stripped, make sure it is completely dry.
3. If the grain was raised in the stripping process, sand it down.
4. Make sure the surface is clean and free of wax.
5. Test the stain on an obscure part of the piece to see what it will look like. Make sure that you

Here Is What You Will Need
Materials
• Rags
• Turpentine
• Pigmented wiping stain
• Sandpaper
• Sanding sealer
• Paint thinner
Tools
• Paintbrush

also check an end grain, because the end grain absorbs stain at a different rate than the rest of the surface. If the end grain looks much different than the rest of the piece, you may wish to use a thin wash coat of sanding sealer on it.

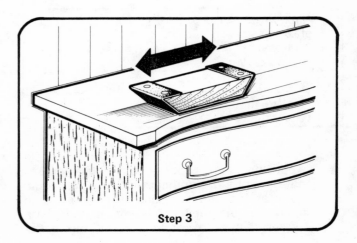

Step 3

6. Stir the stain well before you start, and then stir it frequently as you go. Otherwise, the pigment will settle.

7. Brush the stain on. You need not concern yourself about going with the grain or getting a smooth coat. Just cover all of the surface.

8. When the surface starts to lose the wettish look and begins to dull, wipe with an absorbant cloth. Try to wipe all the stain off. In other words, put some muscle behind your wiping. Turn the rag over frequently to expose a clean part as the other section gets loaded.

9. If you do not like the results, you can start over. Paint thinner on a rag will remove nearly all of the stain. You must rub hard, though. If the problem is just that the piece is not dark enough, you need not remove the stain. Put on another coat and let it stay on a little longer before wiping. You can, of course, always try adding a darker stain to the original mix.

10. When you achieve the right color tone, wipe down the furniture with a clean rag to remove any more surface matter. Then let it sit for at least 24 hours before you apply the finish.

100. Antiquing Furniture

THE TECHNIQUE of furniture refinishing called antiquing first started when paint companies brought out antiquing kits a few years ago. While kits are still available, you can save money and be much more creative by purchasing the required materials separately. As far as the paint is concerned, any semi-gloss enamel will do. The antiqued effect results from a glaze applied over the paint. You can buy different kinds of glazes in many shades and colors. In addition, you can make your own glaze by mixing thinned artists oil colors into a varnish or other clear sealer that will take oils. The entire antiquing process is simple if you follow these directions.

Step 1

Here Is What You Will Need

Materials

- Antiquing kit or latex semi-gloss enamel and glaze
- Deglosser
- Wiping cloths

Tools

- Paintbrushes
- Toothbrush

1. Apply the base coat as you would for any other paint job. You need not remove the old paint as long as it is sound, but you should make sure that the finish is smooth. Moreover, as with any paint job, you will obtain better adhesion if you degloss the surface before painting it.

2. Let the base coat dry. If the coverage is incomplete, put on a second coat. Paint a scrap the same color to use for experimental pur-

poses. The scrap will let you see just how to attain the glaze effect you want.

3. Make sure that the paint is completely dry before applying the glaze.

4. Brush on the glaze, but take no pains other than to be sure you cover the entire surface.

5. When the glaze starts to look dull, wipe it off. How much you wipe away and what you wipe with determine the furniture's final appearance. A soft cloth removes more glaze than a coarse one, and very coarse material — like burlap or a carpet scrap — will leave streaks.

6. As you wipe the glaze away, take more off in the center than in the corners to give the finish an aged look.

7. For a simulated wood grain finish, drag a dry brush or a carpet scrap across the piece (going with the grain) after you wipe the glaze. This technique takes practice before you can expect professional results.

8. Another popular treatment is called spatter-dashing, which means leaving little dark dots over the surface. Dip a toothbrush into dark (almost black) paint and hold the brush close

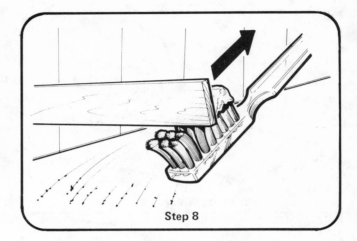

Step 8

to the surface with the bristles pointed upward. When you draw a stick across the bristles toward you, you will cause the paint to spatter on the furniture. Since spatterdashing is usually done after the base coat and before the glazing, you must make certain that the glaze you buy will not dissolve your dots.

101. Furniture Finishing

THE FINISH ON a piece of furniture is put there to protect the wood and also to make the piece look its best. Although there are many types of finishes, the three basic surface finishes are shellac, lacquer, and varnish. Learn the advantages and disadvantages and how to apply each, and then you can make up your mind about which finish to use on your furniture.

Shellac is the easiest finish to apply and provides a very high degree of shine. The big disadvantage is that shellac offers little resistance to water and alcohol. That means you would not want to use shellac in a kitchen, on a coffee table, or on a bar top. If you do have furniture you want to finish with shellac, though, here is how to do it.

1. Make sure that the shellac is fresh. Most makers stamp the date of manufacture on the lid. Never buy any shellac that is more than four months old, and never buy more than you need because you cannot keep it long.

2. Stir the shellac, but avoid making waves. Never shake shellac to mix it because shaking causes bubbles.

Here Is What You Will Need
Materials
• Shellac, lacquer, or varnish
• Denatured alcohol
• Sandpaper: 220 and 240 grit
• Steel wool: 4/0 (0000)
• Lacquer thinner
• Pumice and rubbing oil
Tools
• Paintbrush
• Tack rag

3. Use a very thin shellac for the first coat. Shellac is thinned with wood alcohol, also called denatured alcohol.

4. Apply the shellac with a well-loaded, soft-bristled, and fairly wide brush. You want to put the shellac on fairly rapidly. Use as few strokes as possible, but do not stroke fast. Overlap each stroke against the wet edge. Lap marks will tend to even out.

5. After the first coat dries (in an hour or so), sand with an open coated 220-grit sandpaper.

6. Clean the furniture and apply the second coat. Put on another thin coat; several thin coats are much better than one thick coat.

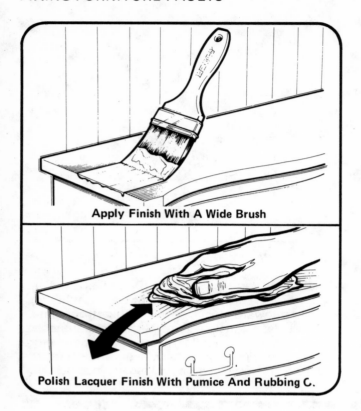

Apply Finish With A Wide Brush

Polish Lacquer Finish With Pumice And Rubbing O.

7. When dry — the second coat usually takes a little longer than the first to dry — sand with a 240-grit paper.
8. Keep adding coats to suit your taste. Some people stop at two, while others go to five or six. For all subsequent coats, use 4/0 (0000) steel wool instead of sandpaper for smoothing.
9. If you plan to wax the furniture, wait at least 24 hours after the last coat.

Lacquer has an advantage that is often a disadvantage: it is very fast drying. To a pro, fast drying is an advantage; but to an amateur, this can spell disaster. Lacquer can be sprayed or brushed, but spray equipment is expensive and it is not something you use without experience. Although aerosol cans of lacquer work well and are easy to use, they are far too expensive for finishing a large piece of furniture. If you plan to brush on the lacquer, be sure to ask for brushing lacquer. The type used in a spray rig would be dry before you could move the brush from the can to the furniture. Buy as much thinner as you buy lacquer; you will need to keep the lacquer thin and free flowing. Here is how to apply it.

1. Select a clean, wide brush for faster coverage.
2. Flow the lacquer on with the grain. Work fast and always against a wet edge.
3. Although lacquer dries to the touch in a few minutes, consult the label to find out how long to wait between coats. Sanding is unnecess-

ary because each subsequent coat dissolves the covering layer of the previous coat and fuses them together. Therefore, sand only for smoothing, not adhesion.
4. After the last coat, apply a very fine abrasive such as pumice and rubbing oil to provide a high polish.

Varnish is the most popular finish of the three basic types. Available in glossy or satin finishes to suit your taste, varnish is tough, water resistant, and heat resistant. The biggest disadvantage with varnish is that it is very slow to dry. A long drying time means that varnish has longer to gather lint — and it does. It is more difficult to apply than the other two, and if not done right, a varnish finish ends up with bubbles and brush marks. The new synthetic varnishes are much faster drying and easier to apply, with the most popular type for furniture seeming to be the polyurethane. Here is how to do the best possible job with varnish.

1. Try to eliminate the dust problem as much as possible before you start to apply the varnish. Pick a dust-free room with no drafts (including no heat vents), but make sure that the room has some ventilation. Vacuum the room, and then wait a couple of hours for the dust to settle.
2. Wear synthetic, lint-free clothes.
3. Work your brush against your hand before you start to make sure there are no loose bristles.
4. Go over the entire piece of furniture with a tack rag right before you start. A tack rag can pick up minute particles of dust and lint.
5. Work opposite a light source so that you will not skip any spots as you apply the varnish.
6. Learn how much varnish to get from each dip of the brush in the can. You want to avoid having to rake the brush across the can to remove the excess because raking creates bubbles. Flow the varnish on in long, slow strokes, using as few strokes as possible. Work against the wet edge at all times, and brush with the grain.
7. Pick up the brush at the exact moment you reach the edge. If you pause, you will leave a ridge of excess varnish along the edge.
8. Be sure to let each coat dry completely before even thinking about a second coat. Test by pushing your thumbnail into the finish on an obscure part of the piece. If your nail leaves any indentation, wait some more.
9. Fine sanding between coats will take off the gloss and give better adhesion. Use a 4/0 (0000) steel wool for sanding.
10. Before applying the next coat, go over the piece with your tack rag.

Two or three coats of varnish are recommended. Although it takes time and care, varnishing usually yields a fine finish in the end.

Making Your Own Tack Rag

A TACK RAG is a cloth with a tacky varnish touch that removes dust and lint as you run it lightly across a surface. It is very helpful when preparing a piece of furniture for an application of varnish. In fact, you will find no better way to clean a surface before varnishing or before applying any finish than to wipe it with a tack rag. While these rags are available at the paint store, you can make your own easily and save some money. Here is how to do it.

Here Is What You Will Need
Materials
• Lint-free cloth • Turpentine • Varnish • Sealed jar
Tools
• None

1. Select a well-washed lint-free piece of cloth. An old diaper, part of an oxford cloth shirt, a piece of cheesecloth, an old handkerchief, or anything similar will do.
2. Dip the cloth in warm water.
3. Wring it out as completely as possible.
4. Now soak it with turpentine.
5. Wring it out again.
6. Lay the cloth on a flat clean surface.
7. Drip varnish over the surface until the cloth has small dots of varnish about two inches apart all over it.
8. Fold the cloth over, and then roll it up and wring it out to distribute the varnish. Keep doing this until the cloth — when unfolded — is uniformly coated with varnish. It should feel tacky, but not leave any varnish on your hand.
9. Between uses, store the tack rag in a sealed jar.
10. From time to time, sprinkle small amounts of turpentine and water on the rag to restore its tackiness.

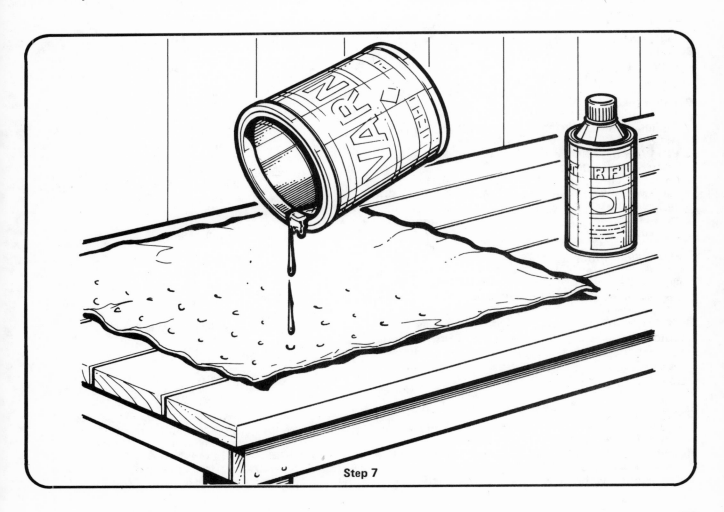

Step 7

Directory of Manufacturers

MANY OF the firms listed below will be glad to send literature about their products. Some may supply basic information, such as a simple color chart. Others may have comprehensive colorful idea booklets and installation sheets. It is suggested that you examine the various types and styles of materials at a convenient retail store. Pick up whatever catalogs the dealer may have available. For additional information not available at the store, write direct.

FLOOR MATERIALS

Resilient Tiles & Sheet Flooring:

American Biltrite Rubber Co., Inc.
575 Technology Square
Cambridge, MA 02139
Armstrong Cork Co.
Liberty & Charlotte Sts.
Lancaster, PA 17604
Azrock Floor Products
P.O. Box 531
San Antonio, TX 78292
Congoleum-Nairn, Inc.
195 Belgrove Dr.
Kearny, NJ 07032
Flintkote Co.
Building Materials Div.
480 Central Ave.
E. Rutherford, NJ 07073
GAF Corporation
140 West 51st Street
New York, NY 10020
Johns-Manville
Greenwood Plaza
Denver, CO 80217
Kentile Floors, Inc.
58 Second St.
Brooklyn, NY 11215
National Floor Products Co.
Industrial Park
Florence, AL
Sears, Roebuck & Co.
Sears Tower
Chicago, IL 60684

Carpeting:

Armstrong Cork Co.
Liberty & Charlotte Sts.
Lancaster, PA 17604
GAF Corporation
140 West 51st St.
New York, NY 10020
Hercules, Inc.
9th & Market
Wilmington, DE 19899

Ozite
1755 Butterfield Rd.
Libertyville, IL 60048
Montgomery Ward
619 West Chicago Ave.
Chicago, IL 60607
Roxbury Carpet Co.
Framingham, MA 01701
Sears, Roebuck & Co.
Sears Tower
Chicago, IL 60684
Viking Carpets
10 W. 33rd St.
New York, NY 10001

Wood Tiles and Wood Flooring:

Arco Chemical Co.
717 Fifth Ave.
New York, NY 10022
E. L. Bruce Co., Inc.
Democrat Rd.
P.O. Box 16902
Memphis, TN 38116
Harris Mfg. Co.
P.O. Box 300
Johnson City, TN 37601
Montgomery Ward
619 West Chicago Ave.
Chicago, IL 60607
Olinkraft
Jonesboro Highway
West Monroe, LA 71291
Sears, Roebuck & Co.
Sears Tower
Chicago, IL 60684
Tibbals Flooring Co.
P.O. Box A
Oneida, TN 37841
Wood-Mosaic Co.
5000 Crittenden Dr.
Louisville, KY 40213

Seamless Flooring:

Dur-A-Flex Seamless Floors
100 Meadow St.
Hartford, CT 06114

The Electo Co., Inc.
1000 45th St.
Oakland, CA 94607
Lohn & Fink Industrial Products
(Hallemite)
225 Summit Avenue
Montvale, NJ 07645
Sears, Roebuck & Co.
Sears Tower
Chicago, IL 60684

Ceramic Tile:

American Olean Tile Co.
Div. of National Gypsum Co.
1000 Cannon Ave.
Lansdale, PA 19446
H & R Johnson, Inc.
1270 Avenue of the Americas
New York, NY 10020
Montgomery Ward
916 West Chicago Ave.
Chicago, IL 60607
Sears, Roebuck & Co.
Sears Tower
Chicago, IL 60684

WALL MATERIALS

Ceramic Tile:

H & R Johnson Co.
1270 Avenue of Americas
New York, NY 10020

Pomona Tile Co.
Div. of American Olean Co.
216 S. Reservoir St.
Pomona, CA 91766
Montgomery Ward
916 West Chicago Ave.
Chicago, IL 60607
Sears, Roebuck & Co.
Sears Tower
Chicago, IL 60684

Wallcoverings:

Columbus Coated Fabrics
7th & Grant Ave.
Columbus, Ohio 43216
Combeau Industries
2 Decker Sq.
Bala-Cynwyd, PA 19004
Montgomery Ward
916 West Chicago Ave.
Chicago, IL 60607
Sears, Roebuck & Co.
Sears Tower
Chicago, IL 60684
Standard Coated Products
120 E. 4th St.
Cincinnati, OH 45202
Thomas Strahan Co.
Heard & Maple
Chelsea, MA 02150

Metal Tile:

Montgomery Ward
916 West Chicago Ave.
Chicago, IL 60607

False Brick:

Dacor Mfg. Co.
65 Armory St.
Worcester, MA 01601

GAF Corporation
140 West 51st St.
New York, NY 10020

Lustre Tile Corp.
373 Executive Blvd.
Elmsford, NY 10523

Masonite Corp.
29 N. Wacker Dr.
Chicago, IL 60606

Montgomery Ward
916 West Chicago Ave.
Chicago, IL 60607

Plastic Laminates:

Formica Corp.
120 E. 4th St.
Cincinnati, OH 45202

Montgomery Ward
916 West Chicago Ave.
Chicago, IL 60607

Sears, Roebuck & Co.
Sears Tower
Chicago IL 60684

CEILING MATERIALS

Suspended Ceilings:

Armstrong Cork Co.
Liberty & Charlotte Sts.
Lancaster, PA 17604

Gold Bond
Div. of National Gypsum
325 Delaware Ave.
Buffalo, NY 14202

Johns Manville
Greenwood Plaza
Denver, CO 80217

Montgomery Ward
916 West Chicago Ave.
Chicago, IL 60607

Sears, Roebuck & Co.
Sears Tower
Chicago, IL 60684

Ceiling Tile:

Armstrong Cork Co.
Liberty & Charlotte Sts.
Lancaster, PA 17604

Congoleum-Nairn, Inc.
195 Belgrove Dr.
Kearny, NJ 07032

Gold Bond
Div. of National Gypsum Co.
325 Delaware Ave.
Buffalo, NY 14202

Johns-Manville
Greenwood Plaza
Denver, CO 80217

Montgomery Ward
916 West Chicago Ave.
Chicago, IL 60607

False Beams:

Applied Molding Co.
Culpehockes St.
Reading, PA 19601

DIRECTORY OF PLYWOOD MANUFACTURERS

Abitibi Corporation
1400 North Woodward Avenue
Birmingham, Michigan 48011

Boise Cascade Building Products
One Jefferson Square
Boise, Idaho 83701

Celotex Corporation
1500 North Dale Mabry Hwy.
Tampa, Florida 33607

Evans Products Company
1121 S.W. Salmon Street
Portland, Oregon 97208

Forest Fiber Products Company
P.O. Box 68
Forest Grove, Oregon 97116

Georgia-Pacific Corporation
900 S.W. 5th Avenue
Portland, Oregon 97204

Masonite Corporation
29 North Wacker Drive
Chicago, Illinois 60606

Pope & Talbot, Incorporated
1700 S.W. 4th Avenue
Portland, Oregon 97210

Superior Fiber Products, Inc.
North Fifth Street and Bayfront
Superior, Wisconsin 54880

Superwood Corporation
14th Ave. West and Waterfront
Duluth, Minnesota 55802

United States Gypsum Company
101 South Wacker Drive
Chicago, Illinois 60606

U.S. Plywood
777 Third Avenue
New York, NY 10017

Weyerhaeuser Company
Tacoma Building
Tacoma, Washington 98401

DIRECTORY OF HAND-TOOL MANUFACTURERS

Black & Decker Mfg. Co.
Towson, MD

Billings & Spencer Co.
12 Laurel
Hartford, CT 06106

Channellock, Inc.
1306 Main St.
Meadville, PA 16335

Cooper Industries
P.O. Box 728
Apex, NC 27502

Crescent Tool Co.
P.O. Box 728
Apex, NC 27502

Duro Metal Products
2649 N. Kildare
Chicago, IL 60639

Graham Co., John H.
617 Oradell Avenue
Oradell, NJ 07649

Great Neck Saw Mfgrs. Inc.
Mineola, L.I., NY 11501

Greenlee Tool Co.
2136 12th St.
Rockford, IL 61101

Irwin Auguer Bit Co.
100 Grant
Wilmington, Ohio

Masterform Tool Co.
9909 Franklin Ave.
Franklin Park, IL 60131

Millers Falls Co.
Greenfield, MA 01301

Owatonna Tool Co.
376 Cedar Avenue
Owatonna, MN 55060

P & C Tool Co.
Box 22066
Milwaukee PO, WI

Petersen Mfg. Co., Inc.
De Witt, Nebraska 68341

Proto Tool Co.
Washington & Santa Fe
Los Angeles, CA 90054

Simonds Saw & Steel Co.
Intervale & Mack Roads
Fitchburg, MA 01420

Stanley Tools Div.
Stanley Works
New Britain, CT 06050

Stevens Walden Inc.
499 Shrewsbury
Worcester, MA 01604

True Temper Corp.
1623 Euclid Ave.
Cleveland, Ohio 44115

Upson Tools Inc.
99 Ling Rd., P.O. Box 4750
Rochester, NY 14612

Wiss & Sons Co.
400 W. Market St.
Newark, NJ 07107

X-Acto, Inc.
48-41 Van Dam Street
Long Island City, NY 11101

Xcelite Inc.
1972 Bank St.
Orchard Park, NY 14127